Educational Interventions for Students with Autism

Educational Interventions for Students with Autism

Peter Mundy
and
Ann M. Mastergeorge,
Editors

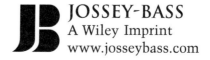

JOSSEY-BASS
A Wiley Imprint
www.josseybass.com

Published by Jossey-Bass
A Wiley Imprint
One Montgomery Street, Suite 1200, San Francisco, CA 94104-4594—www.josseybass.com

Jossey-Bass books and products are available through most bookstores. To contact Jossey-Bass directly
call our Customer Care Department within the U.S. at 800-956-7739, outside the U.S. at 317-572-3986,
or fax 317-572-4002.

Wiley publishes in a variety of print and electronic formats and by print-on-demand. Some material
included with standard print versions of this book may not be included in e-books or in print-on-
demand. If this book refers to media such as a CD or DVD that is not included in the version you
purchased, you may download this material at http://booksupport.wiley.com. For more information
about Wiley products, visit www.wiley.com.

Library of Congress Cataloging-in-Publication Data

Educational interventions for students with autism / Peter Mundy and Ann Mastergeorge,
editors. – 1st ed.
    p. cm. – (The U.C. Davis M.I.N.D. Institute Autism for Educators series)
  Includes bibliographical references and index.
  ISBN 978-0-470-58486-6 (pbk.)
  1. Autistic children–Education–United States. 2. Autistic youth–Education–United States.
3. Learning disabled children–Education–United States. I. Mundy, Peter. II. Mastergeorge, Ann.
  LC4718.E45 2012
  371.94–dc23

                                                 2012001577

Printed in the United States of America

FIRST EDITION

PB Printing   10 9 8 7 6 5 4 3 2 1

CONTENTS

The UC Davis MIND Institute
Autism for Educators Series

ACKNOWLEDGMENTS

This volume and the Autism for Educators series grew out of concerns raised in 2007 by Dean Harold Levine of the School of Education at UC Davis and Robert Hendren, former director of the UC Davis MIND Institute, regarding the need to foster a better integration of education and learning science. This integration was rooted in research efforts conducted at the MIND Institute on behalf of children and families affected by autism spectrum disorders (ASD), and a new emphasis area in learning and mind sciences in the School of Education. Of course, the families of the children in the Davis and Sacramento community and across the nation played a major role in raising this awareness at UC Davis. Their collective voice has been driving the national agenda as well as much of the progress in the study and treatment of autism we have realized over the past decades. Many parents deeply appreciate that progress and recognize that biomedical research may ultimately provide the key to unlocking ASD. However, they also recognize there is much to do now, through advances in education, to improve the lives of children with ASD and their families. Their vibrant efforts to raise awareness of the need for more research on education for school-age children with ASD have sent large and small ripples through our science. One of the larger effects of their advocacy includes the Institute of Education Sciences's support for the National Center for Special Education Research specific to improving education for children with ASD. One smaller effect, but hopefully a significant one, was the development of this book. With this and subsequent volumes we hope to communicate the progress and challenges we face as more concerted national research efforts are targeted toward advancing education for children with ASD. Thus in many ways the parents who never stop encouraging the world to take notice of and help their children are the genesis of this book. We'd like to acknowledge their seminal contribution to this volume and to all of the sciences of ASD. Close behind the voices of parents have been the tremendously articulate efforts of the authors of the truly state-of-the-art chapters herein. Heartfelt appreciation is also extended to our publishers at Jossey-Bass, Marjorie McAneny, Tracy Gallagher, and Justin Frahm, who have taken the time to scaffold and shape the development of this book in numerous constructive and perceptive ways. Last but not least we sincerely recognize the tremendous support and encouragement received from the administration of the UC Davis MIND Institute and School of Education at every step of this project.

Peter Mundy and Ann Mastergeorge

ABOUT THE EDITORS

Peter Mundy, PhD, is a developmental and clinical psychologist who has been working on defining the nature of autism for the past thirty years. He has published over a hundred empirical and theory papers on the nature of the development of social attention and social cognition in children with autism and children with typical development. His efforts in this regard began in 1981 at UCLA, where his work with collaborator Marian Sigman contributed to the current understanding that joint attention impairments are a fundamental feature of the social deficits of children with autism. This work has contributed to significant advances in both diagnostic and intervention methods for young children with autism. He currently is the Lisa Capps Professor of Neurodevelopmental Disorders and Education at the UC Davis Department of Psychiatry and School of Education. He is also the Director of Educational Research at the MIND Institute. In the last ten years Dr. Mundy has also begun a program of research designed to advance the understanding and treatment of problems in learning, social, and emotional development in higher-functioning children with autism. In 2006 he began a National Institute of Mental Health (NIMH)–supported program of research devoted to understanding neurocognitive, motivational, and social processes that affect individual differences in the expression and outcomes of autism in school-age children. In 2009 NIMH awarded funding to enable his research group at UC Davis to develop a multidisciplinary virtual reality laboratory for research on the role of social attention in the social learning disabilities of school-age children with autism. This laboratory is a joint venture of the faculties of the UC Davis MIND Institute, the Center for

Mind and Brain, and the UC Davis School of Education, as well as researchers at Stanford University and the University of Southern California.

Ann Mastergeorge, PhD, is a developmental and educational psychologist who has been working in the area of education and developmental disabilities for the past twenty years. She has published in the areas of early intervention, autism, and classroom inclusion for students with disabilities. Over the past several years, Dr. Mastergeorge has focused her research program in the areas of parent-mediated early intervention for young children at risk and young children with autism and interventions related to social communication and joint attention. Her collaborations have been funded by the National Institutes of Health, NIMH, the Administration on Developmental Disabilities, the U.S. Department of Health and Human Services, the U.S. Department of Education, the Office of Education, and the Institute of Education Sciences. She is currently an investigator on the Autism Phenome Project at the MIND Institute, studying the behavioral phenotypes of autism, and an investigator at the National Professional Development Center on Autism Spectrum Disorders funded by the Institute of Education Sciences. She is a faculty member of the MIND Institute at the UC Davis Medical Center, and is currently an associate professor at the University of Arizona in Family Studies and Human Development, and chair of the Early Childhood Initiative in prevention, early intervention, risk, and disabilities at the Frances McClelland Institute for Children, Youth, and Families.

ABOUT THE MIND INSTITUTE

The UC Davis MIND Institute is an internationally known research organization committed to excellence, collaboration, and hope, striving to understand the causes of and develop better treatments for neurodevelopmental disorders, starting with autism. Through their education division, the MIND Institute strives to deliver the latest in cutting-edge research and evidence-based practices to special educators, parents, and others working with children with autism.

ABOUT THE CONTRIBUTORS

Marianne L. Barton, PhD, is associate clinical professor of psychology at the University of Connecticut (UCONN), in Storrs. She is also director of clinical training for the clinical psychology program at UCONN and director of the Psychological Services Clinic. Dr. Barton's research interests focus on the early detection of autism spectrum disorders (ASD), the identification of varied developmental trajectories in children with autism, and the identification of early social deficits. She is also a licensed clinical psychologist whose interests include the diagnosis and assessment of ASD as well as early developmental psychopathology and the development of attachment relationships in early childhood.

Robyn M. Catagnus, EdD, BCBA-D, is adjunct professor of education at Arcadia University, with additional adjunct experience at Temple University. She holds degrees in psychology (BS); curriculum, instruction, and technology in education (MSEd); and special education (EdD). She is a Board Certified Behavior Analyst with extensive expertise in autism, behavior disorders, and positive behavioral support. As founder and former owner of a special education services agency, she clinically supervised cases, developed staff training programs, and conducted regular workshops and training events. Her current work includes the use of the Internet for distance education supervision, online course development, and instruction in Arcadia University's Autism Certification and Behavior Analysis Certification programs. Her research interests include classwide interventions, action research, online professional development of teachers, e-collaboration for education and behavioral health teams, and staff performance. She currently works as vice president of professional development at

Rethink Autism, an educational technology company serving families and professionals worldwide.

Jenna K. Chin, MEd, is currently pursuing her doctoral degree in school psychology at UC Santa Barbara. She has worked with children with autism in various settings, including public schools, homes, and partial hospitalization programs, in which she has gained experience in behavioral therapy, counseling, assessment, and parent education. Ms. Chin enjoys working with children with behavior, emotional, and developmental problems, and their teachers and families. Ms. Chin's research interests include school-based mental health, early intervention, and family and cultural influences. Consequently she has been involved with research projects for First 5 Santa Barbara, Project ACT Early: Advancing the Competencies of Teachers for Early Behavioral Interventions of At-Risk Children, and schoolwide positive behavioral support initiatives in the Santa Barbara School District.

Deborah Fein, PhD, is a clinical neuropsychologist who has been doing autism research for thirty-five years at Boston University School of Medicine and at the University of Connecticut. She is currently Board of Trustees Distinguished Professor in the Departments of Psychology and Pediatrics at the University of Connecticut. She has investigated numerous topics in the area of autism, including biochemical abnormalities, brain waves, language and memory, cognitive skills, sensory abnormalities, outcomes, early detection and screening, recovery from autism, and theoretical issues concerning diagnosis. She has published many articles and chapters, mostly on autism, and she is the coauthor of a book for teachers, *Autism in Your Classroom* (2007), as well as a widely used screening tool—the Modified Checklist for Autism in Toddlers. She served on the board of directors of the American Association for Clinical Neuropsychology, was secretary of the International Society for Autism Research, and is currently on the science advisory board of Autism Speaks. She is also the associate editor of the journal *Neuropsychology*.

Ellen L. Franzone, MS, CCC-SLP, earned her undergraduate degree in speech and hearing science from the University of Illinois at Urbana-Champaign, and went on to receive her MS in speech and language pathology from the University of Wisconsin-Madison in 1998. Prior to joining the National Professional

Development Center on Autism Spectrum Disorders, Ms. Franzone worked as a speech and language pathologist with children from birth to age twelve and their families. Ms. Franzone has worked with students with ASD and their families at pivotal life moments: prior to and at the time of diagnosis, at the transition to school-based services, and at the transition to middle school. She is particularly interested in ensuring that all students receive programming that takes their individual strengths, needs, and personalities into account. She has worked to develop programs that allow students with disabilities to participate meaningfully in their school and community. Ms. Franzone is thrilled to participate in work that allows her to balance her professional life with her family life.

Cynthia M. Herr, PhD, is an assistant professor and research associate in special education at the University of Oregon. She has directed and taught in personnel preparation programs in special education for over twenty-five years. She currently directs a grant-funded personnel preparation program in autism. Dr. Herr has taught children and adults with a wide variety of disabilities in elementary school and community college, and at the University of Oregon, during her thirty-seven years in special education. Dr. Herr is a nationally recognized author and expert in special education law. She has consulted with school districts and has also served as an advocate for parents of children with disabilities. She has conducted workshops on individualized education program development as well as social skills training for community agencies. Dr. Herr has published in the areas of special education law, autism, and secondary transition.

Brooke Ingersoll, PhD, is an assistant professor of clinical psychology at Michigan State University (MSU), where she directs MSU's Autism Research Laboratory. Dr. Ingersoll's research and publications are focused on the development of social communication skills in young children with ASD, with an emphasis on intervention. Dr. Ingersoll has published a parent training curriculum for families of children with ASD and is the principal investigator of a Department of Defense–funded research grant that is developing a parent training program for families of children with ASD that can be delivered remotely via the Internet.

Brittany L. Koegel, MA, is a doctoral student at UC Santa Barbara, with an emphasis in special education and developmental disabilities risk studies. Her interests are socialization skills for young adults with Asperger syndrome and academic motivation for children with autism.

Lynn Kern Koegel, PhD, the clinical director of autism services in the UCSB Koegel Autism Center and the director of the Eli and Edythe L. Broad Center for Asperger Research, has been active in the development of programs to improve communication in children with autism, including the development of first words, grammatical structures, pragmatics, and social conversation. In addition to her published books and articles in the area of communication and language development, she has developed and published procedures and field manuals in the area of self-management and functional analysis that are used in school districts and by parents throughout the United States, as well as translated into other major languages. Dr. Lynn Koegel is the author of *Overcoming Autism* (2004) and, most recently, *Growing Up on the Spectrum* (2010, with parent Claire LaZebnik), available in most bookstores.

Robert L. Koegel, PhD, has focused his career in the area of autism, specializing in language intervention, family support, and school integration. He has published over two hundred articles and papers relating to the treatment of autism. He is presently editing two books on the treatment of autism and positive behavioral support, and is the editor of the *Journal of Positive Behavior Interventions.* Models of his procedures have been used in public schools and in parent education programs throughout California, the United States, and other countries. He has trained many health care and special education leaders in the United States and abroad.

The Koegels are the developers of pivotal response treatment, which focuses on motivation. They were the recipients of the first annual Children's Television Workshop Sesame Street Award for "Brightening the Lives of Children" and the first annual Autism Speaks award for "Science and Research." In addition, Dr. Lynn Koegel appeared on ABC's hit show *Supernanny,* working with a child with autism. UC Santa Barbara received a $2.35 million gift to expand the physical space of the UCSB Autism Research Center, which was renamed the UCSB Koegel Autism Center in recognition of the Koegels' work on behalf of children with autism, and a large gift from the Eli and Edythe L. Broad Foundation to start the Center for Asperger Research, which is now part of the UCSB Koegel Autism Center.

Suzanne Kucharczyk, EdD, coordinates the Frank Porter Graham Child Development Institute at the University of North Carolina at Chapel Hill site of the National Professional Development Center on Autism Spectrum Disorders. Dr. Kucharczyk began her work with children with autism and their families in elementary, middle school, and high school classrooms. Suzanne has continued to work closely with classrooms as she has moved to work at the program, school, and other organizational levels. Over the years her work has focused on the professional development of education providers and the development of organizational supports for the implementation of effective practices. She received her EdD from Teachers College, Columbia University, in adult learning and leadership and her BA and MA from the University of Illinois at Urbana-Champaign in special education and educational policy studies. Her dissertation study explored how schools are implementing an inclusive education program for children with autism that involves organizational learning and knowledge sharing.

Wendy Machalicek, PhD, BCBA-D, is an assistant professor in the Department of Rehabilitation Psychology and Special Education at the University of Wisconsin-Madison. Her scholarship focuses on the assessment and treatment of challenging behavior in children with autism and related developmental disabilities. Her research emphasizes the development of novel ways to support and educate parents and teachers of these children to teach appropriate communication, social, play, and functional life skills. To date, Dr. Machalicek has authored or coauthored thirty-two peer-reviewed research articles and four book chapters.

Nancy S. McIntyre, BS, MSTC, is a doctoral student in the learning and mind sciences at the School of Education at UC Davis. Over the past twenty years she has worked with a wide variety of students from preschool through high school. Ms. McIntyre is currently involved in research in the Social Attention Virtual Reality Lab at the UC Davis MIND Institute. Her main research interest is the academic achievement, particularly reading comprehension development, of school-age children with autism and its relationship to their developmental differences.

Jamie Pagliaro, MBA, is executive vice president and cocreator of Rethink Autism, an educational technology company headquartered in New York City. He has spent the past fifteen years working in homes, schools, and clinical settings serving individuals with autism and severe behavior disorders. Prior to Rethink Autism,

Mr. Pagliaro was founding executive director of the New York Center for Autism Charter School. The school has received national recognition as a model public program. At Rethink Autism he oversees all content and product development, and collaborates extensively with public school systems implementing the company's Web-based technology. Mr. Pagliaro earned a BA with honors in psychology from Wesleyan University and an MBA from Villanova University. He also volunteers and serves as board chair for the national nonprofit Music for Autism.

Sarah R. Reed, MA, is a doctoral student in the Autism Intervention Research Program at UC San Diego and Rady Children's Hospital, San Diego. Her research focuses on the implementation of evidence-based treatments in community environments and how to optimally translate intervention research across service delivery settings. Ms. Reed is particularly interested in examining intervention implementation with groups of students, as this is the service reality for many community settings. On a clinical level, she has extensive experience implementing naturalistic behavioral interventions with children with autism as well as providing training to parents, clinicians, and students in these methods.

Laura Schreibman, PhD, is Distinguished Professor of Psychology at UC San Diego, where she has been on the faculty since 1984. She earned her PhD at UCLA, where she focused on the field of behavior analysis and treatment of childhood autism. She currently directs the federally funded UC San Diego Autism Intervention Research Program, which focuses on the experimental analysis and treatment of autism. She is a codeveloper of pivotal response treatment, an empirically validated naturalistic behavioral intervention. Her general research interests include the development and investigation of naturalistic behavioral intervention strategies, the development of individualized treatment protocols, translation of empirically based treatments into school settings (classroom pivotal response treatment), generalization of behavior change, parent training, and issues of assessment. She is the author or coauthor of four books and over 150 research articles and book chapters. Her latest books are *The Science and Fiction of Autism* (2005) and *Classroom Pivotal Response Teaching (CPRT): A Guide to Effective Implementation* (2011).

Aubyn C. Stahmer, PhD, is the research director of the Autism Discovery Institute at Rady Children's Hospital, San Diego and a research scientist at the Rady

Hospital Child and Adolescent Services Research Center of UC San Diego. She has conducted clinical and research programs in the area of autism for the past fifteen years. She has published many scholarly articles on inclusion and early intervention services for children with autism and leads two grants examining collaborative adaptation and implementation of interventions for children with autism in community programs. Her current interests include the study of early intervention systems for children with autism and the translation of evidence-based practices in community settings, including schools.

Jessica Suhrheinrich, PhD, is a postdoctoral researcher at UC San Diego and the Child and Adolescent Services Research Center at Rady Children's Hospital, San Diego. Her primary area of research involves examining the use of evidence-based practices for children with autism in school settings and improving the quality and availability of training for teachers of children with autism. Prior to undertaking her graduate work in experimental psychology, Dr. Suhrheinrich was a classroom teacher herself, and she has firsthand understanding of the barriers to translation of evidence-based practices to classroom settings.

Lisa Sullivan, PhD, is the project coordinator for the National Professional Development Center at the MIND Institute at UC Davis. Dr. Sullivan recently completed the doctoral program in learning and mind sciences at the School of Education at UC Davis. Her dissertation research examined the role of joint attention in learning and school readiness. Dr. Sullivan's research also includes a year-long study on the impact of an autism training program on teacher practice and competency. She is a former classroom teacher specializing in using cooperative learning groups. She was a Teacher Education Fellow at UC Davis, supervising middle school teachers in the credential program. Her main area of interest is in working with educators to translate research into practice that will improve student outcomes.

Kate Szidon, MS, is a graduate of Lawrence University in Appleton, Wisconsin. Ms. Szidon earned her MS in special education from the University of Oregon's Specialized Training Program in transition in 1996. Following her certification program, Ms. Szidon taught for twelve years in the state of Oregon. Her experiences in special education include providing technical assistance and support to a medium-size school district. She was also a special education teacher in a variety of settings and roles including high school transition coordinator, autism teacher for both elementary and middle school, and reading and math support teacher for all levels of school-age students. Ms. Szidon joined the National Professional Development Center on Autism Spectrum Disorders at the University of North Carolina in summer 2009. She has worked with students with ASD as a classroom teacher, transition coach, and camp leader. Her work interests include program development in autism, transition, applied behavior analysis, and functional behavior assessment. She is excited to be able to participate in a project that is focused on improving school outcomes for students with autism.

Bridget A. Taylor, PsyD, BCBA-D, is cofounder and executive director of Alpine Learning Group and senior clinical adviser for Rethink Autism. She has specialized in the education and treatment of children with autism for the past twenty-five years. She is a Board Certified Behavior Analyst and a licensed psychologist. Dr. Taylor is active in the autism research community and has published numerous articles on effective interventions for individuals with autism. She serves on several editorial boards for journals including the *Journal of Applied Behavior Analysis, Behavioral Interventions,* and *Behavior Analysis in Practice.* She is also a member of the Autism Advisory Group for the Cambridge Center for Behavioral Studies, is a board member of the Association for Science in Autism Treatment, and serves on the professional advisory board for the Association of Professional Behavior Analysts.

Allison Wainer, MA, is a graduate student at Michigan State University, working toward a PhD in clinical psychology. Her most recent research has focused on the use of technology to disseminate training in evidence-based intervention techniques. Her additional research interests include early autism intervention, parent training, and the broader autism phenotype.

FOREWORD

The past three decades have witnessed tremendous changes in how we think about autism and the ways in which we provide services for children affected by autism and their families. Once thought to be a rare disorder, autism as we now know occurs in 1 out of every 110 children. This dramatic increase in prevalence is at least partly due to improvements in the instruments available for the identification and diagnosis of children with autism. It is also due, however, to the recognition that the expression of autism varies greatly among children. As Lorna Wing recognized nearly thirty years ago, autism can be expressed as aloof withdrawal in some children but as a tendency to display active but unusual patterns of social engagement in others. In addition, about 40 percent of children with autism are affected by intellectual disabilities, whereas 60 percent have average to above-average intellectual abilities. So we now understand that children with autism present with a heterogeneous array of symptoms—and that the causes of autism may be equally varied. To recognize this fundamental point, we now refer to the autism spectrum of disorders.

In terms of services for individuals on the autism spectrum, considerable progress has been made with respect to interventions for preschool children. Thirty years ago many scientists and clinicians believed effective treatments were not possible for children with autism. However, as we have come to understand more about the nature, causes, and consequences of autism, we also have begun to develop effective interventions that target the social, cognitive, and behavior problems that impede learning and development in many children during the preschool years. Recent, carefully controlled studies of intervention effectiveness suggest that behavioral and developmental approaches to early intervention with two- to five-year-olds can, at a minimum, decrease the risk for intellectual disability in childhood for many children with autism spectrum disorders (ASD).

Here at the MIND Institute we are extremely proud to be conducting research that is on the cutting edge of improving early intervention services for children with autism. However, we also realize that early intervention is only the beginning of what we need to do to optimize the development of children with ASD. Indeed, there is a pressing need to improve intervention services for school-age children on the autism spectrum. To that end, the MIND Institute has developed a strategic partnership with the UC Davis School of Education to advance education for school-age children with autism. The book you hold in your hands is the first tangible product of that partnership. It reflects the expertise of scientists and educators who are engaged in the next wave of research on autism spectrum disorders. This book is designed to advance the national discussion and research agenda and—most important—to raise educational methods for school-age children with ASD to a level comparable to the achievements evident in recent work with preschool children. Of course, one book alone cannot accomplish this goal, but it does represent an important beginning. I applaud the editors and contributors of this work for taking on the challenge and moving us forward in ways that will benefit individuals with autism spectrum disorders and their families.

October 2011

Leonard Abbeduto, PhD
Director, MIND Institute
Tsakopoulos-Vismara Endowed Chair,
Department of Psychiatry and Behavioral Sciences,
UC Davis School of Medicine
Sacramento, California

Educational Interventions for
Students with Autism

PART ONE The Educational Needs of Children with Autism

Effects of Autism on Social Learning and Social Attention

Peter Mundy, Ann M. Mastergeorge, and Nancy S. McIntyre

Most often autism is regarded as an early-onset disorder that affects the development of social interaction and communication abilities and that has a significant negative impact on the quality of life and outcomes of individuals affected by autism and their families.[1] Although valid, the standard "social impairment" perspective on autism may not readily speak to the needs of educators who are charged with promoting academic achievement in reading or math for students with autism. Consequently there is the perception of a gap between clinical research and educational practices for school-age children with autism.[2]

This chapter addresses the gap by describing how the social impairments of autism affect learning in children. Indeed, we will argue that in regard to education for children with autism, this syndrome may be accurately and usefully conceptualized as a form of social learning disability. First, to understand fully what we

| 1—Very rarely | 2—Rarely | 3—Occasionally |
| 4—Somewhat often | 5—Often | 6—Very often |

Questions:

1.	I like being around other people.	1 2 3 4 5 6
2.	I find it hard to get my words out smoothly.	1 2 3 4 5 6
3.	I am comfortable with unexpected changes in my plans.	1 2 3 4 5 6
4.	It's hard for me to avoid getting sidetracked in conversation.	1 2 3 4 5 6
5.	I would rather talk to people to get information than to socialize.	1 2 3 4 5 6
6.	People have to talk me into trying something new.	1 2 3 4 5 6
7.	I am "in-tune" with the other person during conversation.	1 2 3 4 5 6
8.	I have to warm myself up to the idea of visiting an unfamiliar place.	1 2 3 4 5 6
9.	I enjoy being in social situations.	1 2 3 4 5 6
10.	My voice has a flat or monotone sound to it.	1 2 3 4 5 6
11.	I feel disconnected or "out of sync" in conversations with others.	1 2 3 4 5 6
12.	People find it easy to approach me.	1 2 3 4 5 6
13.	I feel a strong need for sameness from day to day.	1 2 3 4 5 6
14.	People ask me to repeat things I've said because they don't understand.	1 2 3 4 5 6
15.	I am flexible about how things should be done.	1 2 3 4 5 6
16.	I look forward to situations where I can meet new people.	1 2 3 4 5 6

FIGURE 1.1 Examples of Items from the Broad Autism Phenotype Questionnaire[3]

These items represent *some of the behaviors and dispositions* that may be observed in many people at moderate levels of expression. However, autism is characterized by more extreme levels of expression of these otherwise typical behaviors. People affected by autism exhibit different subsets and levels of these behaviors, hence autism's characterization as a range or spectrum of presentations (also known as autism spectrum disorders).

mean when we use such terms as *disability, impairment,* and *disorder,* we must recognize that autism is a part of human nature.

The characteristics associated with autism can be observed in many people in the general population. This is called the *broad autism phenotype* (see Figure 1.1).[4] For example, the social interactions and social learning of people with autism may be diminished by a tendency to focus on or even obsess about a restricted range of interests. However, this type of behavior is not limited to people with autism. For example, artists, scientists, or businesspeople can obsessively, but productively, focus on a narrow range of interests that have limited appeal for many other people. Because the broad autism phenotype is part of human nature, some argue that "autism" is not a disease or a disorder, but rather one of the many expressions of human diversity.[5]

THEY ARE CHILDREN FIRST: UNDERSTANDING THE AUTISM SPECTRUM OF DISORDERS

This human diversity perspective reminds us that children affected by autism are more similar to than different from their peers. They are children first, not a category unto themselves. Like all children they display a wide range of abilities and personalities. Taking pleasure in getting to know and engage each child and his or her idiosyncrasies can be immensely rewarding for teachers. Moreover, this approach provides the fundamental and necessary building blocks for optimizing education for children with autism in classrooms and schools.

> Getting to know, engage, and prize the differences that make each child a unique student is as essential to the effective education of a child affected by autism as it is for any other child in a classroom.

It stands to reason then that the better that teachers and school administrators can understand the development and idiosyncrasies of children with autism, the better they can engage these students, interpret their behaviors, and instruct or guide them in the classroom. Of course this may be challenging. Autism weakens students' ability to engage interpersonally with teachers and peers in expected ways. For example, some children and adults may be so extremely fixated on their own interests that it is hard for them to pay attention to the immediate interests of another person, such as a task assignment described by their teacher. This can lead to the perception that the child or adult is aloof, oppositional, or even unreachable.

When problems of this magnitude occur—and they chronically disrupt learning and the quality of life for children and parents—we refer to autism using the terms *disorder, impairment, and disability.* Of course autism is no different from other "disorders" of human nature in this respect. Many people may often mispronounce words, talk to themselves, or feel sad. However, if those behaviors become sufficiently extreme as to hinder one's ability to learn to read, to engage in social interactions, or to work, we may infer that an individual is affected by a *reading disability,* a *psychotic disorder,* or a *mood disorder,* respectively.

Diversity Within the Spectrum

The term *autism spectrum disorders* (ASD) is now used to acknowledge that children can present with many different patterns or combinations of symptoms within the broad autism phenotype. To illustrate this point, note that at various times research has emphasized that autism is characterized by the following:

- A specific inability to think about the mental states (thoughts) of other people (also known as the "Theory of Mind" hypothesis)[6]
- A deficit in the planning and execution of complex actions and thinking (also known as the "Executive Function" hypothesis)[7]
- An inability to focus on broad, comprehensive sets of information as opposed to a limited set of details (also known as the "Weak Central Coherence" hypothesis)[8]

Each hypothesis holds more than a grain of truth about autism. However, when Pelicano[9] examined the degree to which these "core" deficits characterized six- and nine-year-olds, she observed that only twenty-two of thirty-seven six-year-olds with autism (60 percent) displayed evidence of deficits in all three cognitive domains (Theory of Mind, Executive Function, and Weak Central Coherence). Moreover, by nine years of age only seven of thirty-seven children

(19 percent) displayed deficits in all three domains. At no point in this age range did all children with autism display the same pattern of "core" cognitive difficulties, but all children displayed impairment in at least one domain.

Related to this point, Lorna Wing long ago observed that there are at least three behavioral subgroups of children with autism:[10]

- Some children display an aloof behavior pattern.
- Some display a passive but responsive behavior pattern.
- Some are characteristically active but odd in their frequent social interactions.

This diversity of expression can make autism difficult to recognize, especially among higher-functioning children with active but odd behavior patterns. It probably reflects biological differences that occur across all people in the relative tendency toward very active patterns of behavior or more inhibited patterns of behavior.[11]

This type of temperament-related variability in autism is of more than passing interest, though, because active children may present greater behavior challenges but also a greater responsiveness to interventions. For example, recent reports have suggested that three- to six-year-olds affected by ASD who are more active in toy play and in approaching other people are more likely to be responsive to early, intensive, discrete trial behavioral intervention[12] as well as pivotal response treatment.[13]

Accommodating ASD Diversity in Education

The wide range of characteristics of children with autism makes it necessary to provide a wide range of services in schools. The Institute of Education Sciences (IES)[14] estimated that 296,000 children with autism were served by public schools across the United States in 2007–2008. That figure represents about 4.5 percent of all children served under the Individuals with Disabilities Education Act (IDEA). However, this was only about 0.6 percent of the population of school-age children. We say "only" because that is significantly less than the current Centers for Disease Control and Prevention[15] estimates of prevalence obtained from a large sample of elementary school students with autism, which is about 1 in 110, or 0.9 percent of the population. It is likely that the increased identification of children with autism had not had its full impact on the K–12 student population at the time of the IES estimate. Nevertheless, the IES[16] data also indicated the following:

- 35 percent of identified children spent 80 percent or more of their time in regular classrooms.
- 18 percent spent 40 to 79 percent of their time in regular classrooms.
- 37 percent spent less than 40 percent of their time in regular classrooms.
- The remaining 10 percent were in separate public, private, or home-based education settings.

How Autism Affects Learning

So if autism is diverse in its presentation, how can teachers and professionals understand the syndrome in a way that facilitates their ability to engage and instruct these students? One way is to consider the effects of autism on learning.

From its earliest presentation in preschool children, autism exhibits the characteristics of a social learning disability. To illustrate the utility of this social learning disability perspective, we will do the following in this chapter:

- Describe how autism affects learning in the first thirty-six months of life
- Discuss the history of autism research and describe how research on the early development of children with autism in the first thirty-six to sixty months of life has advanced diagnostic methods
- Describe how research on the early development of these children has led to the social attention and social learning disability perspective on autism
- Discuss the similarities and differences of the learning difficulties of school-age children with autism compared to those of other children who receive services under the auspices of IDEA, such as children affected by attention deficit hyperactivity disorder (ADHD)
- Consider how the social learning disability perspective on autism can inform and improve educational interventions

BRIEF HISTORY OF RESEARCH ON AUTISM

Unlike specific learning disabilities or ADHD, autism is apparent in many children well before they enter school or even preschool. The very early onset of autism is similar to that of intellectual and developmental disabilities (IDD, formally known as "mental retardation"). However, *autism is not a form of intellectual disability.* For people with IDD, most (or all) domains of cognitive development (for example, language, visual-spatial skills, and reasoning) are equally delayed or disturbed from early in life. By definition they display uniformly lower performance than peers on measures of vocabulary, verbal and nonverbal analogies, language comprehension, memory, and mental rotation of abstract figures that are common to intelligence tests. As a consequence, their test scores or intelligence quotients (IQs) are lower than 70 to 75. Based on the scores of thousands of children in a normative sample, an average score on an IQ test is about 100, and 98 percent of all children receive a score above 70.

Many, if not most, school-age children currently identified as affected by autism have an IQ estimate greater than 75. The most recent data on this come from the new Centers for Disease Control and Prevention (CDC) national surveillance network on autism, called the Autism and Developmental Disabilities Monitoring (ADDM) Network. In 2006 the ADDM Network gathered data on 307,790 eight-year-olds in public schools across eleven states and identified 2,757 children, or 1 in 110, affected by autism.[17] Equally important, albeit less well recognized, the CDC also reported that 59 percent of the identified children with ASD had average to above-average intelligence quotients.[18]

By comparison, in the 1980s we believed that about 1 in 2,500 children were affected by autism, and only about 25 percent to 30 percent of these children had IQs higher than 75. So both the total number of children identified as having autism *and the proportion of children with ASD without intellectual disabilities* have gone up noticeably in the last thirty years.

These findings have important implications for advancing education for children with autism. For example, much of the available research on adapting instruction for school-age children with autism involves children who are also affected by intellectual disabilities.[19] Yet the CDC data suggest that we must develop effective evidence-based interventions for children with autism with average or above-average, as well as below-average, intellectual competencies. That, obviously, is no small task.

The notion that autism displays a pattern of cognitive development that is different from those of IDD began to emerge in the 1980s. Surprisingly, little was known about the development of autism at that time, even though it had been forty years since the syndrome was initially described.[20] In the 1980s, however, people like Geraldine Dawson, Marian Sigman, and Sally Rogers, among many others, began to recognize the value of applying new insights from infant developmental science to the study of autism. As this began to occur, the conceptualization of ASD, the diagnostic instruments used to identify ASD, and intervention methods used with children affected by ASD gradually began to improve.

One thing that immediately became apparent was that young children with autism displayed a distinctive pattern of strengths and weaknesses in cognitive development when compared to children with IDD, such as those affected by Down syndrome. Preschoolers with autism seemed to learn about solving problems that involved object manipulation, such as puzzles, relatively quickly, but their ability to attend to and engage with people developed relatively slowly. For example,

- They readily learned *object permanence,* or that objects do not cease to exist when they are moved out of view and can often be recovered by searching.[21]
- They could even find objects in difficult tasks that required searching in multiple locations.[22]
- They came to understand that an intermediary object (such as a stick) could be used as a means to obtain a goal, such as an out-of-reach toy.[23]
- They didn't display specific problems with using gestures and eye contact to request assistance from adults.[24]
- They could recognize themselves in a mirror.[25]
- They displayed clear evidence of attachment to a specific caregiver.[26]

However, preschool children with autism displayed significant delays or impairments in paying attention to people compared to children with IDD or typical development. For example, although young children with autism would make eye contact with an adult to nonverbally request a toy, they did not readily use spontaneous eye contact with an adult to socially share their enjoyment while playing with the toy (see Figure 1.2 for an illustration of this type of behavior).[27] They also did not automatically follow the gaze direction when an

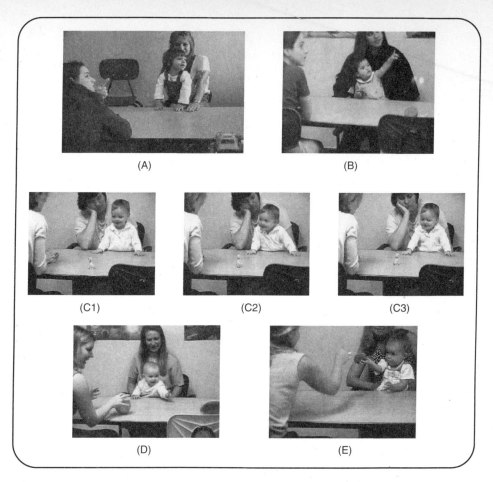

FIGURE 1.2 Examples of Social Attention Coordination or Joint Attention Preverbal Behaviors That Develop in the First Nine to Twelve Months of Life[28]

These examples include the following: (A) responding to joint attention or following another person's line of regard to share the experience of an object or event; (B) initiating joint attention or initiating attention coordination with pointing or showing, with the goal of sharing an experience with others; (C1, C2, C3) initiating joint attention by alternating the gaze between an object or event of interest and another person; (D) initiating a request for a behavior, and coordinating attention, with the goal of eliciting aid in obtaining an object or event from others; and (E) responding to a behavior request and coordinating attention with that of another person in order to correctly respond to the request, such as with an open-palm, "give it to me" gesture. Children with autism develop D and E relatively well. They develop A, B, and C more slowly. Often before preschool they become relatively proficient at A. However, B and C can remain problematic through the school-age years. In preschool assessment little alternating eye contact to share pleasure in an event is a red flag for autism. Improving this type of behavior can lead to improved learning in children with autism.

adult looked away from them and pointed to direct their attention to an object or picture in the room. Children with IDD, including children with Down syndrome, shared interests and followed gaze much more readily.

Together these observations indicated that children with autism displayed the following behaviors and patterns:

- A specific developmental impairment in the tendency to coordinate their attention spontaneously with that of other people, or to use *joint attention* to share experiences and information with others
- Reticence to share experiences with other people by imitating their actions[29]
- A tendency not to respond to their parent's voice or their name being called,[30] or to process information from people's faces[31]

The pattern of evidence was very consistent with what Kanner[32] had described in 1943 as the essential quantitative and qualitative impairment of social-emotional contact with other people in children affected by autism. In addition, for the first time the research of the 1980s indicated that this type of impairment could be precisely measured in young children, such that children with autism could be discriminated from children with other developmental disorders. Finally, the results of research in the 1980s also indicated that compared to children with IDD, young children with autism were characterized by a pattern of relative strengths and in social as well as cognitive development.

Prior to the 1980s, the lack of evidence-based descriptions of the behavioral characteristics of autism had a profound and negative effect on diagnosis and identification. It was not until 1980 that a description of autism appeared in the third edition of the *Diagnostic and Statistical Manual of Mental Disorders* (DSM-III) of the American Psychiatric Association.[33] This very positive step forward, however, was also problematic: the highly influential DSM-III was released just as developmental science began to advance our understanding of autism, but before the benefits of that science could be realized. DSM-III suggested that the behavior of children with autism could be characterized as consistent with a pervasive lack of responsiveness to others, even though nascent research suggested that autism was characterized by individual differences in social behavior[34] and a pattern of relative strengths and weaknesses in cognitive development. The DSM-III description was at best imprecise and at worst misleading.[35]

Such a broad description could not accurately describe children across age groups, because the social behaviors associated with autism were shown to frequently change and improve over time.[36] Studies also indicated the following:[37]

- Many children with autism responded when adults imitated their behavior.
- They displayed greater attention to others in structured rather than unstructured situations.
- They enjoyed physical play with caregivers.
- They systematically expressed some types of nonverbal communication with eye contact.
- They displayed clear evidence of caregiver attachment.

The perception that children with autism displayed a *pervasive lack of responsiveness to others* was simultaneously too broad to apply to different age groups of children and too narrow and imprecise to identify accurately many children who had profound impairments in social development but yet were still responsive to other people. These limits contributed to conceptual confusion about the nature of autism and to the tendency to identify relatively few children with this disability through the end of the twentieth century.

It wasn't until the publication of the fourth edition of the DSM in 1994 and its "technical revision" in 2000 that more precise, evidence-based behavioral descriptors of autism were provided.[38] One advance was the explicit recognition that the course and characteristics of autism could present quite differently across children. For example, individuals with "Asperger's Disorder" were described as having a "higher-functioning" variant of autism. These individuals did not display intellectual disabilities or problems with some aspects of language and communication development. Problems in the conceptual validity and diagnostic reliability of the distinction between "Autism Spectrum Disorder" and "Asperger's Disorder" have been such that it is unlikely that the latter term will be retained in the fifth version of the DSM.[39]

Nevertheless, the explicit recognition that children with autism differ in terms of social and cognitive course, and that many children achieve higher-functioning (average and above-average IQ) outcomes, will remain in DSM-5. These differences will be described in DSM-5 in terms of three severity ratings based on children's manifest need for support.

With the improved evidence-based behavioral descriptions of autism, powerful new "gold standard" standardized diagnostic instruments were developed in the latter part of the 1990s, such as the Autism Diagnostic Inventory[40] and the Autism Diagnostic Observation Schedule.[41] These advanced methods allow true cases of autism to be recognized by more people within a wider range of children. Its increased recognition led autism to be added as a category that qualifies for special education services in 1990, when the Individuals with Disabilities Education Act was authorized. Equally important, the increased precision of the diagnostic description reflected a subtle but telling shift in our conceptualization of autism: the description of the social impairments of autism now emphasized problems in the spontaneous initiation of behaviors to share information with other people, rather than emphasizing a pervasive lack of responsiveness to other people.

EARLY DEVELOPMENT, SOCIAL ATTENTION, AND LEARNING

Exemplifying the shift to an emphasis on impairments in the tendency to initiate adaptive social behaviors in ASD, DSM-IV describes a fundamental social symptom of autism as "a lack of spontaneous seeking to share enjoyment, interests, or achievements with other people (e.g., by a lack of showing, bringing, or pointing out objects of interest)."[42] The critical role of impaired initiations in the developmental course of autism has become clear as we have begun to adopt a developmental social learning perspective on the symptoms of autism. This perspective is perhaps best represented in what has become known as the social attention model of autism (see Figure 1.3).[43] A basic premise of this model is that the early and robust disturbance of the typical development of social attention significantly disrupts the normal process of social learning in preschool-age children with autism, and this impairment is likely to also be expressed in school-age children and adults as well. This model is well illustrated by details from research on the role of joint attention in typical development and in cases of autism.

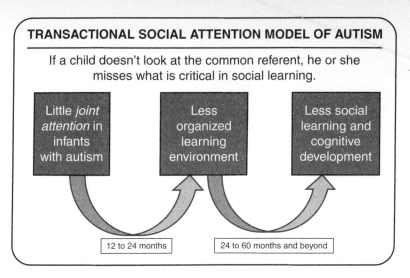

TRANSACTIONAL SOCIAL ATTENTION MODEL OF AUTISM

If a child doesn't look at the common referent, he or she misses what is critical in social learning.

| Little *joint attention* in infants with autism | Less organized learning environment | Less social learning and cognitive development |

12 to 24 months   24 to 60 months and beyond

FIGURE 1.3 An Illustration of the Social Attention Model of Autism

Prioritizing attention to people—and learning to coordinate attention with that of other people in particular—is a major milestone of early development. This type of joint attention skill development helps young children adopt a common frame of visual reference with others that facilitates social engagement, symbolic and language development, and social cognition (learning about people). Children with autism have a syndrome-specific deficit in joint attention development. This deficit not only is a symptom of autism but also is part of the disorder of autism, hindering children's ability to readily share information with other people and easily benefit from social learning opportunities. Left untreated, this deficit can lead to significant delays in cognitive development and perhaps even have an impact on early neurocognitive development. Even when treated, many children with autism continue to struggle with joint attention and with adopting a common frame of reference with others. This can impede their capacity for learning in the classroom.

Joint Attention's Role in Typical Development and in Cases of Autism

One of the primary reasons why human learning is unique and expansive is that we are highly capable and highly motivated when it comes to sharing information with each other. But how do we learn to share information? Certainly, speech and language development, as well as our capacity for mental and symbolic representation, are central to our ability to share information. We use language and symbols (such as the written word) to establish a common point of external physical reference (for example, "Today we are going to count all the different types of leaves we can collect outside") or internal mental reference ("Who can describe a beautiful leaf they found yesterday?"). Establishing a common frame of reference is essential to the meaningful and useful exchange of information.

So, how do we learn to establish a common frame of reference with other people? Does language or symbolic development enable this, or do we learn to establish a common frame of reference before we learn to process language and symbols? The latter increasingly appears to be the case. Indeed, the preverbal ability to establish a common frame of reference with others is likely to provide critical aspects of the cognitive scaffolding needed to build language and symbolic skills.[44]

Infants are not born with this ability, but rather gradually develop it in their practice of joint attention. Two types of joint attention behaviors develop in the first year of life:

- Responding to joint attention
- Initiating joint attention

Responding to joint attention (RJA) refers to infants' ability to follow the direction of the gaze and gestures of others to share a common point of reference (see Figure 1.2). RJA development begins between two and four months of age, is associated with activity in the frontal as well as posterior (parietal and temporal) brain areas by five months, and exhibits stable individual differences across children by nine months.[45] At first joint attention is effortful for infants. At nine months it takes the typical infant about 2 seconds to process the shift of attention of an adult and then successfully follow that adult's direction of gaze. By eighteen months of age this type of social information processing on average requires about 0.8 seconds.[46]

Initiating joint attention (IJA) reflects infants' spontaneous sharing of experience by directing the attention of adults to their experience of objects or events through the use of gestures (for example, showing) and eye contact (see Figure 1.2). Stable individual differences in joint attention development also emerge by nine months of age, and there is evidence that both the frontal and posterior brain areas begin to work together to advance the development of this type of skill in the second year of life.[47] Ultimately, by adulthood IJA and RJA are associated with activity in common brain systems as well as in systems that distinguish IJA from RJA.[48]

The development of joint attention abilities is vital to advances in the rate and quality of social learning most infants begin to experience with respect to language and social cognitive development beginning at six months of age.[49] Parents do not intentionally teach infants and toddlers all the words they need to learn through daily, structured language instruction. Indeed, it is the rare parent who sets aside a day to systematically instruct his or her twelve-month-old on all the names for different types of cutlery in the kitchen ("This is a fork," "This is a knife," and so on). Instead, during the course of daily interactions parents spontaneously refer to novel objects or events by name, and in this way they provide innumerable, unstructured, incidental word learning opportunities for their infant (see Figure 1.4).

Infants have an advantage regarding these incidental opportunities if they are active partners in establishing a common frame of reference with caregivers. Baldwin[50] suggests that they do this by actively and spontaneously coordinating their visual attention with that of their parent or caregiver. That is, they follow the direction of their parent's gaze to understand the most likely place to look, thereby increasing the chances that they will identify the correct target in novel word learning situations. In other words, infants actively use responding to joint attention (see Figure 1.2) to self-organize the flow of information in incidental word learning opportunities to reduce referential mapping errors.[51] This is not to belie the observation that parents (or teachers) actively scaffold the learning of their young children. Nevertheless, the benefits that infants receive from scaffolding are amplified as they begin to develop the facility of mind (joint attention ability) that increases their likelihood of establishing a common frame of reference with parents.[52]

Initiating joint attention also has positive effects on infants' social learning. The associated behaviors, such as showing an object, spontaneously and clearly express a child's attempt to share his or her immediate interest with a parent or other potential teacher. When parents respond to such behaviors by providing object labels or other information, they do so at a time when their child's interest and attention are optimal for learning.[53] So both types of joint attention serve a self-organizing role in infant learning.

This learning function of joint attention develops slowly in infancy but *continues to operate throughout our lives.*[54] Indeed, without the well-honed capacity for joint attention, success in many pedagogical contexts would be difficult.

FIGURE 1.4 Illustration of the Role of Joint Attention in Social Learning[55]

In this image an eighteen-month-old has the opportunity to learn a new word, *Rooster.* However, the possibility of a referential mapping error exists (that is, incorrectly associating the new word, *rooster,* with the wrong entity, the lizard). To decrease the likelihood of this error and increase correct word learning, the infant may be an active partner in the social learning process. She may look in the direction of her parent's gaze and turn in the correct direction toward the rooster. This is a simple illustration of a larger and vital element of social learning: children must actively coordinate their attention with that of others to adopt a common frame of reference in order to avoid referential mapping errors in most direct instruction situations. If children, such as those affected by autism, struggle with adopting a common frame of reference with others, their learning can suffer. Recognizing this issue goes more than halfway to providing improved educational opportunities for children with autism.

Imagine the school readiness problems of a five-year-old who enters kindergarten but is not adept at coordinating attention with that of teachers or peers. Similarly, children, adolescents, and adults who cannot follow, initiate, or join with the rapid-fire changes of shared attention in social interactions may be impaired in any social learning context, as well as in their very capacity for relatedness and relationships.[56]

In their cogent paper on bridging the gap between research and practice in intervention for autism, Dingfelder and Mandell[57] argue that one problem has been that although the mission of schools is to promote academic achievement in such content areas as reading and math, efficacy studies of intervention for autism tend to focus on "measures of the symptoms of autism (e.g., joint attention, imitation, challenging behaviors) or IQ, which may not directly relate to outcomes of interest" to teachers and schools.

Now imagine a child who has significant delays or impairments in the development of joint attention by early in the second year of life, when language development typically begins to accelerate. Such is the case for children with autism. Observations of parents' interactions with children with autism indicate that they provide as many incidental learning opportunities to their children as do parents of other children.[58] However, young children with autism are much less likely than other children to play an active role in establishing a common frame of reference with parents using joint attention, and they are far less capable of doing so. In recent years we have begun to study the development of autism in infants before they receive a diagnosis. Infant siblings of children with autism are more likely to develop autism than are infants in the general population. Working with large numbers of infant siblings of children with autism, researchers are able to observe when and how some infants begin to display subtle problems early in life, before clearly developing autism between twenty-four to thirty-six months. New data from these *infant sibling studies* indicate that many siblings who go on to show symptoms of autism at age three first show developmental impairments in joint attention by twelve to fifteen months.[59] Interestingly, at least one study indicates that children with autism whose parents tend to follow their children's line of regard and provide learning opportunities matched to their demonstrated interests develop language significantly better than do children with autism whose parents tend to present learning opportunities that require them to follow their parents' frame of visual reference.[60]

In addition, the degree to which young children with autism develop facility with RJA affects the degree to which an increase in the intensity of early intervention correlates with an increase in effectiveness in promoting their language development.[61]

> Young children with autism are less likely to benefit from spontaneous social learning opportunities in parent-child interactions than are typically developing children, or even children with other developmental disorders. This is because symptoms of autism (that is, joint attention deficits) lead to impairments in children's capacity to establish a common frame of reference with other people, which hinders their ability to readily acquire information in social learning opportunities. This, in brief, is the idea behind the social attention and social learning model of autism (see Figure 1.3).

Why Does Autism Affect Social Attention?

We don't yet fully understand why autism affects the development of social attention and joint attention. However, research suggests there are two primary possibilities.

Neural Interconnectivity

One hypothesis is that children with autism fail to develop the ability to engage in joint attention. For example, research has suggested that children with autism are most vulnerable to difficulties in the development of complex mental processes that require several widely separated brain areas to work together. This is called the neural *interconnectivity hypothesis* of autism.[62] Current research also suggests that joint attention places a high demand on connectivity between and within frontal and posterior brain networks for its development, even in young children.[63] So it is possible that problems in neural connectivity lead directly to the development of a *disability* of children with autism to engage in joint attention with other people. In this regard, the frontal networks are thought to play a primary role in the development of children's capacity to monitor and regulate their own attention, and the posterior system is involved in monitoring and mentally representing other people's attention and behavior. Interconnectivity allows these two systems to work together so that children and adults can engage in the *triadic tasks* of monitoring, comparing, and aligning one's own attention in relation to that of another person or other people.

> If a disability significantly decreases the tendency of a child to align his or her attention with that of other people, this can also significantly decrease his or her opportunities to learn from others, share information with others, or express and enjoy engagement with others at any age. Such is too often the case for children with autism.

One other point about the interconnectivity hypothesis is noteworthy. Current research suggests that several other problematic aspects of human nature, such as difficulties with self-regulation, attention deficit hyperactivity disorder, or obsessive-compulsive disorder, and even specific learning disabilities, involve connectivity problems in brain systems that overlap with those observed in autism. This may be one reason why behaviors associated with these aspects of human nature are also often part of the broad autism phenotype.

Motivation and Social Attention

An alternative to the idea that autism is associated with an *inability* to engage in joint attention is presented by the *social motivation hypothesis*.[64] According to this hypothesis, sharing attention and experiences with other people may be intrinsically rewarding. Consequently, internal motivation may play a major role in joint attention, such as the motivation that moves us to bring an interesting event or object (for example, a magazine photo) to the attention of a family member. If motivation affects the frequency with which we engage in joint attention, then low motivation may play a role in the reduction of joint attention in autism.

A motivation deficit associated with joint attention may occur if social attention is aversive for children with autism. This may be true for some children, some of the time. However, it does not generally appear to be the case. Many children with autism enjoy physical play with adults, they display attachment behaviors, and they direct eye contact and gestures to people to make requests. Yet these same children display joint attention impairments. Such observations have long suggested that an aversion hypothesis does not readily explain joint attention disturbance in autism.[65]

Alternatively, social stimuli may not necessarily be aversive, but they could be less interesting (*less positively rewarding*) than is typical, and nonsocial objects and events may be more interesting (*more positively rewarding*) than is typical. In the latter case, idiosyncratic preferences or interests may be expected to chronically divert children with autism from effectively sharing attention with people. If unusual motivation toward nonsocial objects or events is prominent in guiding attention in early development, this could contribute to joint attention deficits and impaired social learning in children with autism. By and large, this possibility currently has the best support in research with young children.

Evidence for the social motivation hypothesis has been provided by the comparative study of responding to joint attention versus initiating joint attention behaviors. Differences in internal motivation may more strongly influence the tendency to initiate behaviors than the tendency to respond to the behaviors of others. This is what we see in autism with respect to joint attention deficits: many children with autism attend to and respond to the joint attention bids of others, at least in the later preschool years. However, they continue to exhibit difficulty in initiating joint attention.[66] It also seems that, even when they do initiate joint attention, they smile and take pleasure from the experience of joint attention less frequently than do other groups of children.[67] The social motivation hypothesis of joint attention gained additional support in a recent brain imaging study, which indicated that the brain systems associated with IJA more clearly involve the activation of reward centers of the brain than do those associated with RJA.[68]

Of course the social motivation hypothesis has implications for teachers. Imagine what this difference in basic social motivation could be like for the child with autism in the classroom. We all get frustrated when, from time to time, our schedules interrupt the pursuit of our own interests and goals. Fortunately, many of us often experience sufficiently clear rewards in shifting away from our own preference to collaborate with others, so we can relatively easily learn to regulate our frustration with being distracted. However, what if sharing attention and collaborating with others were not clearly rewarding, and our own pattern of interests and attention priorities rarely matched the proclivities of those around us at home, school, or work? Multiple daily expressions of frustration in having our attention diverted to things of less intrinsic reward value and meaning might become routine. That pattern of behavior and emotional expression in the classroom and elsewhere can be common at any age for children with autism.

What sounds singularly like a problem, though, can also be viewed as an opportunity for educators. Recall that children who initiate more may be more responsive to interventions.[69] Teachers may effectively guide that motivation to initiate toward improved learning. Indeed, that has become a basic principle that is central to both effective preschool intervention and pivotal response treatment. In both cases educators first react to or create instructional opportunities that recognize the interests of the child, and then use the child's interests as a fulcrum to increase his or her tendency to engage in social learning.[70] Although it may not be possible to engage in such child-directed episodes of instruction all the time in a classroom, education for children with autism is enhanced by recognizing and using their different motivations and interests.

We will return to this important perspective on social motivation in joint attention and autism when we discuss interventions later in the chapter. For the moment, though, let us consider in more detail how joint attention disturbance or difficulty with adopting a shared frame of reference with other people—and other problems—may affect elementary- and secondary-age students with autism.

EFFECTS OF AUTISM ON ATTENTION IN SCHOOL-AGE CHILDREN

In 2007 a story was published in the *New Yorker* called "Parallel Play: A Lifetime of Restless Isolation Explained."[71] In this story Tim Page provided the following recollection of the life of a very bright second-grade student in the 1960s who was affected by ASD:

My second-grade teacher never liked me much, and one assignment I turned in annoyed her so extravagantly that the red pencil with which she scrawled "See me!" broke through the lined paper. Our class had been asked to write about a recent field trip, and, as was so often the case in those days, I had noticed the wrong things.

"Well, we went to Boston, Massachusetts through the town of War-renville, Connecticut on Route 44A. It was very pretty and there was a church that reminded me of pictures of Russia from our book that is published by Time-Life. We arrived in Boston at 9:17. At 11 we went on a big tour of Boston on Gray Line 43, made by the Superior Bus Company like School Bus Six, which goes down Hunting Lodge Road where Maria lives and then on to Separatist Road and then to South Eagleville before it comes to our school. We saw lots of good things like the Boston Massacre site. The tour ended at 1:05. Before I knew it we were going home. We went through Warrenville again but it was too dark to see much. A few days later it was Easter. We got a cuckoo clock."

It is an unconventional but hardly unobservant report. In truth, I didn't care one bit about Boston on that spring day in 1963. Instead, I wanted to learn about Warrenville, a village a few miles northeast of the town of Mansfield, Connecticut, where we were then living. I had memorized the map of Mansfield, and knew all the school-bus routes by heart—a litany I would sing out to anybody I could corner. But Warrenville was in the town of Ashford, for which I had no guide, and I remember the blissful sense of resolution I felt when I certified that Route 44A crossed Route 89 in the town center, for I had long hypothesized that they might meet there. Of such joys and pains was my childhood composed.

I received a grade of "Unsatisfactory" in Social Development from the Mansfield Public Schools that year. I did not work to the best of my ability, did not show neatness and care in assignments, did not cooperate with the group, and did not exercise self-control. About the only positive assessment was that I worked well independently. Of course: then as now, it was all that I could do.

This recollection poignantly illustrates one fundamental problem for many children with autism and their teachers in elementary and secondary classrooms. The information of interest, or the objects and events that "grab" their attention, are often very different for students affected by autism than for most other students in any given classroom. Of course, all students have idiosyncratic momentary interests or pursuits that divert them from task engagement in the classroom every day, but they are also possessed of the motivation and ability to recognize the consensual focus of attention with teachers and peers, and to become sufficiently interested in the common topic or achievement goals to return to the collaborative learning process. However, a biologically based difficulty with the motivation and ability to adopt a common frame of reference and topic of interest with others may chronically impede classroom learning and be regarded as a defining feature of the social learning disability of autism.

In a student with an average or above-average IQ the behavior associated with autism may lead teachers to perceive the student as oppositional and may mystify if not alienate peers. This chronic negative impact the child's social learning disability may have on his or her interactions with peers and teachers can contribute to an overlay of frustration and emotional and self-regulation difficulties that make matters worse for the student.

Because this pattern of behavior is often perceived as a failure in a child's ability to pay attention to class tasks and assignments (and as a sign of oppositionality), autism in higher-functioning students is often mistaken for ADHD. In fact, some symptoms of ADHD are often evident in children with autism.[72] It is important to identify these children because the presence of higher levels of ADHD symptoms can negatively affect social attention, cognition, and academic achievement in children with autism.[73] By and large, though, children with ADHD and higher-functioning autism can be distinguished by using both a measure of ADHD symptoms, such as the Conners 3 parent and teacher report scales,[74] and the Autism Spectrum Screening Questionnaire.[75]

Oddly enough, research has yet to provide a clear and evidence-based conceptual definition of the differences in the attention problems of school-age students with autism and school-age students with ADHD. Nevertheless, the following provisional distinctions can serve as a guide. The attention problems of children with ADHD may be characterized by difficulty inhibiting off-task sensory and mental distractions. If their attention is diverted from a task by distractions, children with ADHD may also have problems in remembering what the task is (working memory weakness) when attempting to return to the task after their attention to distracters has diminished or has been actively inhibited. Attention regulation problems in many children with ADHD may also occur with a tendency for high levels of activity (hyperactivity), which increases the likelihood of distraction and further decreases the likelihood of returning to tasks with the cessation of distraction.

Alternatively, although they are not immune to distraction, a more fundamental issue for children with autism is a tendency to (over)focus on their own interests or visual and auditory stimulus preferences. This and the reduced motivation or ability to routinely become engaged and interested in a common topic or frame of reference with others combine to lead to a high frequency of off-task behaviors. Their off-task behaviors may be complicated by hyperactivity less often than in ADHD, although hyperactivity can be an issue for some children with autism. So in some sense ADHD may be characterized as a tendency to adopt but then lose track of the common topic or social-cognitive frame of reference during classroom tasks and assignments, whereas autism may be characterized as a tendency to have difficulty initially adopting, recognizing, or finding interest in a topic or common social-cognitive frame of reference (coordinated focus of social attention) required by tasks or assignments in the classroom.

INTERVENTIONS AND CHILDREN WITH AUTISM

When evidence-based interventions for autism first began to be developed, researchers did not explicitly recognize problems in initiating versus responding behaviors, or problems with adopting a common frame of reference. Early interventions for autism were primarily based on operant models for learning verbal behaviors that were prominently available in the 1960s and 1970s.[76] Experimental group studies have provided compelling evidence supporting these applied behavior analysis (ABA) approaches. At minimum, they can be very effective in reducing the risk for intellectual disabilities in preschool children with autism (for example, see Figure 1.5). ABA approaches primarily rely on reinforcing and shaping children's responses to task demands using adult-directed instruction trials. The systematic use of discrete adult-directed instruction trials gradually increases desired behavior targets while reducing problematic behaviors in many children.

The ABA approach provides a very important and effective foundation for interventions for children with autism. But because it seeks to rehabilitate the impairments of children one behavior at a time, it is labor intensive (requiring thirty to fifty hours per week for one or more years) and costly. Moreover, it is primarily designed to improve the ability of children with autism to respond to

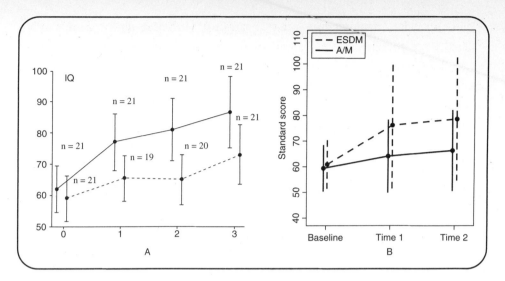

FIGURE 1.5 Comparison of Intervention Outcomes for Intense Preschool Applied Behavior Analysis Intervention (Panel A) and Intense Preschool Developmental Intervention (Panel B)[77]

Panel A depicts the change on a preschool IQ assessment for children receiving ABA intervention (solid line) and those receiving community standard preschool interventions (dotted line). The graph shows development over years of intervention (1, 2) and a one-year follow-up (3). At the one-year follow-up, most of the children who had received ABA intervention had IQ estimates above the average for the range of intellectual disabilities (greater than 70), but few children in the sample who only received standard preschool interventions had comparable cognitive outcomes. Panel B depicts a group of children who received the Early Start Denver Model (ESDM) preschool intervention versus a community standard control. The control group was referred to as the Assess and Monitor (A/M) group. ESDM uses discrete adult-directed instruction trials, as does ABA intervention, but it adds incidental trials that are based on following the attention and behavior of the child to identify a momentary interest and then presenting learning opportunities vis-à-vis the child's expressed interest. This type of hybrid intervention has an impact on cognitive outcomes that is comparable to that of ABA, but it requires fewer hours of intervention. In both studies preschool IQ was measured with the Mullen Scales of Early Learning.

adult directives in instructional settings. Autism is, however, characterized as much by impairments in the ability to spontaneously adopt a common frame of reference and actively initiate and engage in learning with other people as by deficits in children's tendency to respond to directives. Therefore, even the best practitioners recognize that ABA approaches may need to be augmented by other methods to target social attention and the initiation of self-organizing behaviors in learning situations among children with autism.[78]

In response to this perceived need, intensive "developmental interventions" have been fashioned that attempt to balance the adult-directed, child-responsive format of ABA methods with increased use of child-directed incidental learning trials. In the second approach, interventionists and parents are trained to spontaneously modify instruction by following the child's direction of gaze or activity and presenting learning opportunities related to the object or event of a child's immediate, manifest interest. The incidental learning trials are included to promote greater child engagement and self-initiated, active learning. An outstanding example here is a report of a recent randomized controlled study of preschool intervention using the Early Start Denver Model (Figure 1.5, Panel B).[79] The results of this study indicated that this hybrid combination of discrete and incidental learning trials in early intervention may be just as effective as the pure ABA approach to reducing risk for intellectual disabilities in preschool children with autism but require less time in intervention.

Another approach to preschool intervention has explicitly tested the hypothesis that targeting social attention may promote a type of self-initiation that is pivotal for learning.[80] At UCLA, Kasari et al. first developed effective intervention methods for increasing IJA in young children with autism. These methods largely involve determining the interests of a child by following the direction of his or her gaze, and then entering into joint activity with the child around that interest. One method here is to imitate the child's actions with an object of interest. Interestingly, although preschool children with autism are sometimes reticent to imitate others, they respond with increased social attention when other people imitate their actions. This increased social attention, or the spontaneous sharing of attention while the child and interventionist are engaged with the same toy, is a primary goal of the intervention. The interventionist takes pains to socially reward each episode of initiated social attention with especially clear, accentuated, and positive facial, vocal, and gestural affect. When they have been guided toward sharing attention and clearly rewarded in this way, many young children begin to engage in shared attention more frequently and elaborately with adults.[81]

After developing this intervention for IJA, the UCLA group then implemented a randomized controlled study that compared groups of preschool

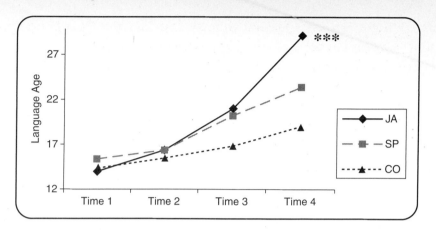

FIGURE 1.6 Impact of Targeting Joint Attention Skills in Preschool Interventions for Children with Autism[82]

Equal numbers of children were randomly assigned to one of three intervention groups. One group received one year of intense ABA intervention (group CO, 1,400 hours per year). A second group received 1,400 hours of ABA plus 30 hours of targeted intervention designed to increase children's spontaneous play behaviors (group SP). The third group received 1,400 hours of ABA intervention plus 30 hours of targeted intervention designed to increase initiation of the types of joint attention behaviors illustrated in Figure 1.2 (group JA). The results indicated that two years after the end of the intervention (Time 4), the group that received the targeted joint attention intervention had continued to learn language at a significantly more rapid rate than children who received either of the two comparison interventions.

children who received thirty hours per week of ABA intervention for one year (1,400 hours per year) with children who received ABA treatment augmented by one hour of IJA treatment, five times per week, for five to six weeks (25 to 30 hours per year). The results indicated that both groups of children displayed significant advances in language development (see Figure 1.6). However, the group that also received targeted IJA treatment displayed greater improvement in expressive language development six and twelve months after all treatment than did the ABA-only group. Moreover, children who showed better development of IJA also had better four-year outcomes in regard to both cognitive advances and symptom reduction. Thus, through a deeper appreciation of the contribution of joint attention disturbance to the learning disability of autism in the preschool period, researchers are beginning to move forward on the identification of targeted treatments that hold the promise of increasing the efficiency and cost-effectiveness of early intervention methods.

Other studies have also shown that improving joint attention in preschool children leads to a cascade of improved learning across other domains.[83] Moreover, the capacity to respond to and initiate social attention bids has been observed to affect the responsiveness of young children with autism to early language intervention.[84] Therefore, impairments in social attention are now widely regarded as pivotal targets for intervention among children with autism.[85] More recently, the National Standards Project of the National Autism Center[86] has listed joint attention intervention as one of eleven evidence-based approaches to treatment for children with autism (see Chapter Eight for the complete list of approaches). Joint attention has even begun to be recommended as a target for teaching and individualized education program development with school-age children.[87]

The increasing recognition of the pivotal role that social, joint attention impairment plays in the learning problems of school-age children with autism is encouraging. At the very least this may help reduce some of the misinterpretations of behaviors that can disrupt teachers' engagement with often challenging students. However, much like in 1997 when we were just beginning to realize the applications of research on social attention to preschool interventions,[88] in 2011 we are only on the verge of developing applications designed to advance education for these children.

One question that comes to mind as we consider education for school-age children with autism is, "Can we expect education and intervention to be very effective throughout the lives of children affected by ASD?" The answer to this question is an unequivocal yes, even though it may appear from the reports of the media and researchers that the preschool period is the main time for effective intervention. The perception of its singular importance comes from the evidence of the success of early intervention and the possible association of that success with brain plasticity. Brain plasticity refers to a period of rapid brain growth and organization of neural functions and connections. Children may be most affected by interventions received during such periods of plasticity, and a major period of brain plasticity occurs in the preschool years. It is not, however, the only significant period of brain plasticity.

Another major period of neural plasticity occurs between eight and eighteen years of age and is associated with significant changes in the cognitive, executive, and social competencies of children.[89] However, the changes in neural plasticity and aspects of cognitive development that are typical in the development of many children between elementary and secondary school are not as clearly evident in the development of children with ASD.[90] These observations are beginning to lead to the recognition of a later elementary to secondary school phase of delay in the development of children with ASD. This reminds us that autism is a *developmental* disorder that continues throughout child development, even after preschool treatment. Fortunately, the recognition of neural plasticity between eight and eighteen emphasizes that the late elementary and early secondary school years probably constitute another sensitive period for effective intervention for many.[91] In this regard, school-age intervention may be as important as preschool intervention for children with ASD. We will probably only see optimal outcomes for children affected by ASD if we can improve the continuity of school-age education programs, making them a form of follow-through for advances begun with preschool efforts.

In this regard, important new approaches to and targets of intervention are beginning to follow from a deeper understanding of the social learning disability of autism. For example, one intervention involves teachers' explicit consideration of the interests of individuals with autism when adapting their curriculum and assignments. Very instructive examples of this pivotal response approach are available from the work of Lynn and Bob Koegel at UC Santa Barbara.[92] Their research group has shown that encouraging children to express their interests by making choices within the confines of academics can lead to improved engagement and writing and better performance of arithmetic tasks.

It is also useful for teachers and school personnel to understand that children with autism may have specific difficulties with reading for meaning. These children can display relatively well-developed word decoding skills, but they often have trouble developing the types of reading comprehension skills that enable them to "read to learn" in later elementary and secondary school grades.[93] This is opposite to the pattern of poor decoding but less impaired comprehension observed in children with specific reading disability.[94] Indeed, 50 to 70 percent of school-age children with higher-functioning forms of autism ultimately display large enough IQ and achievement disparities to qualify for specific learning disability designations,[95] and reading (comprehension) disability is common among these children.[96]

Deficits in social attention may be especially problematic for learning that requires the student to make social inferences or consistently keep track of social referents, as is the case in the development of reading comprehension or written expression skills. For example, practice in reading comprehension requires the student to maintain a clear sense of reference (who said or did what) and to make inferences from information about the behavior of the characters. These types of referential and inferential skills in reading enable most children and adults to adopt and maintain similar background details to establish a frame of reference and meaning that is common to all readers of the same passage of text.[97] However, as we hope is clear at this point, adopting and maintaining a common frame of reference is difficult for children with autism, as is using accrued contextual and background information in problem solving.[98] Other observations also suggest that reading comprehension deficits may be central to the nature and course of autism in many school-age children. Two recent studies have reported that differences in the intensity of the social impairments of autism are either concurrently correlated with reading comprehension difficulties[99] or predictive of the development of reading comprehension difficulties in school-age children with autism.[100]

Fortunately, a sufficiently detailed literature is emerging to guide teachers and schools in their attempts to improve reading comprehension instruction for students with autism. These students' reading difficulties may involve problems with identifying relationships between causal antecedents and consequences, generating and answering questions while reading (self-monitoring), and locating referents and rereading to repair understanding.[101] Adapted instructional methods may help teachers systematically address each of these problem areas. Three informative reviews of research on and methods for delivering reading comprehension instruction for children with autism are now available.[102] Interestingly, one observation in this literature is that cueing students to pay attention to and remember the best referent word of a given pronoun was one of the most effective strategies for improving reading comprehension.[103] In addition, Flores and Ganz[104] provided a small sample of children with concentrated instruction (twenty minutes per day) to increase their ability to interpret analogies, attend to and recall facts from a passage they read, and practice explaining the details of events they read about in short passages. These authors found that instruction in these three mental processes significantly improved reading comprehension in elementary school children with autism.

TO SUM UP

Studies of intervention for autism tend to focus on "measures of the symptoms of autism (e.g., joint attention, imitation, challenging behaviors) or IQ, which may not directly relate to outcomes of interest" to teachers and schools.[105] There is therefore a gap between the concepts that receive the most attention in research on autism and the needs of schools. We believe we are on the verge of closing that gap, however, and have tried to illustrate that belief with a discussion of the relevance of joint attention to the education of children with autism.

We hope that several main points are clear from this discussion:

- Children with autism are more similar to than different from their peers.
- What distinguishes them in large part is a reduced tendency to readily adopt a shared frame of reference with other people in the classroom. This begins with joint attention differences in preschool and continues to be expressed in different patterns of interests that guide their attention in elementary and secondary classrooms.
- We must recognize the biological basis of the different patterns of interests and social attention that are characteristic of children with autism.
- We must attempt to join with their patterns of interests to cultivate reciprocal engagement with others; this may be one component that is common to all effective methods for advancing education for children with autism.

The preparation for this was partially supported by the UC Davis Lisa Capps Endowment for Research on Neurodevelopmental Disorders and Education, as well as NIMH grant 1R21MH085904 on social attention in school aged student with ASD.

Evidence-Based Instructional Interventions

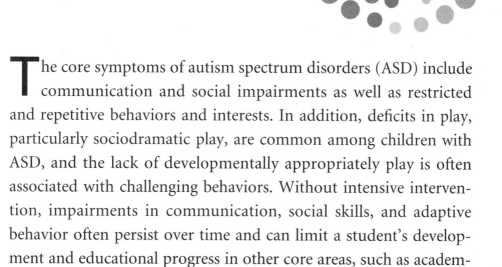

Wendy Machalicek

The core symptoms of autism spectrum disorders (ASD) include communication and social impairments as well as restricted and repetitive behaviors and interests. In addition, deficits in play, particularly sociodramatic play, are common among children with ASD, and the lack of developmentally appropriately play is often associated with challenging behaviors. Without intensive intervention, impairments in communication, social skills, and adaptive behavior often persist over time and can limit a student's development and educational progress in other core areas, such as academics and age-appropriate play and leisure skills. Accordingly, researchers have recommended that instruction for students with ASD target these curricular areas:

- Academic skills
- Communication and social skills
- Functional life skills
- Play and leisure skills

There is an extensive body of intervention literature evaluating instructional strategies and supports for addressing each of these skills in classroom settings. For each curricular area, a number of intervention strategies have demonstrated effectiveness in teaching targeted skills to children with ASD. However, there is a continued need for future research to determine the most effective strategies for the acquisition, generalization, and maintenance of these essential skills.

This chapter provides an overview of targeted curricular areas and a selective review of recent school-based research evaluating the effectiveness of interventions designed to address the academic skills, communication and social skills, functional life skills, and play and leisure skills of students with ASD, ages three to twenty-one.

This chapter's first section, *Instructional Interventions for Targeted Curricular Areas*, provides an overview of targeted skills and intervention procedures within each curricular area. The *Overall Findings from the Literature* section evaluates trends across the reviewed studies in regard to the targeted skills, effective instructional strategies used across curricular areas, and participant characteristics. The *Implications for Practice* section provides suggestions for teachers when research on teaching a particular skill is lacking. *The To Sum Up* section provides a brief summary of findings and offers suggestions for future research.

INSTRUCTIONAL INTERVENTIONS FOR TARGETED CURRICULAR AREAS

In each of the following subsections, one study is described in detail to illustrate the instructional procedures that characterize interventions in a particular curricular area.

Academic Skills

A small number of studies have evaluated the effectiveness of interventions to teach academic skills to students with ASD. These studies have targeted a variety of skills across several areas, including the following:

- Reading or related literacy activities[1]
- Story writing[2]

- Mathematics[3]
- Student task engagement or task completion[4]
- Test-taking skills[5]

In one study, Soares and colleagues[6] examined the effectiveness of computer-aided self-monitoring to increase academic task completion and reduce the challenging behaviors of a thirteen-year-old student with Asperger syndrome in a special education classroom. The intervention consisted of teaching the student to use a computer-based visual schedule and self-monitoring sheet to keep track of and self-reward completion of three academic tasks. The student showed completed assignments to his teacher, and he undertook self-rewarded task completion by using the computer mouse to move an image of Mickey Mouse to the empty box underneath the name of the completed activity. Effects of the self-management strategies on task completion and challenging behaviors were evaluated using an "A-B-A-B design." This allows a researcher or teacher to better understand the *causal* relation between intervention and performance by gathering information on the baseline ability of the child during a set of initial observations (A); then observing if behavior or academic performance improves with a period of intervention (B_1); then seeing if the behavior or academic performance worsens when the intervention is removed for a trial period (A); and, finally, determining whether the behavior or academic performance improves again when the intervention is reinitiated (B_2).

Prior to intervention, the student completed 22 percent of daily assignments, and teachers reported high rates of challenging behaviors. During intervention, the student completed 92 percent of academic tasks, and challenging behavior decreased during the last intervention phase (B_2). In addition, the data indicated a strong association between periods of intervention and improved performance versus performance during periods without intervention.

Communication and Social Skills

Some studies have aimed to improve social initiations with peers in general, for example by encouraging positive comments; intentional, positive physical contact; and responses to peer initiations.[7]

Other studies have taught a variety of specific social communication skills. Students with ASD have been taught such conversational and social skills as the following:

- Commenting, initiating, joining in, maintaining conversations, or giving compliments[8]
- Engaging in cooperative, social behaviors, such as helping others[9]

Pivotal behaviors are prerequisites that serve as "keys" to improve other behaviors that rely on the development of these skills. Acquisition of pivotal behaviors can increase the overall level of reinforcement available to a child and improve a child's motivation to learn. Students with ASD have been taught the following pivotal skills:

- Gaining perspective[10]
- Using empathetic statements appropriately[11]
- Responding to and initiating bids for joint attention[12]

Other interventions have sought to improve basic communication skills by doing the following:

- Increasing the vocalizations of young children with ASD[13]
- Improving key communication behaviors, such as requesting a preferred item, help, or attention[14]
- Teaching children to ask, "What's that?" when presented with novel stimuli[15]

In one study, Argott and colleagues[16] evaluated the use of script-fading procedures to teach empathetic statements to three adolescents with autism. Intervention consisted of providing students with scripted written responses to say when the researcher demonstrated a gestural and affective expression of a particular emotion (for example, hurt, tired, happy, excited). The researcher demonstrated one of the three nonverbal affective stimuli (for example, clapping while smiling) and presented a written prompt within one second. If the student responded incorrectly, or failed to respond to the written prompt, the researcher physically prompted the student to point to the script and read it aloud. Once the student read the scripted statement aloud, the researcher delivered reinforcement (that is, praise and a token). After students responded to 100 percent of scripted responses for five consecutive sessions, scripts were systematically faded.

The effects of script fading on students' use of scripted and unscripted empathetic verbal statements were evaluated using a multiple-baseline research design across participants. Multiple-baseline designs across participants include baseline assessment of participant performance followed by intervention across multiple participants. The intervention is implemented in a time-staggered fashion to control for external variables (for example, maturation) that might affect participant performance. In this study, during baseline assessment, none of the students responded to the presented nonverbal affective stimuli. During intervention, two students demonstrated acquisition of the scripted statements, and their use of unscripted statements increased following script fading. One participant required additional prompts and fading procedures, but eventually demonstrated acquisition of the appropriate verbal responses and responded in the absence of prompting. Although responding was variable, each of the students demonstrated generalization of responses to novel instructors, and a follow-up assessment six weeks after intervention suggested that results were maintained.

Functional Life Skills

Studies have examined the effects of instruction on the acquisition of a variety of functional life skills routines for students with ASD.[17]

Targeted routines have included the following:

- Purchasing items in a store[18]
- Hand washing[19]
- Preparing meals[20]
- Practicing vocational skills[21]

One study taught students to avoid abduction by strangers.[22] In another study, Ayres and colleagues[23] evaluated the use of computer-based video modeling to teach meal preparation to two nine-year-old students with autism.

Intervention consisted of computer-based intervention and the use of video models based on software developed by the researchers. During instruction, students viewed two first-person-perspective video models of the targeted routine (that is, setting the table, making soup, or preparing a sandwich), and then participated in computer-based intervention whereby they virtually completed the targeted routine. Computer-based intervention consisted of providing the student with images of each step of the targeted routine and asking the student to begin the routine (for example, "Make a sandwich"). Students used their computer mouse to drag and drop each of the steps to the correct location in the routine. If the student responded incorrectly or failed to respond, the computer used a system of least-intrusive prompts (that is, auditory response prompts, model prompts, stimulus prompts, and computer completion of the correct steps) with a ten-second constant time delay between prompts. There was no programmed reinforcement following correct responses, but a computer game was available noncontingently following the students' completion of instruction. Once students responded correctly to 90 percent of the steps of a targeted routine in at least three nonconsecutive sessions, the researchers assessed students' ability to complete the targeted routine in real life.

The effects of computer-based intervention on students' ability to give correct responses during computer-based intervention and on generalization of meal preparation skills to school routines were evaluated using a multiple-probe design across behaviors. Multiple-probe research designs are a type of multiple-baseline research design whereby baseline and intervention assessments of participant performance are conducted intermittently over time. During baseline assessment, each of the students demonstrated variable responding, but neither student was able to complete the targeted routines independently. During intervention, one student demonstrated independent completion of each targeted routine, and the student maintained these skills when computer-based intervention was removed. The second student improved in her independent completion of her two targeted routines, but she did not achieve complete independence. Both students' performance following withdrawal of the intervention suggested partial maintenance of the sandwich-making routine and maintenance of the table-setting routine at levels of independent completion similar to those obtained during intervention.

Play and Leisure Skills

Students with ASD have been taught to play appropriately in the following areas:

- Playing with toys, leisure items, and peers[24]
- Choosing an activity[25]
- Engaging in a leisure activity or playing with toys in a functional manner[26]
- Improving cooperative play skills[27]
- Improving sportsmanship[28]

Machalicek et al.[29] evaluated the effects of an activity schedule intervention on task engagement and challenging behaviors during playground recess for three boys with moderate to severe autism, ages six, seven, and twelve. Prior to intervention, each child demonstrated low levels of activity engagement and engaged in challenging behaviors during recess. The intervention consisted of classroom teachers assisting students to use a photographic activity schedule to guide their play during recess. To create the activity schedule, the teachers took color photographs of eight playground activities (for example, the slide, monkey bars, and swings). One large photograph of the playground activity was attached to the corresponding playground equipment. The activity schedule consisted of a clipboard with smaller photographs of each playground activity and four out-lined squares labeled 1 through 4 on the bottom of the clipboard. Prior to recess, the teacher placed four photographs of playground activities on each child's clipboard. At the beginning of recess, the teacher called participants over one at a time and asked them to review their schedule ("What are you going to play today?"). Using graduated guidance, the teacher prompted each child to point to and say each activity, and then prompted him to remove the photograph of the first activity, match it to the corresponding larger picture attached to that piece of playground equipment, and play in the designated area. After two minutes of playing, the teacher praised the child and delivered a small edible. These procedures were repeated until the child had played for two minutes on each piece of equipment according to his activity schedule. Effects of the activity schedule intervention on activity engagement and challenging behaviors were evaluated using a multiple-baseline design across participants. Results showed that each child improved in his ability to use the activity schedule correctly, each student's task engagement improved, and challenging behaviors decreased when the activity schedule was present.

OVERALL FINDINGS FROM THE LITERATURE

Within each curricular area, researchers have described a variety of instructional strategies aimed at improving the academic, communication and social, functional life, and play and leisure skills of students with ASD. However, the breadth of skills targeted within each curricular area varies. Within some categories (for example, communication and social skills, play and leisure skills) studies have evaluated the effects of interventions on a range of targeted skills, and in some cases two or more studies have evaluated the same or similar targeted skills. It should be noted that there are relatively few studies evaluating academic or functional life skills, considerably restricting the depth of research on targeted academic or functional skills. Given that the majority of children with ASD demonstrate communication and social delays and limited play skills, it is not surprising that a large proportion of recent intervention research has evaluated interventions aimed at improving social or communication skills[30] and play skills.[31] However, children and youth with ASD often have concomitant difficulties acquiring academic concepts and functional life skills. This section discusses the degree to which the reviewed literature has addressed these skills and suggests reasons for broadening the focus of classroom-based intervention research to include academic and functional life skills.

Academic Skills

The No Child Left Behind Act (2002) and the Individuals with Disabilities Education Act (2004) mandate access for all students to the general education curriculum, including reading, mathematics, writing, and science instruction. Basic academic skills are required if a student is to acquire more complex academic concepts and skills, but they are also prerequisites to functional life skills, such as telling time, making everyday purchases, budgeting, and banking.[32] However, research on interventions to teach these basic academic skills to students with ASD is lacking. For instance, the National Reading Panel, in a review commissioned by the National Institute of Child Health and Human Development,[33] reported that phonemic awareness, phonics, fluency, vocabulary, and comprehension were critical for students to develop into successful readers. However, only a few studies included in this review addressed these skills.[34]

Similarly, the National Council of Teachers of Mathematics recommends K–12 mathematics instruction in numbers and operations, algebra, geometry, measurement, and data analysis and probability,[35] but none of the higher-order concepts were covered in the reviewed studies. Within the academic skills category, researchers have targeted pointing to numerals,[36] three-digit by three-digit addition,[37] and single-digit addition and problem-solving skills using number line and touch-point strategies.[38]

Finally, the National Research Council published the *National Science Education Standards* in 1996 to encourage the development of grade-level science standards for all students, including those with disabilities.[39] These standards include science as inquiry, physical science, life science, earth and space science, science and technology, science in personal and social perspectives, and the history and nature of science. Among those studies reviewed, one study compared the use of constant time delay and simultaneous prompting during embedded instruction to teach science definitions to a thirteen-year-old student with autism.[40] Courtade, Spooner, and Browder's review[41] of interventions that aimed to address the National Research Council's call for science standards for students with significant disabilities, including ASD, found few studies addressing science standards, suggesting a need for further research and practical guidance for teachers.

Functional Life Skills

When compared to other curricular areas, a small number of studies have aimed to teach functional life skills to students with ASD. Past research suggesting that daily living skills were relative strengths for children with ASD when compared to communication and social skills[42] may have contributed to researchers' focus on communication and social skills. These findings may in part be explained by the possibility that the adaptive behavior skills, including daily living skills, of children with ASD improve as they mature.[43] However, more recent research suggests that young children with ASD are likely to need explicit instruction to develop age-appropriate daily life skills, such as bathing, grooming, dressing, and taking care of one's health.[44] Difficulties in practicing these independent self-care skills appear to continue into adulthood for individuals with autism or pervasive developmental disorder-not otherwise specified (PDD-NOS) diagnoses.[45] Moreover, diagnosis of autism appears to be correlated with worsened adaptive skills compared to the skills of individuals with PDD-NOS or intellectual disabilities alone.[46] Alternatively, the lack of classroom-based intervention research addressing functional life skills may be in part explained by the location of the research. Researchers may primarily be evaluating instructional strategies to teach daily living skills in residential or outpatient rather than school settings.[47] Nevertheless, many students with ASD will continue to require systematic instruction to become independent in daily living and self-care skills, and schools may play an important role in helping students to achieve these goals.

Effective Instructional Strategies Across Curricular Areas

The studies reviewed in this chapter suggest that a variety of instructional strategies exist to improve the academic, communication and social, functional life, and play and leisure skills of students with ASD. Although some intervention strategies are more commonly used within specific curricular areas (for example, social stories, a type of antecedent manipulation, to teach social skills), the majority of intervention strategies are not specific to a curricular area. Rather, a number of intervention strategies have been used across the curricular areas with positive results. These intervention strategies include antecedent manipulations, behavioral teaching strategies, self-management strategies, instructional delivery modification, naturalistic or social-emotional instruction, peer instruction, reinforcement-based strategies, and technologically enhanced strategies. In addition, one-to-one and small-group instructional arrangements have been evaluated. This section discusses those instructional strategies (that is, antecedent manipulations, behavioral teaching strategies, and technologically enhanced strategies) most commonly used in classroom settings and summarizes findings regarding one-to-one and small-group instruction.

Antecedent Manipulations: Social Stories and Social Scripts

A large number of studies have used antecedent manipulations before or during problematic situations to teach and occasion desired student responses.[48] Antecedent manipulations are strategies that have the purpose of preventing the occurrence of challenging behavior or proactively prompting and encouraging desired, appropriate behavior. In the context of instruction, antecedent manipulations are interventions that are used prior to students' encountering difficulty and that serve to teach or prompt desired behaviors. They have most often been used to teach social skills and improve task engagement or transitions between or within activities. For instance, social stories are personalized stories read to students prior to situations in which they have experienced difficulty in relating to or understanding others. The stories teach the students behaviors that are expected during problematic social situations and may help them learn and remember the social expectations relevant to those situations.

A number of studies have evaluated the following:

- Social scripts[49]
- Activity schedules[50]
- Visual cues[51]
- Social stories[52]

Other studies have evaluated the following:

- Social stories in combination with visual schedules[53]
- Powercards[54]
- Keys to play[55]

Although antecedent manipulations have been shown to have positive effects on targeted skills, they are generally paired with another type of instructional strategy for maximum effectiveness. Teachers should implement antecedent manipulations to "set the stage" for student learning, but students with ASD will often require additional instruction involving behavioral teaching strategies and reinforcement-based strategies to learn new skills.

Behavioral Teaching Strategies: Prompting and Chaining Procedures

Within the category of behavioral teaching, students have learned a variety of targeted skills through the use of systematic prompting and chaining procedures. What typifies this category is the use of operationally defined procedures that include antecedent prompts, specific instructor-delivered prompts to elicit the desired student response with or without the use of time delay, and reinforcement or error correction contingent on student responding. In addition, complex skills and routines are often broken down into their discrete, individual steps, and students are taught one or more steps at a time using chaining. Each step is thought of as a link of the "chain," and the consequence, or next "link" following a step, serves as the discriminative stimulus for the next step. Teachers plan specific prompting for each step according to student performance and may teach the initial step in the routine first (forward chaining), the last step in the routine first (backward chaining), or all of the steps in the first-to-last step order in which they are generally practiced (total task chaining). As steps are mastered, the student is required to complete progressively more steps in the chain until the entire routine or skill is achieved.

A number of studies have evaluated the following:

- Least-to-most prompting[56]
- Most-to-least prompting[57]
- Time delay[58]

Other studies have evaluated the use of the following to positive effect:

- Adapted response prompting, such as no-no prompting[59]
- Echoic prompting paired with constant prompt delay[60]
- Direct instruction[61]
- Discrete trial teaching procedures[62]

It is important to note that studies employing other instructional strategies (such as naturalistic instruction) have also used systematic instruction to teach new behaviors[63]—instruction that includes using antecedent prompts and specific instructor-delivered prompts to occasion desired student responses as well as reinforcement or error correction following student responses. The evidence for the benefits of using systematic instructional strategies for teaching students with significant disabilities is strong, but such approaches often require time-intensive, one-to-one instruction.

Technologically Enhanced Strategies: Video Modeling and Computer-Based Intervention

Some alternatives to one-to-one instruction that provide systematic prompts and reinforcement include computer-based intervention (CBI);[64] other telecommunications technology, such as personal digital assistants (PDAs);[65] and video modeling.[66]

A number of studies have evaluated the following:

- Video modeling[67]
- Video self-modeling[68]

Other studies have evaluated the use of the following to positive effect:

- Video modeling versus video self-modeling[69]
- CBI[70]
- CBI (with a nonverbal reading approach)[71]
- PDAs (to complete assignments)[72]
- Tactile prompting[73]
- Vibrating prompt[74]

CBI can provide students with systematic instruction (that is, instruction using prompts, time delay, reinforcement, and error correction) much like that provided by a teacher during one-to-one instruction.[75] In a similar way, video modeling[76] may provide students with supplemental instruction when the teacher is working with other students, or may provide parents with easy-to-use strategies they can use at home to generalize skills learned at school. Many studies have used video modeling to effectively teach social communication or other skills to students with ASD, making video modeling an evidence-based strategy.[77]

One-to-One and Small-Group Instruction

Best practices for the instruction of students with ASD include direct instruction delivered in one-to-one settings, so it is not surprising that the majority of studies have evaluated the effects of one-to-one rather than group instruction.

However, teachers may find the use of one-to-one instruction difficult in both segregated special education classrooms and inclusive general education classrooms. In general education classrooms, teachers often take on the responsibility of delivering whole-group instruction and managing the classroom, while paraprofessionals support students with disabilities or provide one-to-one instruction to those students. In segregated special education classrooms, differing abilities often necessitate one-to-one instruction for most students, but this may not be possible due to high student-to-teacher ratios. Although students with ASD may each have an assigned paraprofessional to support their learning, paraprofessionals are neither qualified nor specifically trained to implement evidence-based instruction in academic, communication and social, functional life, and play and leisure skills. Perhaps more important, inadequate (for example, one-to-one, once-a-week) instruction in these skills is not likely to lead to improved student outcomes. Accordingly, instructional strategies that can supplement or replace one-to-one instruction, such as small-group instruction, computer-based intervention, or video modeling, may be especially well suited for delivering instruction to students with ASD in both general and special education settings.

Several recent studies have examined the effects of providing instruction to small groups of students.[78] For instance, Leaf and colleagues[79] demonstrated that teacher-implemented group instruction based on teaching interaction procedures resulted in improved social skills for each of the five study participants, and these skills were maintained at eight weeks following the termination of instruction for four of the five participants. Moreover, the participants were able to generalize the majority of social skills to a novel teacher without reminders or reinforcement. For the social skills that participants failed to generalize to novel teachers, priming alone or priming paired with reinforcement resulted in generalization.

These preliminary findings suggest that small-group instruction may be one way for teachers to improve the quantity and quality of classroom-based instruction for students with ASD. In addition to potentially decreasing the need for one-to-one instruction, group instruction provides children with structured opportunities to observe multiple positive examples of social skills exhibited by their peers, and it may give teachers a chance to plan cooperative learning activities that offer naturally occurring opportunities for reciprocal social interactions. Further, providing instruction during naturally occurring interactions might improve generalization of social skills. Recent research evaluating the use of group instruction to teach social skills has demonstrated that group instruction may benefit children with autism, but questions concerning the degree to which acquired social skills generalize to other settings or persons remain unanswered.[80]

INSUFFICIENT EVALUATION OF INTERVENTIONS FOR OLDER STUDENTS OR STUDENTS WITH SEVERE ASD

Although studies involving interventions aimed at improving academic, communication and social, functional life, and play and leisure skills have reported positive results for a range of school-age children with ASD, the majority of published intervention research involves younger children with ASD, and children with a diagnosis of autism.[81] Fewer studies have evaluated the use of interventions to improve these targeted skills with older children and young adults, ages ten to twenty-one, or children with severe autism or concomitant intellectual and developmental disabilities (IDD).

OLDER STUDENTS

The majority of participants in the reviewed studies have been nine years of age and younger. Few students ages ten and older have been included in the reviewed intervention literature, and a very small number of studies have included secondary-age (fourteen years and older) students as participants.[82] Evidently, empirical evaluations of interventions addressing a number of essential skills and interventions for older students are lacking. The explanation for this is less clear, however.

The disproportionate representation of younger students in the literature might in part be due to a shift during late childhood and adolescence toward daily living and vocational—rather than academic—objectives. However, given the persistent instructional needs of students with ASD as well as the increased complexity of grade-level curricula and social roles in secondary settings, these findings suggest the need for evidence-based strategies to deliver instruction to older students.

In addition, within each of the curricular areas there are a number of age-appropriate skills that secondary-age students should acquire. For instance, choosing and engaging in leisure activities (for example, using a computer, taking pictures, playing educational video games) independently or in small groups are socially important skills for older students with ASD. Leisure activities may offer meaningful social opportunities for older students to interact with peers and learn essential social and communication skills. In addition, leisure activities may be effective reinforcers of appropriate behavior when students gain access to their preferred activity contingent upon completion of schoolwork. However, if a student does not have the skills to independently engage in a preferred leisure activity, that student is unlikely to find the activity engaging or rewarding and may engage in disruptive behavior because he or she is bored.

Moreover, the development of leisure skills is perceived as a socially important step during adolescence and throughout adulthood, providing opportunities for relaxation, enjoyment, social interactions with others, and improved self-esteem. Acquiring such skills can often improve vocational skills (for example, the same skills used for browsing the Internet for fun can be used to read classified ads online) or other functional living skills (for example, cooking a meal or making gifts for others). However, few studies have demonstrated the use of interventions to improve the play or leisure skills of older students with ASD.

Machalicek and colleagues[83] evaluated the effects of an activity schedule intervention on the playground behaviors of one twelve-year-old student with severe autism. Ganz and colleagues[84] evaluated the effects of visually cued imitation on the play of one thirteen-year-old student. Blum-Dimaya and colleagues[85] taught four children with autism, ages nine through twelve, to use activity schedules with embedded video modeling to learn age-appropriate leisure skills (for example, playing video games).

Although the research involving older children with ASD has reported positive results, without further research concerning this population it is difficult to determine the degree to which the instructional strategies used to teach younger children with ASD would translate into successful interventions for older students. These findings suggest the need for further evaluations of intervention strategies targeting age-appropriate skills for older students.

STUDENTS WITH SEVERE AUTISM

Similarly, reported participant diagnoses varied from the most commonly reported diagnoses of autism (51 percent). Some participants were described as having both autism and IDD (19 percent). Fewer participants were reported to have diagnoses of PDD-NOS, or autism and PDD-NOS (13 percent). Other participants (17 percent) were described according to the severity of their ASD diagnosis (mild, moderate, severe); of these participants, half were reported as having mild to moderate autism, and half were reported as having severe autism. The reported severity of a student's disability does not seem to contribute to less successful outcomes of instruction. However, some researchers reported adapting instruction to better meet the needs of students who initially progressed less favorably than did other participants.[86] For instance, Krantz and McClannahan[87] reported adapting instruction for the study participant with the lowest IQ in response to that participant's lack of progress.

These findings and our current understanding of ASD suggest that some students may require more or less support in some curricular areas. Students with a more severe level of ASD will often benefit from additional support during intervention, and in some cases from different intervention strategies or targeted skills. Students with concomitant IDD, for example, may require systematic instruction in functional life and functional academic skills, whereas students with mild to moderate autism may instead require social skills interventions, with less emphasis on functional skills.

Also, children with severe autism or concomitant IDD may engage in challenging behaviors that counter teacher attempts at instruction, resulting in less favorable treatment results. It is important to note that differential responding to interventions is also a common issue for students who share similar mild autism diagnoses, and the reasons for these differential outcomes are often unclear.

IMPLICATIONS FOR PRACTICE

Several gaps in the literature require further research to expand our current understanding of the types of classroom-based interventions that are effective in teaching students with ASD across common curricular areas. There is a large body of research evaluating strategies to teach students communication, social, and play skills in classroom settings, but fewer studies have targeted academic or functional life skills or involved older students with ASD or children with concomitant IDD. In addition, classroom intervention research may not approximate the contexts and available resources of today's schools. For instance, classroom teachers may be unable to implement one-to-one instruction for the majority of the school day due to high student-to-teacher ratios.

These evidence gaps and contextual fit issues may pose unique problems for teachers of students with ASD who are charged with identifying and implementing evidence-based interventions that are known to produce positive student outcomes. When currently available interventions lack sufficient evidence, or when none have been found to be effective for a particular group of students, teachers should look to the broader applied behavior analysis literature examining the effects of academic and functional life skills instruction on the skills of students with intellectual disabilities.[88] Although these strategies have not, for the most part, been explicitly evaluated with students with ASD, the principles of applied behavior analysis that underlie instruction for students with autism are the same as those used to teach new behaviors and skills to individuals with intellectual disabilities. Moreover, when selecting an intervention, teachers should rely on their understanding of the principles of systematic instruction to determine its potential efficacy, and when implementing an intervention they should closely follow their data on student performance to make decisions about ongoing instruction and supports. In this way, teachers may carefully evaluate the effects of interventions and instructional arrangements that have proven efficacy with younger students with ASD or with another student population.

TO SUM UP

The National Research Council[89] describes the need for interventions to teach children with ASD academic and cognitive, communication, social, functional life, and play skills and to decrease challenging behavior. This chapter reviewed recent school-based research evaluating the effectiveness of interventions designed to address these essential skills with students with ASD, ages three to twenty-one. The reviewed research suggests that effective interventions exist across each of the reviewed curricular areas. However, we are unable to draw strong conclusions about the effectiveness of many of the interventions because of the variability among participants, targeted skills, and intervention procedures.

In light of these findings, there are a number of ways that future research can extend the current literature. Following is a brief summary of key findings and suggestions for future research.

- The current literature on teaching academic concepts and functional life skills offers few relevant examples of how best to teach these essential skills to students with ASD. Given the difficulties that some students will have in acquiring and generalizing these skills, there is a continued need to evaluate classroom interventions targeting academic and functional life skills.
- Evidence suggests that the use of small-group instruction, CBI, and video modeling is an effective way for teachers to provide instruction that is less time intensive to students with ASD. However, the majority of the studies reviewed here have used systematic instruction, and many researchers have developed their own software for CBI or videos for video modeling. Consequently, teachers may not yet have access to commercially ready resources and may spend long hours creating instructional materials.
- It is unlikely that small-group instruction, CBI, and video modeling can replace one-to-one instruction by a teacher. Nevertheless, their application in conjunction with other commonly used antecedent and behavioral teaching strategies, such as the use of social stories, video modeling, and discrete trial training, is supported by past applied behavior analysis intervention research and may enhance positive outcomes. In addition, the use of systematic instructional procedures in small groups may provide teachers with an efficient way to supplement or replace one-to-one instruction for children with autism in classroom settings.
- Future research should include an analysis of the components of instructional packages to identify which specific strategies are essential in promoting the acquisition of targeted skills and their generalization to novel settings, peers,

and adults. This information may assist teachers in streamlining instruction and making more informed decisions about which instructional strategies to abandon in the face of time and resource constraints.

- Further research is needed to demonstrate the successful use of interventions found to be effective for students with a less severe diagnosis (that is, mild autism) when applied to students more severely affected by their diagnoses.

- Researchers should report the severity of a study participant's autism diagnosis and other characteristics (for example, play, communication, and social skills; and IQ) that may affect treatment outcomes whenever possible to aid practitioners and other researchers in identifying appropriate classroom interventions. This information may also contribute to the further development of individual behavioral profiles that are predictive of treatment outcomes.[90]

- Given the large body of research involving young children with ASD, researchers should adapt and systematically evaluate the use of intervention strategies that have proven efficacy for this population for use with older students.

This chapter was funded in part by a grant from the University of Wisconsin-Madison, Wisconsin Alumni Research Foundation.

Summary and Synthesis

The educational needs of young children, school-age children, and adolescents with autism are described in Part One. A common theme depicted throughout Chapters One and Two is the need to promote the well-being and meet the educational needs of children with autism by recognizing and bridging the gap between research and practice to align what is known and ultimately what is done in classroom contexts. Although the mission of school practice is often to promote academic achievement, Chapter Two discusses the evidence that academic skills must be addressed in the context of understanding the symptoms of autism, such as those pertaining to joint attention skills, imitation skills, challenging behaviors, adaptive behaviors, communication, as well as leisure and social skills. Social impairment—a hallmark symptom of autism—affects children with autism in the context of classroom learning, and autism may be conceptualized as a social learning disability. This construct is described in detail in Chapter One and depicts the relevance of understanding the social deficits in children with autism that distinguish their behavior in an illustration of the social attention model of autism. Further, in order to understand the diversity among these children, it is important for classroom teachers to consider them as individuals, recognizing that they encompass a wide range of abilities, idiosyncrasies, and personalities. This approach of engaging children with autism as *individuals* provides the fundamental and necessary building blocks for providing optimal educational settings.

Given the diversity among children with autism, teachers and professionals need to consider the effects of autism on learning, as well as how the social learning disability perspective can both inform and improve educational interventions. Although we currently do not understand why and how autism affects the trajectory of social and joint attention, evidence in the research literature suggests two possible hypotheses: the interconnectivity hypothesis and the social motivation hypothesis. Understanding the conceptual underpinnings of these hypotheses can provide effective principles of instruction, helping educators create instructional opportunities that recognize the interests of the child and use these interests as a mechanism to increase the child's engagement in social learning. Students with autism exhibit a biologically based difficulty with motivation, and often lack the ability to adopt a common frame of reference and focus of shared attention with teachers and peers. Without specific targeted interventions, therefore, issues of frustration and off-task attention as well as self-regulation difficulties may become marked patterns of classroom behavior. Although children may be most affected by interventions occurring within periods of rapid brain growth during the preschool period, it is known that another major period of neural plasticity occurs between eight and eighteen years of age. The elementary and secondary school years, which are associated with significant changes in cognitive, executive, and social competencies, constitute a sensitive period for effective educational interventions. For example, some of these interventions have been shown to lead to improved writing and math task performance, encouraging students with autism to initiate and express their academic interests by making choices using pivotal response approaches and cueing students to focus on particular referents to improve their attention during reading comprehension activities. Although children with autism express different patterns of interests that guide their attention in classroom environments, teacher-led interventions that focus on integrating their patterns of interests to cultivate shared interests are necessary. Attenuating their off-task attention to academic shared-interest tasks appears to be a component that is critical to implementing effective classroom interventions.

Targeted curricular areas have been described and the effectiveness of interventions has been reviewed in many empirical studies on teaching both academic and social skills to children with autism. Although some intervention strategies are designed to be used within specific curricular areas, Chapter Two describes how the majority of intervention strategies are commonly implemented across curricular areas. These include antecedent manipulations, behavioral teaching strategies, self-management strategies, instructional delivery modification, naturalistic or social-emotional instruction, peer instruction, reinforcement-based strategies, and technologically enhanced strategies. The effectiveness and utility of these interventions can also be measured using self-management strategies that allow the teacher to understand the causal relationship between the provided intervention and the individual with autism's performance. Teachers can teach pivotal behaviors that serve as key indicators to improve overall levels of reinforcement and motivation and enhance learning and systematic instructional contexts. Effective intervention strategies—whether implemented through naturalistic, targeted, or direct instruction—incorporate the principles of systematic instruction. Teachers should use these principles to guide intervention approaches while monitoring student performance to determine the success of the implementation of strategies and the overall efficacy of these interventions in the classroom.

PART TWO Educational Best
Practices and
Interventions
for Children
with Autism

Educational Interventions for Children with Autism Spectrum Disorders

Marianne L. Barton and Deborah Fein

The history of educational intervention in autism has been shaped by the evolution of conceptual models and practices in two parallel fields. In the field of psychiatry, changes in the conceptualization of autism spectrum disorders (ASD), their diagnostic criteria, and their prevalence rates have directly affected the extent and nature of educational services. In the field of education, changes in instructional practices have dramatically affected the ways in which educators provide services to these children. We will consider these parallel lines of development to provide a context in which to examine educational treatments for children with autism and the data available in support of these interventions.

BRIEF HISTORY OF ASD

A distinct syndrome called autism was first identified in 1943 by Leo Kanner,[1] who described a group of eleven children with a striking profile of social and behavioral features, including "autistic aloneness" and insistence on sameness. Kanner believed autism to be distinct from intellectual disability and language disorders, a view which probably influenced diagnostic conceptualizations of the syndrome. In the same year the Austrian physician Hans Asperger published a paper in which he described a group of children with similar characteristics, although Asperger's work was not translated into English until many years later. Kanner noted "disturbances of affective contact" in the infancies of the children he described, and he alluded to atypical social presentations in their parents as well.[2] He argued that the atypical behaviors he observed seemed likely to be rooted in an innate inability to form emotional relationships with others, suggesting a biological model for the syndrome, but the prevailing view of mental disorders at the time was rooted in traditional psychoanalytic theory and favored a psychogenic model. As a result, autism came to be defined as a disorder of maternal deprivation occasioned by the emotional coldness of mothers, referred to as "refrigerator mothers."[3] That conceptual model of autism led to treatment based on psychoanalytic principles, and in its most extreme form required the complete separation of the child from his or her mother for extended periods of time.

In the early 1960s a variety of studies directly challenged the prevailing psychoanalytic models. Rimland[4] argued that autism is a neurodevelopmental disorder and that many of the symptoms of autism can be understood as resulting from developmental processes gone awry. Among the evidence in support of this view were the frequent co-occurrence of seizure disorders and the very high incidence of intellectual disability in the population of children with autism. Equally important, a series of studies of parenting style revealed no significant differences between the parents of children with autism and the parents of typically developing children.[5] That marked the beginning of a radical shift in our understanding of autism that directly influenced ideas about treatment. If autism could be understood as a neurodevelopmental disorder with a clear presentation, biological origins, and a long-term course, treatment might be defined as largely educational, and not psychiatric in nature. Intervention might include a variety of behavioral strategies based on traditional learning theory, as well as strategies based on models of typical social-emotional development.

CHANGES IN THE PREVALENCE OF ASD

Autism was initially regarded as a rare condition, estimated to occur in 4 in 10,000 children; today autism is believed to occur in about 1 in

110 youngsters.[6] Although it is not possible to rule out the possibility that there has been a real increase in the incidence of autism spectrum disorders, there are conflicting reports regarding the evidence of increase as well as potential causes for the rise in incidence. Investigations of many environmental factors, including the widespread use of vaccines, have revealed no association between known environmental factors and an increased incidence of autism spectrum disorders. Instead, the increase in incidence rates seems most closely associated with changes in the diagnostic criteria for the disorder and growing public and professional awareness of ASD.[7] Autism is defined solely on the basis of observed behaviors. As a result, as diagnostic methods change and definitions of the disorder evolve, changes in incidence rates can be expected.

Autism was initially described as a single syndrome until 1987, when it was defined as one of several related conditions called pervasive developmental disorders (PDD). That view recognized increasing variability in both the kinds of symptoms required for diagnosis of the disorder and the severity of those symptoms. The broad category of PDD included the most severe form of the disorder, known as autistic disorder, and a milder variant, called pervasive developmental disorder-not otherwise specified (PDD-NOS). The boundaries of the spectrum were further broadened with the publication of the *Diagnostic and Statistical Manual of Mental Disorders* (DSM-IV) in 1994,[8] such that some children who once might have been considered intellectually disabled now fell under the broader rubric of pervasive developmental disorders. Asperger syndrome was also added to the DSM in 1994, and as a result children with much less severe social symptoms and without significant language delays were included in the broad category of PDD.

Although DSM-IV remains the diagnostic standard, autism is now conceptualized as a spectrum of disorders, and many clinicians no longer attempt to make distinctions among the specific disorders included under the broad rubric of pervasive developmental disorders, now more often called autism spectrum disorders. The DSM will include further changes to the conceptualization of autism spectrum disorders and may eliminate specific subcategories under the broader diagnosis of ASD.

Along with changes to diagnostic systems, the past twenty years have witnessed dramatic growth in the number of parent and professional organizations designed to support children with ASD and their families. Those groups have contributed to increased awareness of autism spectrum disorders in the professional community as well as concurrent efforts to screen for ASD in younger children and subsequently provide early diagnosis and treatment. Those efforts have also contributed to the increase in reported incidence of autism as well as to an increased need for educators to provide intensive and effective interventions.

CHANGES IN EDUCATIONAL PRACTICES

Changes in psychiatric practices coincided with changes in the field of education. In the 1960s the few children diagnosed with an autism spectrum disorder were treated in special education classrooms, either in public school settings or, more often, in private facilities, and few services were designed specifically for children with autism spectrum disorders. Many children with severe developmental disabilities, including ASD, were treated in residential facilities, where they grew into adulthood. In school settings, most children with special education needs were educated in self-contained classrooms and had little contact with typically developing peers. Beginning in the 1970s those practices began to change. In the early 1970s several educational models were developed specifically for children with autism and related disabilities.

In 1975 the passage of the Education for All Handicapped Children Act mandated that every child is entitled to a free and appropriate public education, and that such education must be provided in the least restrictive environment in which the child can learn. In the years that followed, children with special needs were moved to inclusion classrooms, in which educators sometimes had limited support and limited understanding of the modifications these children might require to learn successfully. Children with autism sometimes struggled to use the opportunities available in inclusion classrooms, in part because their social deficits left them less able to engage with typically developing peers, while their sensory, language, and attention difficulties left them less able to learn in the typical classroom setting.

In 1997 the Individuals with Disabilities Education Act (IDEA) mandated that students with ASD (and all students with disabilities) have access to the general education curriculum. Today only a small minority of children with ASD attend special schools or residential facilities. Many children with ASD are educated in inclusion classrooms, although nearly 40 percent spend more than 60 percent of their day in separate classes.[9]

Although many educators make modifications to the general classroom for children with ASD, specialized services are often provided outside of the inclusion classroom, and there is considerable variation in the amount of time children with ASD spend with typically developing peers. The specification of the most appropriate setting for instruction remains a topic of debate among both educators and parents, and is likely to vary as the child moves through school.

For many children, inclusion is more successful in the earlier grades, in which they are better able to keep pace with academic and social demands. For other children, especially high-functioning children, full inclusion may be appropriate through high school, with limited specialized services (for example, social skills training) provided in addition to classroom modifications. For some children, placement in inclusion classrooms requires the help of an instructional assistant to facilitate their participation in educational activities.

> The role of paraprofessionals has also become a topic of some debate, as educators attempt to balance a child's need for individualized support with the danger of promoting dependence on adults or limiting the child's access to the classroom environment.[10]

In 2004 the reauthorization of IDEA mandated that educators implement evidence-based intervention strategies that have been supported by the National Standards on Evidence Based Practices.[11] Before turning to the literature on empirically supported educational interventions, we will briefly discuss the challenges presented by children with ASD as they move through the education system.

ASD IN THE SCHOOL-AGE POPULATION: IMPLICATIONS FOR INTERVENTIONS

The population of students identified as having ASD not only is much larger and more heterogeneous than it once was but also includes children who are currently more visible in regular education classroom settings. Early studies of the cognitive development of children with autism suggested that 75 percent of children with autism functioned in the intellectually disabled range of cognitive ability;[12] current estimates put that figure at 40 percent.[13] Some children function very well academically and experience more difficulties with adaptive and social skills. In part, the increased heterogeneity reflects the changes in diagnostic criteria and specifically the inclusion of children with milder forms of ASD. These data may also reflect improvements in outcomes attributable to increased early detection of the disorder and increased access to early intervention.

Although all children with ASD present difficulties in the three domains that define the disorder (impaired reciprocal social interaction, impaired language, and restricted or repetitive interests or behaviors), the severity of these difficulties is highly variable. In addition, these difficulties are expressed in very different ways in children of different ages. For instance, in preschool-age children, social difficulties may be manifest in a lack of eye contact and social referencing, in the failure to establish a shared focus of interest (joint attention), and in limited interest or engagement in social games and routines. Very young children may exhibit little interest in interacting with peers and prefer to remain engaged in self-absorbed activity. However, as children enter school and move through the elementary school years, social difficulties are more likely to appear. Some of these issues present themselves in the following ways:

- Difficulty initiating and maintaining relationships with peers
- An inability to engage in reciprocal social exchanges (for example, turn-taking)
- An inability to understand or infer another's perspective
- A lack of awareness of nonverbal communication or social norms

Often children with ASD in elementary school exhibit greater interest in peers than they did as preschoolers, but they may lack the skills required to interact successfully. As children with ASD reach middle school age and social demands increase, their atypical presentation may make them more vulnerable to social exclusion, ridicule, and bullying—experiences that can compound their sense of social isolation.

> Boutot and Dukes[14] suggest that the heterogeneity of children with ASD dictates that teachers use a multitheoretical approach, focusing heavily on behavioral methods. A multitheoretical approach integrates empirically supported tools from multiple approaches to design intervention programs based on each child's individualized needs and responses to intervention. Such programs are not eclectic in that they do not represent a collection of disparate and often unrelated instructional methods. Instead they are most usefully viewed as integrative in that teachers incorporate a variety of strategies in a cohesive model that addresses specific needs and measurable goals.

Some researchers have argued that school-age children with ASD present a variety of behavioral and neuropsychological characteristics, in addition to those required for the diagnosis, that clearly affect their ability to function in the classroom. For instance, many children with ASD have significant attention problems, such that attention deficit hyperactivity disorder and ASD are often diagnosed as comorbid conditions.[15] Further, school-age children with ASD often struggle with organization, which makes keeping track of schoolwork and managing transitions particularly challenging.[16] Sensory processing issues appear to be very common in children with ASD, and these may affect their ability to ignore extraneous information in the classroom setting.[17] All of these emotional, social, and behavioral concerns are likely to affect a child's ability to respond to educational opportunities and require attention, accommodation, and flexibility on the part of educators.

EDUCATIONAL INTERVENTIONS FOR CHILDREN WITH ASD

Recently, several groups have reviewed the available evidence regarding educational treatments for children with autism in order to provide recommendations for parents and educators. Several authors have proposed that treatment approaches should be divided into comprehensive treatment models and specific intervention practices in an effort to clarify the intervention strategies being evaluated:

- *Comprehensive treatment models* are defined as "conceptually organized packages of practices and components designed to address a broad array of skills and abilities for children with ASD and their families."[18] Such models should be well specified and clearly replicable.
- *Focused intervention strategies* are individual instructional strategies that teachers or other staff use to teach specific skills and concepts to children with ASD. These practices may be used in a variety of settings and should have a strong basis of research support.

Several authors have proposed criteria for identifying evidence-based practices.[19] For example, intervention models must have been tested in children diagnosed with ASD using clearly specified and replicable dependent measures. In addition, there must be clear evidence that the intervention was followed by gains in targeted skills, and research must be sufficiently rigorous to ascertain that the changes noted are attributable to the intervention. Further, the most desirable research designs include studies with a clearly specified control group and random assignment of individuals. On the basis of these and similar standards, reviewers classify instructional methods as efficacious if they have been supported by several rigorous and well-controlled studies.

Intervention tools that have received support from less rigorous studies are regarded as promising or emerging treatments. In the absence of such studies, data from a series of single case studies carried out by researchers may be regarded as emerging evidence of effectiveness. Still other treatments are identified as lacking in empirical support or as ineffective.

In their recent review of the literature on evidence-based comprehensive treatment models for children with ASD, Rogers and Vismara[20] identified several models that show clear evidence of efficacy, or success when implemented in carefully controlled clinical trials, including the following:

- Early Start Denver Model[21]
- Learning Experiences: Alternative Program for Preschoolers and Parents (LEAP)[22]

- Lovaas Institute[23]
- May Institute[24]
- Princeton Child Development Institute[25]

Notably, all of the models identified have a strong behavioral component.

Odom and colleagues[26] evaluated models using criteria that were slightly different from those of the Rogers and Vismara study,[27] but they arrived at an identical group of efficacious programs. They also described a larger group of programs that seem promising based on limited data (Autism Partnerships; Center for Autism and Related Disorders; Children's Toddler Program; Douglass; Developmental, Individual Difference, Relationship-based [DIR, or Floortime] Model; pivotal response treatment; responsive teaching; Social Communication, Emotional Regulation, and Transactional Support [SCERTS]; and Treatment and Education of Autistic and Communication related handicapped CHildren [TEACCH]), and still others that are poorly operationalized, have limited outcome data, have not been replicated, or show little evidence of effectiveness (Hanen, Higashi, Eden, Summit, Lancaster, and Son Rise).

National Professional Development Center on Autism Spectrum Disorders

In 2007 the U.S. Department of Education founded the National Professional Development Center on Autism Spectrum Disorders (NPDC on ASD) to review the available data on specific intervention strategies for children with ASD. Odom and colleagues[28] report on the data collected by the NPDC on ASD and identify twenty-four strategies that they label as evidence-based practices based on well-designed research. Several of these, such as prompting and reinforcement, have received empirical support as specific strategies and also are components of more complex evidence-based practices, such as discrete trial training. Similarly, although positive behavioral support is included in the list, so are many of the components of positive behavioral support interventions, such as functional behavior assessments.

National Standards Project

In 2009 the National Autism Center completed the National Standards Project (NSP).[29] The NSP was an effort to articulate a set of standards for effective education and behavioral treatment for children with ASD and resulted in a comprehensive review of the data in support of educational interventions for children with autism. Researchers reviewed both comprehensive treatment programs and specific instructional strategies. The NSP identified eleven interventions as "established" based on rigorous research criteria. Of these, two-thirds were developed from the behavioral literature, including a range of strategies associated with applied behavior analysis. The NSP also identified twenty-two intervention models that have received some empirical support and that are therefore classified as emerging treatments, deserving of further study. Finally, they listed five treatment models that have not been shown to be effective in treating children with autism. These include traditional academic interventions, auditory integration training, facilitated communication, gluten- and casein-free diets, and sensory integration therapy.

THE MODELS

Although it is not possible to review all of the available treatment models for children with ASD, we will present a selective review of evidence-based models most often used in educational settings, which include TEACCH, behavioral intervention models, and cognitive developmental models.

TEACCH

One of the earliest comprehensive programs to focus services on children with autism and related conditions was TEACCH, established in 1972 at the University of North Carolina. The TEACCH model is based on the assertion that children and adults with autism share a unique pattern of neuropsychological strengths and weaknesses.[30]

The premise of the intervention, known as structured teaching, is focused on four broad strategies:

- Attempting to provide an environmental structure that supports the child's ability to understand environmental cues and function independently

- Using visual strengths to compensate for weaknesses in other areas of functioning
- Using the child's special interests to provide motivation to learn a variety of skills
- Supporting self-initiated and meaningful communication

Each of these components has been evaluated in a variety of studies, and there is a considerable base of empirical support for each of them.[31] There have been fewer studies of the TEACCH program as a comprehensive intervention model, and some of the early studies of the model are limited by methodological flaws. Nonetheless, many of the specific strategies designed and tested in TEACCH are widely used in classrooms.

A recent study[32] compared the effectiveness of the TEACCH model when implemented in a residential treatment center, the TEACCH model when implemented in an inclusion classroom, and a third nonspecific treatment model. Results revealed no differences between the two TEACCH models and clear superiority of both of those to the nonspecific model. The authors argue that these data demonstrate the utility of applying TEACCH strategies in inclusion classrooms. Both the National Standards Project[33] and the National Professional Development Center[34] identified several TEACCH strategies, including the use of visual schedules, in their group of empirically supported instructional methods.

Behavioral Intervention Models

The most common intervention models for children with ASD, and those about which the most data are available, are models based on behavioral intervention principles.

Applied Behavior Analysis

Boutot and Hume[35] point out that although the term *applied behavior analysis* (ABA) is commonly applied to these programs, there is considerable misunderstanding about the term's meaning. ABA is often mistakenly assumed to refer only to discrete trial instruction, when in fact it includes a much broader range of behavioral techniques, many of which are used in naturalistic settings.

Dillenburger[36] notes that ABA simply represents the application of the science of learning and behavior change to the education of children with ASD. The essential elements of ABA are to identify, define, and measure target behaviors to be created, increased, or decreased; identify environmental variables that currently sustain or interfere with these behaviors; and then put in place procedures to generalize and maintain these behaviors. Thus ABA includes not only the application of behavioral principles (reinforcement, prompting, and so on) but also the careful assessment of any relationship between those methods and learning or behavior change.

Discrete Trial Training

Discrete trial training (DTT) refers to a highly structured, adult-directed teaching format that includes a teacher prompt, a behavioral response from the student, and an attendant reinforcement from the teacher. The method is often used to teach discrete behavioral responses, such as following a directive or labeling objects, and it was among the first to be used successfully with children with autism.

In 1987 Ivar Lovaas published a controlled intervention study demonstrating that 47 percent of the children who received intensive behavioral intervention (approximately forty hours weekly of individual, discrete trial training for a period of at least two years) made dramatic gains in both cognitive skills and social functioning, such that they no longer met criteria for an autism diagnosis.[37] Children in a control group, who received ten hours weekly of services, made much less progress. The Lovaas study was pivotal for several reasons:

- It demonstrated the effectiveness of discrete trial instruction as a treatment for autism, a condition previously viewed as largely untreatable.
- It demonstrated that intensity of treatment was critical to successful outcomes.
- It suggested that with highly intensive treatment a sizable minority of children could be expected to "recover" from autism, an assertion that has been used to justify the provision of intensive services to children with ASD and that continues to be debated.

Lovaas's data were questioned on several methodological grounds.[38] The children in his sample were more homogeneous and probably higher functioning than many children with ASD. Different IQ tests were used at pre- and post-treatment assessments, making direct comparison difficult. Children were not randomly assigned to intervention or control groups, and the treatment was administered in a clinical setting, which cannot be assumed to reflect the realities of public school classrooms.

In response to those concerns, several researchers replicated Lovaas's work and reported similar, though less dramatic findings.[39] Smith, Groen, and Wynn[40] replicated Lovaas's model in a study that included the random assignment of children to intensive treatment and to less intensive treatment. Participants in the Smith et al. study had lower IQ scores at pretest than the children in Lovaas's study, and the study included children with autistic disorder as well as the milder PDD-NOS, a distinction that was not made in the earlier study. The authors documented significant gains in IQ in the treatment group, as compared to much more modest gains in the control group, but most children in the treatment group continued to function in the intellectually disabled range, and only two of fifteen children achieved "best outcome" status. Furthermore, treatment effects for those children who initially presented more severe and pervasive symptoms of autism were quite limited, such that children with an early diagnosis of autism were very similar posttreatment to children with an early diagnosis of autism in the control group.

These results, and others like them, provide further support for the efficacy of intensive behavioral treatment. At the same time, they suggest that early hopes for "recovery" may be misleading. More recent studies have suggested that a small proportion (3 to 25 percent) of children provided with intensive early intervention services may progress sufficiently that they no longer meet criteria for a diagnosis on the autism spectrum, but those gains are likely to be heavily mediated by child characteristics.[41]

Lovaas's method has also been criticized on conceptual grounds. Discrete trial training is highly effective at teaching specific skills, but those skills may not generalize to new settings unless generalization is taught specifically. Furthermore, some authors argue that although DTT is highly effective for many purposes, it may not be an optimal choice for teaching the full range of adaptive and functional skills children with autism must acquire. Equally important, DTT itself does not address the negative behaviors that can interfere with successful learning in children with autism.[42]

None of these criticisms alters the fact that discrete trial training is highly effective at teaching specific skills. They simply suggest that DTT may be best viewed as one part of a comprehensive ABA program that includes generalization practice, positive behavioral support, and the use of behavioral methods in naturalistic settings.

HOW MUCH INTERVENTION TIME IS REQUIRED?

A question that has generated considerable debate concerns the amount of intervention time required to achieve optimal results. Following Lovaas's model,[43] many practitioners have argued that ABA must be provided for forty hours weekly to be effective. However, several studies have suggested that less intensive programs are also effective, but the gains reported are not as dramatic as those attained by Lovaas. In the Smith et al. study,[44] the researchers reported significant gains in the children provided with twenty-five hours of intervention weekly but much less dramatic progress than reported in the original Lovaas study. Similarly, Eldevick, Eikeseth, Jahr, and Smith[45] compared a treatment group receiving low-intensity (twelve hours weekly) direct trial training to a control group and found significant gains in the treatment group, but not the dramatic progress Lovaas described.

It is difficult to assess the meaning of these data because the children in the later studies were more heterogeneous and lower-functioning at the outset of treatment than the children in the original Lovaas study. Sheinkopf and Siegel[46] found no relationship between intensity of services above twenty-five hours weekly and outcomes, but in their study, children's functioning prior to treatment was the most significant predictor of outcomes.

In a study that evaluated discrete trial instruction in the home setting in a short-term model, Reed, Osborne, and Corness[47] reported that although children in the high-intensity group (twenty to forty hours weekly) generally made greater gains than children in the low-intensity group (ten to twenty hours weekly), those differences were not always statistically significant. Further, Reed et al. note that differences in intensity *within* the high-intensity group (for example, above twenty to twenty-five hours) were not associated with differential outcomes.

Although it seems clear that programs offering twenty-five hours weekly or more are much more effective than less intensive services, no studies to date have reported differential outcomes associated with variations in treatment intensity above twenty-five hours. Thus it is unclear if increasing intensity above twenty-five hours weekly is associated with improved outcomes. Additional research is needed to answer definitively the question of how much intervention time is required, and the answer may well vary for individual children. There is greater clarity in the empirical research to date regarding the duration of treatment, with several studies suggesting that effective treatment should last at least two years.[48]

Positive Behavioral Support

In addition to discrete trial training, a variety of empirically supported behavioral methods now make up the arsenal of intervention strategies for children with autism. Positive behavioral support is a multitiered approach that uses behavioral strategies to address challenging or interfering behaviors in children with ASD; it has been identified as an evidence-based practice for this purpose.[49] Positive behavioral support includes a variety of evidence-based strategies designed to support students in a classroom setting, supplemented by specific strategies, such as the use of functional behavior assessments and functional communication training, designed to reduce negative behaviors. Neitzel[50] reviews the evidence base for the use of positive behavioral support and presents a model for its implementation in classroom settings. She describes a process that begins with the creation of a high-quality classroom environment including environmental modifications designed to prevent the development of negative behaviors. The second stage of her model includes the use of functional behavior assessment to identify the purpose served by maladaptive behaviors and the provision of training to develop alternative skills. Finally, children for whom those levels of intervention are insufficient may be provided with an intensive individualized behavior plan to reduce negative behaviors and teach more functional skills.

Incidental Teaching

Like positive behavioral support, several treatment models use behavioral methods in the context of naturally occurring interactions instead of, or in addition to, highly structured, adult-directed sessions. These more naturalistic efforts were initially derived from an early model known as incidental teaching,[51] in which teachers responded to a child's attempts to communicate in the natural environment by reinforcing and elaborating the child's communications, using a variety of prompts and modeling strategies. Proponents of incidental teaching often alter the child's environment to provide frequent opportunities for communication in an effort to obtain desired objects or activities, and use interaction in the natural environment to practice generalizing skills taught in more structured settings.[52]

Pivotal Response Treatment

Many of the principles of incidental teaching were later modified through the addition of more carefully defined behavioral principles and labeled the natural language paradigm.[53] More recently the model has been elaborated further as pivotal response treatment (PRT).[54] PRT employs behavioral strategies, including careful specification of antecedent cues, modeling, reinforcement, and practice of previously mastered skills to facilitate language development in the context of child-initiated interaction in the natural environment. PRT has received considerable support from rigorous empirical investigations and is considered to be an evidence-based practice.[55]

DISCRETE TRIALS VERSUS NATURALISTIC BEHAVIORAL INTERVENTION

In an oft-cited review, Delprato[56] described ten studies in which discrete trial training was compared to behavioral intervention provided in the context of naturally occurring interactions. Delprato concluded that in all of the relevant studies, instruction in the context of natural routines was more effective than discrete trial instruction alone at facilitating language development. The data reviewed by Delprato is specific to language development and may suggest a larger gap between discrete trial and more naturalistic approaches than actually exists. Most interventions employed in a naturalistic context rely heavily on behavioral principles. Furthermore, modern ABA therapy done by well-trained and skilled therapists places a great deal of emphasis on stimulating positive affect in the child, and on creating a relationship between therapist and child that is infused with positive affect. This not only increases the child's motivation to learn but also stimulates the child's potential for deeper and more meaningful relationships with others in his or her life. Thus the distinction between ABA (when done well) and naturalistic or developmental models is not the clear boundary that it used to be.

Cognitive Developmental Models

Coincident with increased attention to behavior analytic intervention models, a second tradition in the field of educational intervention for children with autism spectrum disorders emerged from research on language development and social-emotional functioning in very young children. Models in this tradition are often labeled cognitive developmental models, and they address broad skills, such as emotion sharing, that are presumed to underlie behavior change.

Cognitive developmental models are strongly rooted in normative child development theory and include a focus on emotional functioning and relationships with caregivers. They also highlight the provision of environmental supports to facilitate children's emotional and communicative functioning.

These models include the DIR, or Floortime Model, developed by Stanley Greenspan and his colleagues,[57] and SCERTS.[58]

Note: Relationship development intervention[59] is also a cognitive developmental model, but because it is primarily a parent-training program it will not be considered here.

Cognitive developmental models are based on empirically supported principles, such as the recognition that in typically developing children, language emerges in the context of meaningful interactions with caregivers. However, critics argue that the unique deficits presented by children with ASD may render those principles insufficient in teaching children with ASD. Indeed, one model of autism[60] suggests that an initial neurological insult exerts its developmental effect by impairing the ability of children with ASD to make use of the experiences that support typical development. Such a conceptual view suggests that although there may be a role for cognitive developmental models in the treatment of children with ASD, such models may not be sufficient to reestablish normative developmental trajectories without the structure and support provided by behavioral methods. In some cases, components of cognitive developmental models have been supported by well-designed research.[61] The models themselves, however, have not been evaluated in controlled studies.

Floortime

The first cognitive developmental model to receive national attention was Floortime, proposed by Stanley Greenspan and Serena Weider. Floortime is a less structured approach that focuses on engaging the child in communicative exchanges and play-based interactions. It is designed primarily for use with young children, and the few studies of the model have been limited to toddlers and preschoolers. The largest study of Floortime was conducted by Greenspan and Weider[62] and included a chart review of two hundred children diagnosed with an autism spectrum disorder or a related but milder disorder known as multi-system developmental disorder (MSDD). Because the MSDD diagnosis is no longer used, it is difficult to fully characterize the children treated by this intervention. The authors report that 58 percent of the children made marked progress such that they no longer met diagnostic criteria for an ASD diagnosis. The authors also note that there was no comparison with other methods, nor was there any attempt to randomize assignment to treatment, and that both factors limit the generalizability of their findings. More rigorous investigations of the model have not been reported. Although these early data may suggest that Floortime offers some promise as an intervention tool, it clearly has not received the kind of empirical investigation that would support its widespread use. Equally important, the model lacks a well-specified curriculum, making consistent implementation difficult.

SCERTS

SCERTS is a multidisciplinary approach to treatment based on a social pragmatic model of communication development. The model focuses on three
broad goals: the development of social communication (SC) skills beginning
with gesture, the development of self-monitoring skills to support emotional
regulation (ER) and consistent engagement with others, and the use of transactional supports (TS) in the environment to facilitate consistent functioning and
promote generalization of skills. SCERTS is defined by its authors[63] as a conceptual framework that permits educators to integrate multiple specific strategies
into an intervention plan. The model includes careful specification of goals and
consistent data collection, and may incorporate behavioral strategies, including
the use of discrete trials, as well as more naturalistic tools. Although efficacy data
is limited to date, several studies are currently under way to evaluate the model.

Early Start Denver Model

The Early Start Denver Model (EDSM) is similar to the SCERTS program in that
it was designed in the cognitive developmental tradition but also includes behavioral methods. In a recent evaluation of the model, Dawson et al.[64] report on
forty-eight children ages eighteen to thirty months who were randomly assigned
to either the ESDM program or community-based intervention for a period of
two years. Treatment services were provided in the natural environment (children's homes) by trained staff and by parents for approximately twenty-five
hours per week. The results indicate that children in the ESDM program showed
significant gains in IQ and adaptive functioning relative to the children in the
control group, and that children in the ESDM program were more likely to shift
from a diagnosis of autism to the less severe diagnosis of PDD-NOS than were
children in the control group.

The Dawson et al. study is significant for several reasons:

- It is among the most methodologically rigorous trials of early intervention yet
  reported.
- It provides clear support for the efficacy of early intervention.
- It demonstrates the meaningful integration of behavioral strategies into a relationship-focused, affectively based model.

There are limitations in the data presented: for example, the teaching model proceeds from naturalistic teaching of a targeted skill with no extrinsic reinforcer, to the use of extrinsic reinforcers (if insufficient progress is made), to the use of massed trials. However, the percentage of children who proceeded along the steps in the model to massed trials or to the use of extrinsic reinforcers is not reported. Therefore, the effectiveness of the different elements of teaching is difficult to gauge.

PROBLEMS WITH ESTABLISHING THE EFFICACY OF MODELS

Odom and colleagues[65] provide a striking critique of the available literature on educational interventions for children with ASD. First, they note that evidence of efficacy is minimal. Only fourteen of the thirty models they describe had published evidence of efficacy in peer-reviewed journals, and in many cases the data in support of the model were quite limited. Furthermore, very few authors attempted to assess the fidelity with which models are implemented. Odom and colleagues describe the difficulty of completing randomized controlled trials, and they also cite a need for careful research that might inform treatment decisions earlier in the process of implementation. In addition, there are few studies that assess the efficacy of intervention for school-age children (as compared to younger children), and even fewer that evaluate outcomes among adolescents. Such ongoing issues as the heterogeneity of the population of children with ASD and the need to identify child characteristics that mediate intervention effects also pose significant obstacles to research progress.

MOVING INTERVENTIONS FROM THE CLINIC TO THE PUBLIC SCHOOL

The difficulties that plague research on treatment outcomes in the clinical setting are significant, but the challenges of implementing evidence-based intervention strategies in public school settings are even more daunting. Despite the fact that many of the intervention models described here are widely used in classroom settings, few studies have looked at their effectiveness there or in the treatment of school-age children.

Eikeseth et al.[66] provide an exception in their study of four- to seven-year-olds who received intensive behavioral intervention (discrete trial training) in the classroom setting. Children in the treatment group received about thirty hours weekly of individual behavioral treatment, supplemented by parent training and placement in a regular education classroom. Children in the control group received individual instruction in an eclectic model. They also participated in an inclusion classroom, but their parents did not receive parent training. At the end of one year, children in the treatment group had made significantly more progress than children in the comparison group, although there were no significant differences in posttest scores between the two groups. This study is helpful in supporting the application of clinic-based treatment methods to the educational settings in which they are likely to be delivered. It also suggests that intensive treatment is effective for older children.

Studies such as this one are critical to assessing the extent to which the promise of models tested in carefully controlled settings will carry over to the less controlled setting of the public school. Although there are several model programs for children with ASD in place in public school settings (for example, in Lancaster, Pennsylvania; Denver; Philadelphia; and Bergen County, New Jersey), efforts to evaluate these programs are just beginning.

Shin, Stahmer, Marcus, & Mandell[67] reported on a randomized controlled study of classroom-based intervention in a large urban school district. They studied 178 children in thirty-nine kindergarten through second-grade classrooms. Classroom teachers were randomly assigned to receive training in structured teaching (ST) or in the Strategies for Teaching based on Autism Research (STAR) program, an ABA-based program that provides individual sessions of discrete trial training and pivotal response treatment in the context of functional classroom routines. The results suggest that students in the STAR program achieved marginally larger gains in IQ scores than did students in the ST Model, but the results did not reach statistical significance.

The authors[68] note that there was a significant interaction between treatment model success and teacher experience. Among teachers with less than three years of experience, there were minimal differences between the two programs; both groups of children gained approximately eight points in IQ scores. Among teachers with more experience, students in STAR classrooms gained more than twelve IQ points, as compared to gains of about three points for children in structured teaching classrooms.

Subsequent analyses of additional data from the same study suggest that efforts to assess the fidelity of implementation of the two methods are critical to understanding outcome data. Teachers were filmed monthly in order to gauge the fidelity of implementation of each model. Only 50 percent of teachers using the ST model were willing to implement the program on taping days (as compared to 100 percent of STAR teachers), and even among those willing to implement the model only 40 percent met the criteria for overall fidelity of implementation.[69]

> Clearly, treatment fidelity is critical both to effective implementation of intervention programs and to meaningful efforts to evaluate the effectiveness of the programs in community settings.

It is possible that adherence to treatment models is especially important for less experienced teachers, who may have fewer intervention strategies at their disposal. Dingfelder and colleagues[70] suggest that teacher implementation of evidence-based practices may be related to the extent to which teachers believe that doing so is expected and rewarded by administrators and other classroom staff. They also describe numerous challenges to the implementation of evidence-based practices in public school classrooms. These include limited time available for staff training, unanticipated changes in classroom staff, and inconsistent communication with administrators.

The limitations described as challenges to the implementation of evidence-based practices are highly consistent with reports from educators and clinicians charged with implementing evidence-based practices in public school classrooms. Most treatment models require intensive training to implement successfully, and those with less detailed manuals and procedures require even more training and staff support. Typically educators have little training in ASD or in intervention models specific to autism.

Further, some studies have suggested that intensive training (up to five days) is associated with improved teacher skills as well as improved student outcomes,[71] but intensive training is expensive to provide, making it especially difficult to offer in the current economic climate. Professional development days may be inadequate for the intensity of training required and are typically too infrequent to permit ongoing monitoring, consultation, or problem solving. Often there is little time in the school day for ongoing supervision or the kind of team-based approach that facilitates problem solving and collaboration. Curricular demands, mandated testing, and time pressures often undermine both the intensity of intervention models and the extent to which they are implemented as intended on a consistent basis. The careful record keeping required to document treatment effectiveness and inform changes in goals and strategies may be seen as an additional demand on instruction time.

> Often teachers seem to feel isolated, lacking in access to experienced mentors or supervisors, and unsupported by administrators and other staff. All of these challenges could be readily addressed with modifications to typical public school practices, but those require time, money, and a willingness to implement innovative teaching strategies.
>
> Although regularly scheduled team meetings are common in many private settings, they are much less frequent in public school settings. The difficulties presented by children with ASD require teachers to undertake creative problem solving as well as to have a background of knowledge and experience. Teachers should have ongoing and frequent access to professionals with expertise in designing and implementing effective programs for children with ASD so that consultants can facilitate proactive programming.
>
> When teachers feel supported, they are more likely to experience the difficulties posed by their students as challenges rather than as barriers, and they are much more likely to discover and enjoy the many rewards of working with students with ASD.

ASD INTERVENTIONS AND PARENT INVOLVEMENT

Any review of educational interventions for children with ASD would be incomplete without discussion of the role of parents. Parent involvement has long been regarded as a critical component of effective intervention programs for young children with ASD.[72] Parents' involvement enables them to receive support and training, helps them learn to promote their child's generalization of skills, and ensures meaningful collaboration between parents and teachers. Most early intervention programs are family focused, with the result that the transition to the more child-focused setting of the elementary school can be jarring and anxiety provoking for parents. In addition, many children with ASD enter the elementary school system with very limited communication skills, which lends additional importance to establishing reliable communication between home and school. Parents of children with ASD often struggle to obtain an early diagnosis, and those difficulties may be even more pronounced in families of minority status.[73] In addition, parents report very high levels of stress in caring for a child with autism.[74] All of these issues highlight the critical importance of frequent, direct communication between teachers and parents. Increased communication between teachers and parents is associated with shared goals and increased trust[75] as well as with increased parent involvement in instructional programs. Fein and Dunn[76] offer some guidelines and suggestions for facilitating parent-teacher communication.

TO SUM UP

A review of the literature related to educational intervention for children with ASD clearly indicates that despite the many gains educators and researchers have made in this area, there remains much that we do not know. It is clear that behavioral methods have received the most consistent support and should be a significant part of all intervention programs. But no single approach is likely to work for every child with autism,[77] and even the most successful approaches are likely to promote gains in only about 60 to 70 percent of children.[78] There are several models that have received a range of empirical support, but the field of autism research is not yet able to specify which model of treatment works best for a given child.[79] The implementation of all models in the public schools, and the consistent collaboration of families in educational efforts, continue to be significant challenges.

In 2001 the National Research Council[80] reviewed the available data on educational interventions for children with ASD and identified a set of characteristics of high-quality instructional programs. Despite the passage of time, many of these recommendations remain relevant and have been elaborated by some of the research reviewed here:

- Successful intervention must begin early and must be intensive.
- Families must be actively involved in their child's intervention, family involvement should include frequent and direct communication between home and school, and there should be numerous opportunities for parent training.
- Staff should be highly trained in multiple intervention strategies and have specific training in ASD.
- Each child's program should include specific, measurable goals, the progress toward which is regularly assessed.
- Instruction should include systematic teaching based on behavioral strategies and careful attention to generalization and maintenance of skills.
- The instructional environment, including the physical setting, the level of structure provided, and staffing patterns, should be flexible, and instruction should include a mixture of structured intervention and more naturalistic strategies.
- The curriculum should include a focus on communication, academic, and social goals as dictated by the needs of individual children.
- Transitions should be carefully planned and supported.

It is critical that researchers continue to subject intervention strategies to rigorous empirical investigations, and equally critical that consumers, teachers, and parents carefully track students' progress to document the effectiveness of the intervention strategies they test every day.

Finally, educators require specific support to develop and implement more effective interventions for children with ASD:

- Teachers need adequate preparation, sufficient staffing resources, and personal support.
- All teachers who work with children with ASD should have training both in instructional strategies appropriate to this population and in the specific needs of children with ASD. Although in-service training can be helpful, often it is too brief and too limited to address the complex issues presented by children with ASD.

- Educators also need time to meet with team members, expert consultants, and parents to consider and investigate new strategies and to design and implement consistent data collection tools.
- Teachers require consistent encouragement from administrators to implement effective instructional programs.

Improving Educational Interventions for School-Age Children with Autism Without Intellectual Disabilities

Lynn Kern Koegel, Robert L. Koegel, Jenna K. Chin, and Brittany L. Koegel

Outcomes for individuals with autism spectrum disorders (ASD), even those with fewer support needs (sometimes referred to in the literature as those with "high-functioning" autism), are not as favorable as we would like, given the large number of empirically based interventions available. Studies[1] show the following about adults diagnosed in childhood with ASD who were verbal and had an intelligence quotient in the average or close-to-average range:

- Only about one-third were able to live independently or semi-independently.[2]
- About a third experienced depression or anxiety.
- About half maintained paid employment.
- More than half had never had an intimate relationship.
- Almost none were married.

Such poor long-term outcomes may be due, in part, to the fact that developing friendships can be challenging for children with ASD. For example, Bauminger and Shulman[3] found that although most children with autism had at least one mutual friendship, the relationships were rarely initiated by the children themselves. That is, most of the friendships were fostered through the help of others, such as the parent of the child with autism. In contrast, among a matched group of typically developing children, only half of the mothers reported helping their children develop friendships. In addition, children with autism were reported to have friendships that were less stable; met with their friends less often; and engaged in more structured activities, such as board games, with their peers. This is quite different from typically developing children, who were more likely to engage in activities that were less structured, preferring to "hang out," and more frequently went on outings outside of the home with their friends.

Furthermore, without the proper intervention, children with high-functioning autism have been reported to perceive their friendships as less close, less helpful, and less intimate when compared with children who do not have autism.[4] This challenge with friendships may be partially due to social communication issues, as children with high-functioning autism have difficulties with conversational flow and demonstrate fewer friendship-related characteristics, such as goal-directedness and positive affect, when interacting with typical peers.[5]

> Difficulties with social communication and pragmatics appear to have a significant negative effect on friendship development in children with ASD and, consequently, lead to poor short- and long-term outcomes.[6]

This chapter will discuss possible reasons why such poor social prognoses and disappointing long-term outcomes persist, despite the many empirically based interventions available for individuals with ASD. Even successful interventions are often used incorrectly or within the wrong context and are therefore ineffective. Minor modifications, however, appear to change the effectiveness of these interventions dramatically, and this chapter discusses adaptations that can be made when problems occur. It also focuses on possible solutions to these problems by describing not only the range of scientifically sound interventions for implementation in school settings but also likely barriers to effective intervention. Finally, we will provide recommendations for improving the long-term outcomes for individuals diagnosed with ASD.

INCLUDING CHILDREN WITH ASD IN REGULAR CLASSROOMS

A marked change in the education and interventions for children with autism relates to increasing efforts to promote inclusion, particularly in the classroom. In the past when children with autism were segregated in special education classrooms, problems occurred, such as fewer social interactions with typically developing peers[7] and lower academic achievement.[8] More recently, however, students with disabilities, including autism, are less frequently being placed in special education schools and classes and increasingly being taught in regular education classrooms by regular education teachers.[9]

Regular education settings provide ideal environments for interactions with typically developing peers who can serve as role models, provide social support, and assist with interventions. Furthermore, included students with autism demonstrate more positive self-concept, greater self-esteem, more frequent interactions with typical peers, better socialization, and more appropriate classroom behavior.[10]

> Students with autism are able to learn social conventions and skills, which can lead to improved mental health, by modeling their typically developing peers in regular education settings.

An accumulating body of research supports the positive effects of systematically implemented inclusion interventions on socialization and social acceptance by typically developing peers. Not only does inclusion improve the academic and social competence of children with autism,[11] but also their classmates are able to be exposed to—and interact and become friends with—their peers with autism. This exposure can lead to less social isolation and stigmatization for the children with autism, and more accepting views among their peers.[12]

Whitehurst and Howells[13] interviewed typically developing, middle school–age children before and after they participated in a two-year extracurricular project with children with autism. Prior to the project, the students had little knowledge about autism and made remarks that referred to children with disabilities in a "dehumanized" way. Some even showed signs of fear and confusion. Following the two-year project, their perspectives changed, and they demonstrated social acceptance of the students with ASD, showing that the inclusive experience had made a positive difference. This study suggests that inclusion can be a good psychoeducational experience for typical children and can lead to social acceptance of peers with ASD.

Kamps et al.[14] studied 203 typically developing elementary school children who had been involved in social skills groups, academic activities, and peer network activities with children with autism. They interviewed the children about their experiences and their likelihood of engaging in such inclusive activities in the future. When asked what they liked most about the groups, the majority of the responses were related to their social and interpersonal aspects. Almost all students stated that they were certain they would want to be involved in the activities again, and 75 to 96 percent stated that they wanted to engage in more activities with children with autism.

The benefits of inclusion for both children with ASD and their typical peers have been well documented. However, it is also well documented that simple physical integration of students with ASD and typically developing students will not result in quality social relationships.

HELPING STUDENTS DEVELOP SOCIAL RELATIONSHIPS

Purposeful, effective interventions are necessary to avoid the stigmatization, isolation, or teasing of students with autism and to assist these students in the development of social relationships. The data suggest that effective social interventions should include working with the students who are typically developing, as well as the students with autism. Cooper et al.[15] describe the importance of preparing mainstream students for the inclusion of their peers with disabilities. A case study was conducted in two classrooms that had students with autism who were being rejected and isolated by their peers. By educating the classmates on autism and having them realize the strengths of the students with autism, the typically developing students became more accepting.

For instance, the "incessant talking" of one of the students with autism was turned into a positive by having the students realize that he had interesting knowledge on topics he was talking about. A part of the social integration curriculum was having the students create a disposition of care; they were encouraged to "become a hero" through caring for other classmates and resisting giving in to negative peer pressure. Students were then willing to learn techniques to reduce the incessant talking when necessary. When the students provided visual cues, the student with autism learned to stop talking. This intervention improved the attitudes of the typical students in the classroom, and the behavior and acceptance of the students with autism. The students, teacher, and principal all reported positive results as a response to the targeted peer intervention.

> School interventions that include both the typical peers as well as the child with autism are likely to be the most effective.

Interventions to Improve Socialization

Many interventions have been empirically documented to instate and improve socialization in children with ASD, but only when they are implemented in the correct contexts. Some of these interventions involve the active participation of typical peers, and create an environment in which the child with autism has frequent and regular opportunities for socialization.

Circle of Friends or Big Buddy Programs

Circle of Friends (CoF) or Big Buddy programs use peer volunteers who are selected to be paired or grouped with peers with disabilities.[16] CoF often focuses less on teaching skills and behaviors and more on psychoeducation and fostering friendships.

In a review of the literature related to CoF interventions, Greenway[17] lists four components of the small-group intervention (similar steps are taken to establish the whole-class intervention, with the difference of using the target student's entire class rather than select students):

- Establishing prerequisites, such as getting parent approval and the commitment of a staff member to lead a weekly circle
- Encouraging children to take an active role in having a successful circle
- Establishing the circle and choosing an appropriate mix of students
- Meeting weekly in a group to discuss problem solving and self-esteem building

> An essential factor of CoF interventions is to acknowledge the strengths of the child with autism as opposed to his or her weaknesses or difficult behavior.[18]

To implement the CoF, the teacher chooses a group of peers with a range of social skills (so the child with autism does not stand out) and that have a friendship with the child with autism. The CoF is organized as a small group to facilitate giving directions to the students. The children participate in an activity that the child with autism enjoys in order to create motivation. During the activities the teacher encourages the children to engage in verbal behaviors, such as singing or talking with one another. The teacher praises the children who engage verbally during the session. The child's paraprofessional typically attends, but only interrupts sessions if the child with ASD is engaging in disruptive behavior.[19]

Small Peer Groups

Morrison, Kamps, Garcia, and Parker[20] implemented a social intervention that placed children with autism in small peer groups, wherein the peers talked to the children with autism about how to ask appropriate questions, make comments, and improve on other conversational areas. These groups, focused on teaching initiations, helped children with autism increase the length of social interactions and increase their initiations. The peer groups were taught appropriate interactions by their regular education teachers through singing songs, playing games, and participating in regular class activities, and were rewarded when they engaged in verbal interactions. Again, these techniques that recruit groups of typically developing peers can improve socialization for children with autism if they are implemented correctly.[21]

Socialization Scripts

Gonzalez-Lopez and Kamps[22] developed a technique that focused on establishing peer groups to teach socialization to children with ASD using scripts. All children (both typical children and children with autism) were taught by the teachers to greet others, talk about appropriate subjects, use imitation, follow simple instructions, share, take turns, and ask for help. The typical peers were taught to give easy instructions to the children with autism, physically show them what to do if they did not understand the instructions, praise good behavior, and ignore disruptive responses. Results of this methodology suggested that the intervention created more involvement between the children with autism and their typical peers, and the typical peers also reported feeling more accepting of children with autism after the intervention.

Cooperative Arrangements

Establishing cooperative arrangements can improve the socialization of children with autism in schools. This technique involves developing activities with at least two players so that the children are placed in a social setting.[23] These age-appropriate and mutually reinforcing activities are designed to require cooperation.

For example, if a class is doing an art project, the activity can be arranged so that students have to work together to create the end product. Instead of having students color individual pictures, for example, the teacher may have the children work in pairs or groups so that they color a picture together. Opportunities for verbal social communication can also be created as part of the activity, for example by having the students ask each other for different colored crayons, decide which parts each will color, compliment and comment on each other's work, and so on.

To encourage socialization both outside and inside the classroom, cooperative arrangements also work well for after-school playdates.[24] Suggestions of compatible typical peers from teachers and school staff can be helpful for parents arranging social activities outside the school.

Antecedent Interventions to Improve Socialization

Many of the techniques in the following paragraphs can be conceptualized as *antecedent interventions,* in which techniques are implemented prior to when an event—such as a social peer activity—is expected to occur in the natural environment. Antecedent interventions can reduce or eliminate the need for direct intervention at times when it might be stigmatizing, embarrassing, or unnatural for the individual with autism to have an interventionist present.

For example, an effective antecedent intervention is *priming,* or having students practice social activities before they occur in natural settings. In one study, Zanolli, Daggett, and Adams[25] primed children with autism both by teaching initiations and by teaching peers to respond to initiations. They did this by selecting a few typically developing peers to remain in the classroom with the children with autism during a break time. During this time, the teacher prompted the children to greet each other, and then allowed them to play whatever they wanted for five minutes without any consequences. If the children with autism made an initiation, then the teacher gave the peer time to respond; if the peer did not respond, then the teacher prompted him or her (for example, "John spoke to you, what did you say?"). After these priming sessions, the child with autism increased unprompted social initiations during all class times.

Priming to increase skill competence has also been used effectively to improve the involvement of children with autism in games with their typically developing peers during recess breaks at school.[26] Specifically, the children with autism were taught to become proficient at an age-appropriate, child-selected game prior to the introduction of the game in a social setting. During the priming sessions, the interventionist, in a nondemanding manner, ensured that the children were knowledgeable about the game's rules. The games were then made available on the playground, but no direct intervention whatsoever was provided at school.

The use of priming with games produced the following results:

- Increased rates of peer initiations
- An increased number of statements by typical peers reflecting the target children's competence
- Peer statements suggesting competence of the target children in regard to their knowledge of the game (for example, peer questions about how to play or about the rules of the game)
- Generalization of initiations to unprimed activities
- Improvements in the children with autism's affect as well as improvements in the typical peers' affect

A benefit of this type of antecedent intervention is that gains are evidenced in the absence of an interventionist. Also, when activities are primed at home, the parents can be an active part of the intervention, resulting in home-school collaboration.[27]

Using *picture cues* can be especially helpful for children with ASD, who are often better visually than verbally. One study focused on activities in which the students could participate during free playtime subsequent to the intervention.[28] The target children were shown pictures of all the available activities in the classroom and were asked to select and verbalize the activities they would engage in. This advance preparation increased their appropriate engagement during the succeeding playtime. Further, when the children with autism were engaged in appropriate behaviors, they were much more likely to have social interactions with other children. Again, benefits were evidenced without the need for continuous direct intervention during the free play period in the natural setting.

Finally, *multiple-component interventions* can be used to ensure greater gains, as no single social intervention has successfully addressed all of a child's social needs. For example, Brookman et al.[29] used a combination of techniques to facilitate social interactions between children with ASD and their typical peers during summer day camp, and this same process could easily be implemented within school settings. The study used priming to prepare the children for activities and games that would occur the next day. In some cases, self-management techniques were used to decrease disruptive behaviors. In addition, a variety of social interaction strategies were used:

- Teaching the children with autism sharing behaviors. For example, treats can be sent with the child with autism to share during snack and lunch.
- Encouraging all children (with and without autism) to ask each other for help, rather than an adult. For example, instead of asking a counselor to open a drink, the child was prompted to ask another child.
- Facilitating social conversations by prompting the children with autism to ask questions and respond to their peers.
- Prompting ongoing social engagement during all activities.

These strategies were quickly and easily taught to paraprofessionals who had minimal formal training in the area of autism, suggesting that their implementation on a large scale should be possible. These combined interventions implemented together resulted in significant social improvements between children with autism and their typical peers.

> Many interventions focus less on teaching social skills per se, and more on attempting to foster social relationships, often through the involvement of peers who do not have disabilities.[30] Therefore, focusing on skill development while simultaneously helping provide the scaffolding to establish and foster peer relationships appears to be of great importance.

Interventions to Reduce Problem Behaviors

Problem behaviors in children with ASD often lead to restrictive school settings, difficulties with socialization, and fewer leisure and extracurricular activities with typical peers.[31] Although problem behaviors in the past were managed using consequences—primarily punishment—more proactive and positive antecedent procedures are now available, so that painful and dehumanizing procedures, which previously were shunned by professionals, are no longer implemented.[32] In the following paragraphs we will discuss some of the interventions available for decreasing problem behaviors.

Functionally Equivalent Replacement Behaviors

Some children with ASD have serious problem behaviors that interfere with learning and social relationships[33] and create challenges for teachers and parents. One relatively new method for dealing with problem behaviors has addressed the importance of determining why the behaviors are occurring and then developing a treatment plan that creates replacement behaviors for the problem behaviors.[34] These new behaviors, which have the same communicative function as the problem behaviors, are often called functionally equivalent replacement behaviors. There are two types of assessments commonly used for this purpose:

Functional assessments analyze the antecedents and consequences of a behavior to develop a hypothesis as to why the problem behavior occurred.[35] Then a treatment plan is developed based on the function of the behavior. Interventions that make use of functional assessments have been shown to reduce problem behaviors significantly and also create long-lasting changes, because the individual can appropriately communicate the same function that was being expressed by the problem behavior.[36]

A functional assessment form can be found in one of our papers.[37] This form allows one to define the problem behavior, and then check boxes related to the setting in which the problem behavior occurred, the time the problem behavior occurred, and the antecedents and consequences of the behavior. The form is simple to use, already listing most common functions.

Understanding the antecedents and consequences surrounding the problem behavior allows one to understand why the behavior occurred (for example, to get out of an activity or to gain attention), allowing the interventionist to develop and teach appropriate replacement behaviors.

The literature also contains a number of consequence-based interventions, such as nonverbal social disapproval procedures that remove the consequences the child is trying to receive.[38] Such strategies, and extinction procedures, wherein the problem behaviors are ignored, can be used while teaching the replacement behaviors so that the problem behaviors become inefficient and ineffective for the student.[39]

Context-based assessments evaluate the contexts in which behaviors occur, looking for trigger stimuli and motivating operations (an environmental variable that alters the reinforcing value of an item or event).[40] This type of assessment is similar to a functional assessment, but it focuses on the antecedent context that might have caused the behavior to occur, whereas a functional assessment looks at both the antecedents and the consequences of the behavior.

An intervention plan can be developed after the function of the behavior is assessed and contextual variables are better understood.

Antecedent Interventions to Improve Problem Behaviors

Generally these interventions involve manipulating the environment to reduce the likelihood of a problem behavior, such as by doing the following:

- Making ecological changes in the environment (altering the seating arrangement, varying the order and predictability of assignments, and so on)
- Making curricular changes (encouraging partial participation, incorporating motivational components into the curriculum, increasing meaningful assignments, and so on)
- Replacing the problem behavior with an appropriate communicative behavior

Other antecedent interventions include the following:

- Environmental fit therapies that modify the task that triggers the inappropriate behaviors[41]
- Contingent escape and instructional fading,[42] which prevents the child from using an escape behavior
- Social stories[43] that provide children with appropriate models through storybooks written from children's perspectives

One type of antecedent intervention involves the implementation of an *environmental fit plan* to decrease problem behaviors prior to their occurrence by modifying the demands placed on the child because avoidance is a common function of problem behavior in individuals with autism. This has been shown to reduce problem behaviors during both motor and academic tasks.[44] Each task that is an antecedent to a problem behavior is made easier for the child.

For example, in one study a child was given the prompt of dotted lines for writing letters as a curricular modification.[45] After six intervention sessions, the child was given the opportunity to try the unmodified task again, which he was able to complete without the prompt and without disruptive behavior. The end goal of the intervention was to have the child complete the task without modifications.

Similarly, an antecedent intervention that reduces problem behaviors when the function is escape and avoidance involves *contingent escape and instructional fading.*[46] This technique includes physically preventing the child from using the escape behavior, while at the same time not removing the task. The child is physically guided to engage in the task for short time periods, and then is given a contingent break. At the start, the child is not required to complete the task as long as he or she makes attempts to perform the task. Gradually and systematically an increased amount of task engagement is required until the child can complete the task with little or no break time.

Social stories are similar to priming techniques, described earlier, in that they give individuals with autism a chance to practice desired behaviors that they will use in mainstream settings.[47] Social stories are read to children and adolescents with autism, describing a situation they find difficult. The story starts by laying out the problem, then describes common responses and reactions of others, and then portrays the feelings of others, which is thought to teach perspective. The story then details an appropriate response to the social situation from which the child with autism may learn.[48] Social stories are around five to ten sentences long and often include visual pictures, which is a preferred method for teaching individuals with autism. Teachers can use social stories as an antecedent intervention to promote prosocial behaviors and decrease problem behaviors. Spencer, Simpson, and Lynch[49] provide examples of social stories, such as "Waiting for My Turn to Talk" and "Center Time." Ozdemir[50] showed that using social stories effectively reduced disruptive behaviors (using a loud voice in class, chair tipping, and cutting in the lunch line) for three children with autism, ages seven to nine. These studies demonstrate how social stories can be incorporated into the curriculum for students with autism as an antecedent intervention to improve their behavior.

Another procedure, *self-management,* can be programmed to occur in natural, inclusive school settings in the absence of an interventionist.[51] That is, self-management is an effective intervention that is less socially conspicuous in that it does not require a one-to-one aide or interventionist teaching and monitoring behavior.[52]

Wilkinson[53] demonstrated an effective self-management program for increasing on-task and compliant behavior in a case study with a student with autism.

This student used a self-recording checklist taped to his desk to self-monitor his on-task and compliant behavior, which was specifically described to him prior to the intervention. The teacher gave him a visual cue when it was time for him to monitor his behavior. At the end of the day, the teacher and student reviewed his progress, and he was praised for his good behaviors. When he met 80 percent of his daily behavioral goals, he was allowed to choose from a group of incentives in which he could engage at the end of the school day, such as computer time or a desired game or activity. He brought the checklist home to review with his parents and to exchange for further rewards based on his recorded behavior. This intervention was implemented for fifteen days, and appropriate behavior was maintained after the self-management program was completely faded, suggesting that the student had successfully learned to self-control his behavior.

Whereas Wilkinson's study[54] aimed at improving behaviors that could result in better social inclusion of the student with autism, Koegel, Koegel, Hurley, and Frea[55] conducted a study to assess whether a self-management intervention targeted at teaching appropriate social skills could help replace disruptive and inappropriate behaviors. Koegel and colleagues' intervention was aimed at increasing verbal initiations for children with autism. The children in this study, ages six to eleven, had a variety of socially undesirable behaviors, including self-injurious behaviors; tantrums; running away from communicative partners; repetitive behaviors, such as spinning in circles and hair twirling; hitting objects; and shouting. The children were each provided with a wrist counter to use in the community, at home, and at school. They were taught how to track appropriate social responses on their wrist counter, and once they achieved a certain number of responses or "points," these were reinforced with a desired reward (usually small edibles). This self-management technique successfully improved the social behaviors of these children, while decreasing untargeted inappropriate behaviors. Again, the benefit of these self-management procedures is the independence associated with the method. The self-management technique is also less intrusive; that is, having a checklist taped to one's desk or a wrist counter is less conspicuous than having a teacher or interventionist providing direct intervention in the child's natural settings.

Although effective, self-management does not necessarily target the function of the behavior. Therefore, long-term decreases in problem behaviors are unlikely if the student is not taught appropriate replacement behaviors. Self-management is an ideal strategy when immediate and rapid behavior changes are necessary, such as when a child is disruptive in an inclusive school setting and is at risk of being transferred to a more restrictive setting. However, simultaneously implementing a functional analysis to determine the causes of a behavior prior to implementing the self-management program is important, particularly if the student doesn't already have a repertoire of appropriate behaviors. Then the self-management program can be implemented immediately, while simultaneously the child with autism is being taught functionally equivalent replacement behaviors, thereby increasing the likelihood that the changes are durable and will be maintained.

Interventions for Older Children with ASD Who Have Comorbid Diagnoses

For children with ASD, other mental disorders, such as depression, anxiety, and attention deficit hyperactivity disorder (ADHD), are much more common than in typically developing children and need to be addressed as an integral part of their program.[56] Effective interventions that schools may be able to offer (in addition to those described earlier) include several types of cognitive behavioral therapy interventions.[57]

In addition, many children on the spectrum are medicated to deal with the presence of a comorbid disorder. For example, Adderall is commonly prescribed for ADHD, and antianxiety or antidepressant medications, such as Xanax, are also prescribed.[58] Although these medications may improve the symptoms for a short amount of time, whether they are long-term solutions is unknown, and there may be negative side effects from these medications over time.[59] Most researchers believe that medication should not be used alone but rather in conjunction with behavioral and psychological therapies.[60]

Positive outcomes have been shown as a result of *cognitive behavioral therapy* (CBT) for comorbid anxiety disorders,[61] attention disorders, and problem behaviors in students with autism. Although different types of cognitive behavioral therapies can be used, they all must be implemented in a social environment.[62] Parent participation is extremely important.[63] The following are key components necessary for successful CBT intervention:[64]

- Psychoeducation (educating parents and children about the disorders and treatment procedures)
- Somatic management
- Cognitive restructuring
- Problem solving
- Exposure prevention
- Relapse prevention

One CBT intervention that was successful in treating anxiety and other co-morbid disorders for children with autism was reported by Wood et al.[65] The intervention was implemented by professionals who had at least one year of experience working with children on the autism spectrum. The children were taught skills in specific social areas to help them with friendship building. This involved teaching the children to give compliments, be good sports, have successful playdates, and be good hosts for playdates. The authors also educated parents and school providers on methods to teach the children to enter into appropriate interactions with peers. These areas were practiced throughout intervention sessions until children felt comfortable engaging in appropriate interactions. The intervention successfully reduced anxiety (as measured by the Anxiety Disorders Interview Schedule) in children with ASD during social conversations.

Wood et al.[66] also addressed attention deficits in children with ASD. The authors used motivation as a key aspect to keep the children interested and alert. Interventionists used individualized special interests to teach therapeutic concepts (for example, a child's favorite movie could be used as the main topic in social conversation during initial sessions). Later intervention was focused on expanding the children's preferred social topics to other interests.

An additional area that Wood and colleagues[67] addressed was problem behaviors, such as aggression, in children with ASD. These behaviors were decreased by using contingency management procedures. For example, children earned points for not engaging in aggressive behaviors for a whole day, and then received a reward at the end of the day for the points they earned. Overall, these types of interventions can reduce anxiety, increase attention spans, and reduce problem behaviors for children with ASD.

BARRIERS TO EFFECTIVE INTERVENTION

Despite the fact that many empirically based interventions are available, numerous variables and barriers interfere with the implementation of effective interventions:

- The broad spectrum of symptom severity in the ASD population presents challenges in both assessment and educational programming.
- Varying levels of disruptive behavior can interfere with student test taking and evaluation.
- Children with autism get very few teaching opportunities throughout the school day.
- Funding issues and poor training of support staff prevent the implementation of intervention strategies.

The heterogeneity of symptom severity in the ASD population presents challenges in both assessment and educational programming.[68] Thus responsiveness to intervention may differ among autism phenotypes. Further, the consistency of the intervention across settings, academic tasks, and interventionists may result in more or less rapid gains.

Related to the heterogeneity of individuals diagnosed with autism are the varying levels of disruptive behavior that can interfere with test taking.[69] The presence of disruptive behavior can result in inaccurate evaluations of the student's cognitive ability and performance, and consequently goals may be developed that do not challenge the child. This may create a situation wherein a curriculum—whether it is academic or social—is inappropriate for the child. Skilled individuals are needed in the schools with the expertise and experience to assess and develop appropriate intervention programs for individuals with ASD. Also, staff members need to regularly monitor the effectiveness of the interventions and the child's response to the interventions being implemented. Hiring skilled personnel for attending to the needs of the rapidly increasing number of children with ASD may be challenging and deceptively expensive in the beginning, even though costs decrease as the interventions help children achieve gains and as procedures that create independence are incorporated.

Finally, barriers to effective intervention may include funding issues as well as the poor training of support staff. As an example, paraprofessionals, who often provide the greatest number of direct hours to the child, report feeling under-trained, and the field of education has done little to change this.[70] The expectations for paraprofessionals are extremely high,[71] and too often they receive inadequate supervision, monitoring, and training.

Paraprofessionals have reported having a moderate level of knowledge of the paraeducational standards,[72] and in one survey more than 60 percent felt they needed more training in all areas of competency, including advocacy, communication, and facilitation of services.[73] Logically, paraprofessionals who reported higher levels of knowledge had more years of experience and more training, when all other variables remained constant.[74] This suggests that experience, coupled with more intensive training, will improve the knowledge and confidence of paraprofessionals. But often there is considerable turnover among paraprofessionals. New paraprofessionals have reported feeling overwhelmed when beginning work[75] and have complained about receiving a "one size fits all" plan, whereby the children they are expected to work with fall on a large spectrum with many different needs and skills.[76]

TRAINING PROGRAMS FOR PARAPROFESSIONALS

Although most of the training of paraprofessionals has been inadequate,[77] a variety of effective training programs for paraprofessionals have been discussed in the literature. Studies show that requiring paraprofessionals to acquire a basic knowledge of the procedures that are effective with ASD as part of their training, as well as providing them with direct feedback while they work with their students, are critical for child gains.

Many individual techniques have been used, including modeling teaching procedures, having the paraprofessional read training manuals, providing written and verbal instructions to the paraprofessional, coaching, and offering on-site practice with feedback. The most successful trainings have used multiple-component programs that include some direct practice with feedback.[78] If professional time is limited, supervision can be accomplished via one-on-one meetings using videotapes of the paraprofessional working with the child. Viewing videotapes can be time-efficient for both the paraprofessional and the supervisor.

For an example of a more direct training, Kohler, Anthony, Steighner, and Hoyson[79] were successfully able to improve the skills of paraprofessionals and teachers by using a combination of a few techniques:

- Meeting with family members, teachers, and paraprofessionals to plan activities
- Implementing in vivo training of paraprofessionals
- Giving postsession process-based feedback
- Giving weekly outcome-based feedback

Kohler et al.[80] began by introducing paraprofessionals to naturalistic teaching approaches with a printed handout that showed seven strategies and descriptions. The paraprofessionals were given a chance to discuss the procedures with an adviser specially trained in these naturalistic approaches. The paraprofessionals then implemented the techniques and were subsequently provided with daily feedback from trained professionals, allowing them again to discuss procedures as well as problems that arose during the sessions.

Paraprofessionals also received in vivo training, whereby a trained professional observed the session and explained when correct and incorrect procedures were used. Paraprofessionals received a checklist that the trainer had completed, which explained where mistakes were made and where procedures were implemented correctly, and then were able to discuss the feedback with the trainer. This multiple-component approach resulted in increased social interactions and engagement among the participants with autism.

Robinson[81] trained paraprofessionals in pivotal response treatment (PRT) using a combination of modeling and video-based feedback. At the start of training, paraprofessionals were able to observe a trained clinician working with a student for fifteen minutes in three consecutive sessions. The trainer made sure to demonstrate PRT strategies in a variety of settings and with different activities to increase the likelihood of generalization. After these three sessions, the paraprofessionals implemented the techniques and were provided with direct feedback. The program resulted in rapid learning by the paraprofessionals and social gains by the students with autism.

TO SUM UP

When they have received systematic intervention, children with autism can be quite successful in school, both socially and academically. However, when systematic, empirically supported interventions are not used correctly, or when staff members are not trained, children with autism are unlikely to receive educational benefit. Only with consistent, coordinated, empirically based programs—implemented in an intensive manner—will children with ASD be able to make the gains necessary to reach their potential. Consider the following issues:

- The social experiences for students with autism at school are few and isolated.
- School programming for socialization needs to be improved.
- Program implementation and staff training are insufficient.
- The development of interventions and the adaptation of existing interventions for older children, adolescents, and adults are needed.
- The translation of research into practical, easy-to-use procedures continues to be important.

Preparation of this chapter and the research reported therein were supported in part by NIH Research Grant Number DC010924 from NIDCD, awarded to Robert Koegel, and by the Eli and Edythe L. Broad Foundation award to Lynn Kern Koegel. We also wish to acknowledge the assistance of Kristen Ashbaugh in the preparation of this manuscript.

Translating Evidence-Based Practices from the Laboratory to Schools: Classroom Pivotal Response Teaching

chapter
FIVE

Laura Schreibman, Jessica Suhrheinrich,
Aubyn C. Stahmer, and Sarah R. Reed

Increasing diagnoses of autism have led to pressure to improve the quality of educational services for children with autism by incorporating evidence-based practices (EBPs) into school programs. However, this process has been difficult, and both autism researchers and educators report frustration concerning the gap between research and practice.[1] Historically, special education and intervention researchers have focused primarily on developing effective interventions, with less attention given to the pragmatics of implementation in the classroom and teacher training.[2] Thus EBPs for educating children with autism exist, but often they are not effectively incorporated into programs serving this population.[3]

Translational research focuses specifically on *how* to adapt empirically validated teaching protocols that have been developed and studied in laboratory settings for use in applied settings where they are more likely to benefit the children who need them. This field has focused not only on adapting the intervention protocols themselves but also on understanding the real-world environments within which these protocols are to be used. Classrooms are often targeted as settings for such applied research because these are the most likely venues for educating children.

Recent research has focused on teachers' use of and attitudes toward EBPs in the classroom. Teachers reported using EBPs with students who have autism, but described using them in a highly modified form, combining several methodologies to develop individualized programs based on each child's specific characteristics and adapting the program from the established training protocol to meet their own needs.[4] In addition, the majority of teacher participants in one study reported that they, and the paraprofessionals in their classrooms, did not receive adequate training. These findings suggest that adaptations to EBPs as well as additional resources may be needed to best fit the needs of classroom teachers and paraprofessional staff.

WHAT IS PIVOTAL RESPONSE TREATMENT?

One EBP developed in laboratory settings for children with autism is pivotal response treatment (PRT). PRT is essentially a child-directed model that emphasizes allowing the child to choose the nature of the educational interaction, the materials involved, and the timing. Further, it involves ensuring child attention, interspersing previously mastered skills, providing reinforcing consequences that are directly related to the child's behavior or response to the instruction, reinforcing response attempts, and encouraging turn-taking with the teacher or other students. Also, PRT incorporates tasks that serve to broaden and "normalize" the attention of the child by teaching responses to simultaneous multiple stimuli.

PRT is a form of naturalistic behavioral intervention, based on principles established via applied behavior analysis (ABA), and is well supported in the scientific literature. Compared to a more highly structured, repetitive-practice form of behavioral intervention, such as discrete trial training (DTT), PRT involves the same behavioral principles but has a more loosely structured and naturalistic format.

Naturalistic ABA-based interventions like PRT have been developed to address some of the limitations associated with such highly structured ABA-based programs as DTT. These limitations include a lack of generalization (use of learned skills in other settings and with other people), poor maintenance (use of skills over time), and reliance on teacher cues to respond.[5] Thus the original PRT protocol was developed to help children respond to different cues, people, and settings; to increase spontaneous responding; to reduce prompt dependency; to increase motivation; and to provide a more flexible teaching format while still relying on the principles of ABA.

> PRT was designed based on a series of empirical studies identifying important treatment elements that address "pivotal" areas of development affecting a wide range of functioning. PRT has been identified as an established intervention in a recent comprehensive review of treatment methods for use with children with autism, conducted by the National Standards Project.[6] Three pivotal areas have been identified:
>
> - Motivation
> - Responsiveness to multiple cues (broadening of attention)
> - Child self-initiations
>
> According to Koegel and colleagues,[7] when these pivotal areas are enhanced, improvement in autonomy, self-learning, and generalization follows.

Improving Communication Skills

Given its importance in so many areas of development for students with autism, communication is a main focus of intervention. We know that when students cannot communicate it interferes with their ability to learn, impedes their social development, affects the development of play behaviors, and prevents them from achieving independence. We also know that early development of communication skills is associated with one's overall prognosis. Children with autism who do learn to communicate successfully demonstrate lower levels of aberrant behaviors, such as engaging in self-stimulation or self-injury, throwing tantrums, and showing aggression.[8] It is clear that a primary goal of early intervention programs for children with autism should be to provide effective communication strategies.

Accordingly, spoken language has been the primary focus of much of the PRT research, and it is clear that PRT is effective at increasing spoken language skills in children with autism.[9] PRT has been shown to improve children's use of a variety of language functions, including speech imitation, labeling, and question asking;[10] spontaneous speech;[11] and conversational communication,[12] in addition to supporting the rapid acquisition of functional speech in previously nonverbal children.[13]

Other Skills Taught Using PRT

Other skills that have been successfully taught using PRT include the following:

- Symbolic play[14]
- Sociodramatic play[15]
- Peer social interaction[16]
- Self-initiations[17]
- Joint attention[18]
- Homework completion[19]

Because PRT was developed in part to improve generalization and maintenance of acquired skills, it is not surprising that it has also been found to increase generalization and maintenance of behavior change in children with autism.[20] Independent reviews of the PRT research base recommend the program as an efficacious, evidence-based intervention for children with autism.[21] In addition, and very important, positive outcomes have been replicated by researchers not associated with the development of the original procedures.[22]

DEVELOPMENT OF CLASSROOM PIVOTAL RESPONSE TEACHING (CPRT)

Collaboration with teachers allowed us to develop a classroom adaptation of PRT. The resulting classroom pivotal response teaching (CPRT) enhances children's motivation and participation in learning; increases the number of learning opportunities they experience each day; and promotes mastery of targeted communication, play, social, and academic skills. CPRT further expands the applicability of the original PRT procedures for use in classroom settings.

> Research examining how special educators usually teach young children with autism in the Southern California region indicated that more than 70 percent of teachers surveyed used PRT, or some variation of PRT, in their programs.[23] Twelve percent of the teachers using PRT reported using it as the primary intervention in their program, although only two of these seven teachers reported using all aspects of the intervention. The remaining 88 percent of these teachers indicated using parts of the intervention or using PRT in conjunction with other treatment methods.

CPRT was developed after research indicated that teachers were not using PRT as specified in the original training manual.[24] In research settings, care is taken to ensure that the protocol for an EBP is implemented correctly and fully—that is, as it was developed and tested by the research team. Deviation from the established protocol will reduce the fidelity of implementation and perhaps reduce the effectiveness of the intervention. Although the high percentage of teachers reporting classroom use of PRT in Southern California was encouraging, the issue of how to improve fidelity and ensure that PRT is maximally effective for the students receiving intervention remained.

Teacher Partnerships to Improve Implementation of PRT

Reports of the need to adapt PRT for the classroom made it obvious that to ensure the correct implementation of PRT, teachers should be partners in improving its usability. Such a partnership would allow teachers to shape intervention protocol into a feasible form for classroom implementation and for researchers to then examine the effectiveness of the adapted intervention.

We began by bringing together groups of teachers to ask them about the benefits and barriers associated with their use of traditional PRT.[25] Preschool and elementary school special education teachers found PRT to be an intuitive, effective strategy for teaching children with autism. Many teachers reported that PRT fit with their idea of "good teaching" and made sense to them. In addition, they reported that it helped children generalize new skills to broader environments. They liked some of the specific components of PRT, including keeping instructions and opportunities clear, simple, and relevant to the child; the use of maintenance tasks to keep child frustration low; the direct relationship between reinforcement and behavior; the ability to honor approximations and goal-directed attempts; and the use of explicit turn-taking.

However, teachers also reported significant barriers to the use of PRT in the classroom. They found it difficult to take the skills they learned in one-on-one training and use them with groups of children, especially in settings like circle time, in large-group activities, and without proper training and support. At times they found it difficult to keep the multiple components straight, and felt that having preliminary knowledge of ABA principles was an important prerequisite to understanding PRT. Teachers also found data collection difficult and were unsure of how to address specific individualized education program (IEP) goals using PRT strategies. They felt this was especially important given that both parents and schools are becoming more data driven and want programs to be determined by the IEP goals. Teachers asked for more information on how to train paraprofessionals in PRT. In addition, teachers reported difficulty using some of the components of PRT correctly. They felt that it was not always appropriate or possible to allow the child to choose the activity, to use direct reinforcement in the classroom, and to take turns with students. Finally, the use of multiple cues, or conditional discriminations (attending to more than one aspect of an item simultaneously), was an area of concern, as this process was difficult to understand and time consuming to implement, and many teachers felt it might not be appropriate for children who are minimally verbal.

Feedback and Continuing Research

Feedback from the teachers indicated potential modifications to the standard PRT protocol. Were all of the PRT components really necessary in order for it to be effective in the classroom? Could they be modified? These are empirical questions, and we are currently addressing these issues experimentally.

Conditional Discriminations

One example from our current research relates to the use of conditional discriminations to broaden attentional focus. Conditional discriminations require a child to respond to stimuli presented in combination—such as by having the child choose a yellow square block from an array of blocks including a yellow square, a yellow circle, a blue circle, and a blue square, thus necessitating that the child identify both color (yellow) and shape (square) to choose the correct block. Prior research[26] demonstrated that many children with autism have difficulty responding to cues in context ("stimulus overselectivity") but can overcome this deficit with training in a series of conditional discriminations. This type of training is the multiple-cues component of PRT. Teachers in our focus groups reported that it was difficult to incorporate conditional discriminations into daily instruction, and they often omitted this component of the protocol. To address this issue we conducted a series of studies to examine the necessity of specifically targeting responsiveness to multiple cues as an element of the CPRT protocol for all children with autism.[27] We designed a discrimination task involving a series of colored blocks to test discrimination learning and responsiveness to multiple cues. A total of thirty-five typically developing children, ages nineteen to fifty months, completed the assessment. Data clearly indicated that children do not reliably attend to multiple cues to make simultaneous conditional discriminations until thirty-six months, and that after that age typically developing children do so quite consistently. On the basis of these data we determined that it is not appropriate for teachers to target multiple cues through CPRT with children with autism who have a developmental age under thirty-six months. In the next stage of this study we conducted the discrimination learning assessment with nineteen children with autism with a developmental age over thirty-six months to look for differences between this group and the typically developing population. Only five children with autism displayed overselectivity, indicating that only a small subset may have difficulty with this skill. However, we retested three of these five children on the same assessment six to ten months later and found that all were able to successfully complete the task.

These results suggest that although the ability to respond to multiple cues is delayed in many children with autism, for some this skill appears to develop over time and without targeted intervention. The intervention methods teachers currently use may already address this skill by exposing a child to many examples of features, such as many circles and many yellow items, across a variety of activities. Thus no specific teaching of the response to multiple cues is required.

Based on these results we have specified that teachers should incorporate multiple examples (rather than complex conditional discriminations as traditionally required) when using CPRT unless children with a developmental age of thirty-six months or older have a specific difficulty with responding to multiple cues. This simplifies the CPRT protocol, as teachers are only required to use the multiple-cues component with a small subset of children with autism in the classroom.

Turn-Taking

A second example of research motivated by feedback from teachers is our investigation of the role of turn-taking in PRT. The turn-taking component of PRT involves teachers' gaining control of an item, modeling a new behavior, and returning the item to the student contingent upon the student's appropriate response. Several teachers in our focus groups reported difficultly implementing this element, either because they forgot to take a turn themselves or because it was difficult to take turns with a child in a group while maintaining the attention of the rest of the group. If turns are important in PRT because they familiarize the child with the back-and-forth flow of interaction, it may be acceptable to facilitate turns among children to fulfill this requirement. However, if turns are crucial because they allow the teacher an opportunity to model behavior at a slightly higher level, then turn-taking among children may not promote the same expansion of skills originally demonstrated by PRT.

To address these issues we are conducting a brief investigation of how the specific components of turn-taking (teacher modeling of a new and appropriate skill and student access to desired materials contingent on correct responding) affect student behavior. Preliminary results indicate that using both modeling and contingency within a session leads to more individual play behaviors and longer duration of play than using modeling alone or contingency alone. These results imply that it is important to maintain the component of turn-taking in CPRT. However, modeling and contingency may not need to be included within the same turn to have a positive effect on play behaviors.

This means that facilitating turns between peers may be one way to include turn taking in the classroom, as long as the teacher is also able to gain control of the materials in other ways throughout the interaction. We will continue to test the validity of these findings with additional participants.

Evaluations of the necessity of conditional discriminations and turn-taking are two examples of research conducted to test adaptations to PRT that teachers have suggested. In addition to investigating these specific adaptations, we also worked with teachers to develop materials and resources that adequately and accurately address the challenges of the classroom.

COMPONENTS OF CPRT

CPRT involves eight critical components, each of which is a procedure of PRT. Each of these components is based in the behavioral model, as noted earlier, and can be understood in terms of *antecedents* and *consequences*. The behavior itself is what we are trying to change. Each of the components described in the following subsections can enhance a student's ability to succeed in the classroom.

Antecedent Components

Antecedent techniques focus on preparing the student for what is about to occur in the classroom.

Component 1: Gain Student Attention

The teacher should gain a student's attention before asking him to say or do something.
Attention refers to where the student is directing his focus. Students with autism seem to pay too little attention to important stimuli (for example, the teacher's instruction) and too much attention to the "wrong" stimuli in their environment (for example, a spinning fan or the wheels of a car). Teachers should therefore ensure that each student is attending to the model or instruction before providing an opportunity to respond. There are several methods that increase the likelihood that a student will pay attention to an instruction.

- *Choose motivating activities.* To increase motivation, the teacher should select activities that interest the child or children. With a little creativity, language, play, social, and academic skills can be taught using many different materials and actions. For example, a block might be used initially to teach constructive play or word imitation, and later as a "cookie" for teaching symbolic play. Even activities that seem to elicit self-stimulatory or stereotyped behavior may be motivating. For example, if a student enjoys watching fans spin, he might ask to turn it on, spin it faster, or pretend it is an airplane engine, providing an opportunity for the teacher to work on communication and initiation goals. If a student enjoys physical activity, he could ask to spin in a chair or bounce on a ball. These objects and activities can be used for teaching even if the student is not using them appropriately.

- *Work close to the student.* Proximity is an important part of gaining attention. Teachers are encouraged to get down to the student's level so that eye contact is possible. If a student is sitting, the teacher might sit with him. If giving the first instruction in the interaction, the teacher may need to touch the student on the arm to gain his attention. Providing an opportunity for close, face-to-face contact will help ensure that the student is able to attend to the instructions and be successful in responding.

- *Be fun and engaging.* The more the teacher enjoys herself, the more the students will enjoy playing with and listening to her. Teachers are encouraged to be playful, silly, and animated, and to watch each student's reaction to these behaviors to determine which ones are working.

- *Keep it natural.* Gaining a student's attention in a natural way should eliminate the need to specifically teach attending. Teachers should avoid repeatedly calling the student's name or asking for attention (for example, "Look at me"). These prompts will be difficult to eliminate if the student forms a habit of waiting for an adult to gain her attention. Instead, teachers can follow some of the suggestions listed earlier to encourage each student to attend naturally.

Component 2: Make Instructions Clear and Appropriate

The teacher should provide clear and appropriate instructions that are easy for the student to understand and are at, or just above, her developmental level.

Identifying a "clear and appropriate" instruction requires knowledge of each student's current ability level. The teacher should know the language, play, and social abilities of the student, her overall ability to attend, whether she has learned the skill being presented, and even how she is performing the day the instruction is provided.

If a teacher decides to provide an instruction to a student, both the student and the teacher should be paying attention to the interaction. It is important to give an instruction at a time when the student's response can be observed and the teacher can provide assistance and feedback. In a group setting, this may mean asking a question of the entire group (for example, "What day is it today?") and responding to the student or students who answer appropriately. Although there will be times when a different student needs immediate attention or other emergencies occur, ideally attention should be provided to the student or group until a response has been made. It is better not to provide an instruction at all than to fail to follow through.

Component 3: Provide a Mixture of Easy and Difficult Tasks

Similar to PRT, CPRT involves using both easy and difficult tasks rather than continuously increasing task difficulty. Tasks that the student has mastered and can produce consistently and easily are called maintenance tasks. Tasks that are new or continue to be difficult for the student are called acquisition tasks. Teachers are taught to use a mixture of tasks, requiring students to play, communicate, and perform both at levels that are easier for them (maintenance) and at more advanced levels (acquisition). Although there is no set rule, a good goal is to use maintenance tasks approximately 50 percent of the time. This can be altered based on the student (a highly motivated student may benefit from more acquisition tasks, and a tired or frustrated student may need more maintenance tasks) or the environment (a student may need a simpler instruction when there are many possible distractions in the classroom). This mixture of task difficulties is important to increase motivation and spontaneous student responding. It is also developmentally appropriate, as this is consistent with the behavior of typically developing children.

Component 4: Share Control with the Student

The teacher should follow the student's lead for her choice of activities and materials and take turns with the student.

Controlling the learning environment refers to choosing the materials, location, and goals for learning. In CPRT, sharing control of the learning environment with the student is another tool to increase motivation. In general, people are more motivated or interested in learning if they get to choose the topic or activity. For example, if we find a physical activity we enjoy, like hiking in the woods, we are more likely to exercise. In the same way, students with autism will be more motivated to interact when engaged with toys, activities, or conversation topics they enjoy. Many students with autism have difficulty attending to their teacher and peers because they lack motivation for social interaction.

A teacher can employ several methods to share control with the students:

- *Incorporate each student's preferred materials.* When preparing to teach a new skill, it will be helpful for the teacher to find materials the student enjoys and that can be used to teach the specific skill. For example, when teaching number identification, a teacher may use a puzzle with numbers, if a student likes puzzles; if a student enjoys scribbling with crayons, a teacher may use crayons and paper to write out the numbers; if a student is highly motivated for computer time, a teacher may use the computer to type out each number in a large font. The key is to provide the student with an opportunity to choose at least a portion of each activity.

- *Follow the student's lead.* It is important to allow the student to help determine when to move from one activity to the next. Thus, if a student initially selects coloring as an activity, continue coloring until he chooses to move on to something else. This creates an opportunity for the student to communicate that he's "all done" or to ask for the new activity (such as playing with a toy car), and it maximizes his motivation.

- *Incorporate turn-taking.* Turn-taking is another way for the teacher to share control with students, involving a give-and-take between the student and another peer or adult. As discussed earlier, preliminary results from our ongoing investigation of the critical components of turn-taking indicate that the teacher should participate in the activity, or facilitate a turn between students that includes modeling and contingent responding to maximize student benefit. If a student chooses to play with a car, for example, the teacher or a peer can take turns rolling, describing, and racing the car with her. Turn-taking allows the teacher to provide appropriate language and play models, demonstrate the give-and-take of social interaction, and regain control of teaching materials.

Component 5: Use Multiple Cues and Multiple Examples of Materials and Concepts

For children with difficulty responding to multiple cues specifically . . .

The teacher should present opportunities to respond that require the student to attend to multiple aspects of the learning materials to give a correct response.

Every time a new skill is learned, it involves associating multiple cues. A cue is a feature of an object or situation that you use to gather information and respond appropriately. When we meet someone for the first time, we hear her name; feel the firmness of her handshake; and observe her hair color, eyeglasses, and style of dress. All of these cues provide critical information about this new acquaintance and help us identify this person the next time we meet. This is how most learning occurs: we learn the association between two or more features of a situation in our environment. Whereas for typically developing children such learning is not a problem, children with autism may have difficulty learning when attention to simultaneous multiple cues is required and thus may demonstrate stimulus overselectivity.

Many children with autism who are initially overselective in their attention can learn to expand their attention to simultaneous multiple cues. As discussed earlier, although PRT recommends using conditional discriminations for all children with autism, our studies have found that some children do not require this level of instruction. This is still being investigated, but we feel that repeated practice with tasks that provide multiple examples, such as learning that the word *car* is associated not just with one toy car, or small cars, but with pictures of cars, big cars, toy cars, and real cars, can help students attend to multiple cues in new tasks. Some students with autism seem to learn this through exposure to multiple teaching materials and through the use of the CPRT steps that encourage spontaneous and varied responding. For students who have continued difficulty with responding to simultaneous multiple cues, teachers can present opportunities to respond that require them to attend to multiple cues, such as shape and size or color and texture (that is, conditional discriminations), to give a correct response. For example, for an art activity, a teacher can use markers, pencils, and crayons of various colors and require students to ask for the writing utensil they want by naming both the color and type (for example, blue crayon, yellow pencil). Remember that the multiple-cues component is not appropriate.

Consequence Components

Once a teacher has presented an opportunity for a student to respond using the antecedent components just described, the next step is to observe the student's behavior in response to that opportunity. How the student responds will determine what the teacher does next. Because CPRT is a naturalistic intervention, opportunities to respond may not require one specific response. Instead, it may be helpful for teachers to think of responses in terms of *appropriate* or *inappropriate* rather than correct or incorrect to keep in mind that a general type of response rather than an exact action, expression, or behavior is expected. After observing the student's response, the teacher should decide whether it is an appropriate or inappropriate reply to the opportunity presented.

Component 6: Provide Direct Reinforcement

The teacher should provide reinforcement that is naturally or directly related to the activity or behavior.

Direct reinforcement is clearly related to the behavior that precedes it. In contrast, indirect reinforcement occurs when the response and the consequence are unrelated. If a teacher holds up a toy car and asks, "What is it?" the student says, "Car," and the teacher says, "Good talking!" or gives the student a cookie, the consequence is not directly related to the response. In contrast, a direct reinforcer for saying "car" would be access to the toy car. Children acquire language because it is an effective way to change their environment, and the natural environment provides direct reinforcement. The problem with using indirect consequences is that the real-world environment does not supply them. It is important to point out that indirect reinforcers can be highly effective in teaching a new skill. However, the skill may only be demonstrated in the setting where it was taught (that is, where the indirect reinforcer is given). Because the natural environment does not provide these consequences, the behavior will most likely be lost. A skill that has been taught with direct consequences will be under the control of natural consequences and should be maintained in the natural environment.

Component 7: Present Contingent Consequences Immediately

The teacher should present consequences immediately, based on the student's response.

One aspect of contingency is that the consequence should be presented immediately after a behavior occurs. The sooner the consequence is delivered after a response, the stronger its effect, whereas the more delayed the consequence is after a response, the weaker its effect. Contingent also means that the consequence depends on the student's response; the consequence would not be presented if there were no behavior. A reinforcer that is presented randomly (in other words, that is not dependent on a behavior) is ineffective at changing behavior. Randomly winning the lottery will not make someone more productive or hardworking, but a bonus for a job well done will increase productivity. In the same way, handing a favorite toy to a student at random intervals will not increase the likelihood that the student will learn to ask for it appropriately, but responding to the student's request for the toy will increase requesting.

Component 8: Reinforce Appropriate Behaviors by Rewarding Attempts

An attempt is a behavior that serves the same function as the targeted skill, without the accuracy or complexity of a "correct" response. In CPRT, teachers are taught to provide reinforcement to the student for trying to answer correctly, even if the attempt is not his best response. Of course the response has to be reasonable in the sense that it is close to what the student has shown he can do. Reinforcing reasonable attempts at responding correctly and thus reinforcing a broader range of responses keeps the amount of reinforcement, and thus motivation, high.

CPRT WITH A GROUP

The components of CPRT are the same whether working with one student or a group of students. However, when working with groups, teachers need to incorporate a broader range of student interests and manage the learning environment more carefully.

The following list offers several tips for incorporating the components of CPRT into group activities.[28]

- *Choose activities that interest all the students in the group.* For example, use learning stations with varied activities, and group students according to their interests.
- *Choose materials that interest each student in the group.* Incorporate the specific interests of each student into a group activity. For example, use flash cards or figurines that match each student's interests to teach counting. As each student counts correctly, he or she gets to play with the preferred items.
- *To reduce frustration for both the students and for you, begin by expecting only brief periods of attention during group activities.* Not all students may need to remain with the group for the entire activity.
- *When leading a large group, be in front of the students or have them situated such that they can all see you clearly.* Place students with the most difficulty paying attention nearest to you or a paraprofessional who can redirect their attention.
- *Provide instructions in a variety of ways.* For example, use both auditory and visual cues when giving a group instruction.
- *Model appropriate behavior for the group by participating in group activities.* Rather than requiring traditional turn-taking between students, larger group activities, such as playing a game of catch or making a mural, may provide opportunities for cooperative action among all students and with you.

DEVELOPING GOALS THAT INCORPORATE CPRT

To incorporate CPRT into the classroom effectively, teachers should consider how IEP goals are written and targeted. Our own research has indicated that one of the main impediments to the implementation of the original PRT protocol in classrooms is that teachers find it difficult to determine how to use PRT to address IEP goals.

The following suggestions offer ideas for how to write goals that can be addressed with CPRT.[29]

- *Write goals to address generalization of skills.* The eventual goal is for students to learn to use their skills in a variety of settings, with many people. Because CPRT is a naturalistic behavioral intervention, it is designed to be used in natural settings and to draw on natural cues in the student's environment. For example, if the student requires a goal that targets giving an appropriate response to yes-no questions, consider the times of day when this will be both a functional skill for the student and one that has a natural reinforcer, and think about different people with whom the skill might be functional. Targeting a yes-no response to needs or wants (for example, "Do you need to go to the bathroom?" or "Do you want a turn?") is a more naturalistic use of this skill than targeting a yes-no response to factual queries that may not be of interest to the student or may not have a natural reinforcer (for example, "Is this a zebra?" or "Is Kevin wearing a blue shirt?"). This will promote generalization so the student can use this new skill at home and in the community.

- *Write goals to target spontaneity.* One of the goals of CPRT for all students is for them to be able to spontaneously and independently use the skills they learn. Initially it may be helpful and necessary to provide support as a student learns a new skill. However, it is important to write goals that include spontaneous, independent demonstration of the skill. This is the best indication that your student will be able to use the skill independently and functionally outside of your classroom. For example, you may want to increase the complexity of your student's requests and comments by having her use an adjective and noun together (for example, a big dog, the princess sticker). Write the goal to focus on the student's independent responses to what she sees in her environment. Instead of designating responses to such questions as "What do you want?" or "What do you see?" as the final goal, target spontaneous requesting and commenting.

- *Write goals that reflect teaching activities that work well in your classroom.* Keep in mind the activities in which CPRT will be best incorporated in the classroom as you develop specific goals for students. If a student needs to learn to interact with peers, and there are opportunities to facilitate play between students with autism and their typically developing peers during snack time and outside playtime, write the goal so it can be targeted during these activities.

For example, students can learn to independently ask for more juice from a peer during snack time and to respond when a peer asks for more raisins. If there is a weekly cooking activity, the focus may be subtraction of fractions in a naturalistic way. If Michael is asked, "The recipe requires $\frac{1}{2}$ cup of flour, and I just added $\frac{1}{4}$ cup of flour. How much more do I need?" the goal might be written as, "Michael will demonstrate addition and subtraction of basic fractions with 80 percent accuracy during functional activities throughout the school day."

Goals for multiple students of varying skill levels can be addressed together using CPRT in group settings. For example, while Michael is working on fractions during the cooking activity, Susie may be learning about measurement and Jovan could be practicing reading skills with the recipe cards. CPRT can and should be used throughout the school day during art, circle time, mealtime, literacy, math, and other teacher-directed activities.

EXAMPLES OF USING CPRT

In our focus groups and conversations with teachers on using traditional PRT in the classroom, many reported that the examples in the current PRT manual[30] seemed out of date and not applicable to classroom environments. The examples were often of one adult interacting with one child, and typically pertained to parents or other family members, as this was the original audience for whom PRT was intended.

Accordingly we have developed classroom-specific examples for use with CPRT to help teachers visualize and understand the application of CPRT in the classroom context. The examples also serve to illustrate the process of incorporating CPRT into both goal writing and group teaching activities, which were two areas of teacher concern.

Each example contains student profiles with accompanying goals, and several classroom activity examples in which the teacher addresses the goals listed for each student. The following information offers one such example.[31]

STUDENT PROFILES, GOALS, AND EXAMPLE GROUP CPRT ACTIVITIES

SCENARIO 2: KINDERGARTEN/1ST GRADE

Student Profile	IEP Goals or Curriculum Area
Jose is a 6-year-old boy who attends a K–2 special day class. He has some intelligible phrase speech which he uses to request and at times to comment, but does not yet use sentences. He can match uppercase letters but does not name them. Jose is at the beginning level of reading sight words. Jose counts to 20 and can give up to 10 objects from a field of 12–15 with 80% accuracy. He requires visuals to augment learning. Jose has difficulty interacting with other students and is often alone on the playground and at lunch.	1. Jose will name the uppercase letters when they are presented in random order, with 100% accuracy on 4 of 5 opportunities. 2. Jose will demonstrate the ability to complete addition sums in single digits with visual support, during 4 of 5 opportunities. 3. Within 1 school year, Jose will spontaneously use simple sentences 5 times in each school day on 6 out of 8 days. 4. Jose will join a group appropriately (by spontaneously waving, saying hello, asking to play, etc.) and will remain in proximity to other students during small group and lunch for 15 min. over 4 of 5 school days.
Sara is a first grader in the same special day class as Jose. She is a 7-year-old girl who uses 5–6 word sentences but does not always express herself well to get her needs met. Sara knows all of the upper- and lowercase alphabet and the sound each	1. Sara will decode simple consonant-vowel-consonant words when shown a variety of printed materials, with 8 out of 10 words correct as measured by interim assessment on 4 out of 5 occasions.

letter makes. She is learning to recognize simple words in print. She prints her first and last names. Sara knows how to do addition for single digit numbers. She is currently working on subtraction skills. Sara has many friends but still has difficulty sharing materials during class activities.

Darren is a second grader. He primarily uses gestures to communicate and makes some inconsistent attempts at single words. He is able to use a picture exchange communication system to make requests with an open-handed prompt. Darren rote sings the ABC song (using approximations) but does not recognize the letters of the alphabet. Darren rote counts to 5 (using approximations) but has not yet developed numeral recognition. Darren parallel plays near peers but has little to no interaction with them. He is often alone and ignores those around him.

2. Sara will demonstrate the ability to do single digit subtraction problems independently, with at least 80% correct on 4 of 5 school days.
3. Sara will, when at an activity with plenty of materials, be able to share with her peers spontaneously for up to 5 turns on 4 of 5 school days.
1. Darren will match the letters of the uppercase alphabet when given 2 sets of letters, with 100% accuracy on 4 of 5 opportunities.
2. Darren will point to the requested numerals to 10, with 100% accuracy during 4 of 5 opportunities.
3. Darren will use words or pictures to communicate at least 20 times without prompting throughout the school day to request objects/activities on 4 of 5 school days.
4. Darren will interact with peers during structured play by turn taking and sharing materials during daily activities with teacher facilitation on 70% of opportunities on 3 days.

Using CPRT at Language Arts with Jose, Sara, and Darren

Activity: Letter and word recognition
Materials: Letter cards, character stickers, writing/matching boards for students, toy animals

The students, Jose, Sara, and Darren, are seated at a small round table with the teacher. She reviews the alphabet with the students by showing them letter cards of all the letters and naming them.

Jose: The teacher shows Jose a letter card. "What letter is this, Jose?" She holds up an S. Jose looks at it and says, "S" (Goal #1). "Good," says the teacher, and gives him the letter, which has a Superman sticker on it (he likes superheroes).

Next, the teacher takes a turn and models a more advanced skill. She writes "all" on her white board and places the "B" card in front of it. "B goes with a-l-l to spell ball."

Sara: Sara is working on "at" words (e.g., bat, cat, hat) and has a board with a blank space followed by "at." The teacher asks Sara if B can be put in front of "at" to make a word. Sara looks at her board and puts the B in front. "What does it say, Sara?" Sara replies, "B-at. Bat!" (acquisition skill, Goal #1). "That's great," the teacher tells her, "it spells bat!" She asks Sara if she would like to take another turn or share her letter with Darren. Sara chooses to give the letter to Darren (Goal #3).

Darren: Darren has a matching board for the capital letters. He places the B from Sara on the correct corresponding letter (Goal #1). He is rewarded by being allowed to choose and play with a toy animal that begins with the same letter.

The teacher continues the lesson in this manner, allowing Jose to name the letters (being rewarded with the embedded stickers), Sara to test them with the "at" board (being rewarded by allowing her to choose to take a turn or share), and Darren to match them to his board (rewarding him with animal toys that begin with the same letter he is matching); the teacher models as needed and gives praise throughout the session.

Using CPRT at Math with Jose, Sara, and Darren

Activity: Number recognition, addition/subtraction
Materials: Number cards, addition/subtraction folder templates (3 squares printed horizontally with + or − and an = between them)

The teacher shows and labels each number card and allows the students the choice of whispering or yelling as they repeat each number after her (maintenance skill). She knows that "being the teacher" is motivating for all her students, so she uses this role to reinforce the students' behavior during a math activity.

Darren: Then the teacher holds up two numbers (3 and 5) and says, "Darren, tell us what numbers these are" (Goal #3). He labels both numbers correctly, and she gives him the corresponding number cards and says, "OK, Darren is the teacher." She helps Darren pass out the numbers. He chooses to give the number 3 to Jose and the number 5 to Sara (Goal #4). Next she holds up 2 more numbers (1 and 2) for Darren and asks, "Where is number two?" Darren takes the 2 card and, smiling, gives it to Sara (Goals #2 and #4). The teacher wants to reward his spontaneous sharing. "That was great, Darren!" she says, "you picked the correct number and even gave it to Sara without being asked! You may choose *two* animals."

Sara: Sara's folder has a subtraction sign between the first two boxes. The teacher tells Sara, "Put your number 5 here" and points to the first box, "and your number 2 here" and points to the second box. She then asks, "What is the answer?" and points to the third box. Sara says, "Five minus two equals three." The teacher announces, "Great job! Now Sara is the teacher." With the teacher's help, Sara gives Jose the number 2 card and tells him to do his math problem.

Jose: Jose makes a nice attempt by reading the numbers on his folder without solving the problem (Goal #2). The teacher praises his effort and he is allowed to flick the number cards with his fingers. The teacher says, "Now I will take a turn" and solves an addition problem on another folder.

The lesson continues in this manner until math time is over.

TO SUM UP

In this chapter we have described a systematic approach to the adaptation and preliminary translation of one EBP for children with autism, PRT. Through the process of enhancing the original PRT procedures and resources to develop a more comprehensive and relevant CPRT, we have noticed several themes:

- Researchers must collaborate with teachers who will be using the strategies to develop an approach that will be used in its entirety to maximally benefit students.
- Researchers need to identify what works for teachers and incorporate useful strategies into the critical components of the intervention.
- Researchers need teachers' help to identify the specific barriers to the implementation of EBPs and how to address them.
- Effective translation of EBPs may require more basic research on existing EBPs to refine them and to determine what components may or may not be appropriate for specific students or settings.
- To inform best practices, these research findings should be used to update previous findings.
- Researchers must continue to investigate the most effective methods for training teachers to use EBPs, such as CPRT, on a daily basis.

The research reported in this chapter was supported by U.S. Department of Education Grant: R324B070027 "Translating Pivotal Response Training into Classroom Environments." The authors are grateful to Patricia Belden, Cynthia Bolduc, Thesa Jolly, Catherine Pope, Linda Reeve, and Lauren Ungar for the resources, guidance, and thoughtful feedback they have provided throughout the course of this research.

Facilitating the Use of Evidence-Based Practices in Classrooms: The National Professional Development Center Model

Ellen L. Franzone, Suzanne Kucharczyk,
Lisa Sullivan, and Kate Szidon

Educators working with students with autism spectrum disorders (ASD) currently receive various forms of training to implement evidence-based practices (EBPs). One of the goals of the National Professional Development Center on Autism Spectrum Disorders (NPDC on ASD; http://autismpdc.fpg.unc.edu) is to increase the number of educators trained in implementing EBPs. To this end, the center has developed a set of high-quality, free professional development materials to facilitate the training of those working with learners with ASD. Although a solid body of research has established the efficacy of specific practices for students with ASD, access to appropriate training and support in how to implement EBPs varies greatly.[1] Challenges arise for educators in determining which practices to implement for individual students and in receiving the appropriate level of training in these practices. In addition, it can be difficult to translate research findings to classroom settings. These challenges are compounded by a lack of resources, especially in terms of time needed by educators to acquire the desired know-how.

To address these challenges, the NPDC on ASD developed criteria for establishing practices as being effective for students with ASD in school settings and reviewed the research literature.[2] Twenty-four EBPs were identified as meeting the criteria established by the NPDC on ASD:

- Antecedent-based intervention
- Computer-aided instruction
- Differential reinforcement
- Discrete trial training
- Extinction
- Functional behavior assessment
- Functional communication training
- Naturalistic intervention
- Parent-implemented intervention
- Peer-mediated intervention
- Picture exchange communication system
- Pivotal response treatment
- Prompting
- Reinforcement
- Response interruption and redirection
- Self-management
- Social skills groups
- Social stories
- Speech-generating devices
- Structured work systems
- Task analysis
- Time delay
- Video modeling
- Visual supports

The center then developed a set of extensive training, monitoring, and evaluation materials to support educators in implementing these twenty-four evidence-based practices in school settings.

This chapter describes the NPDC on ASD model for implementing EBPs for students with ASD and illustrates how each step of the NPDC on ASD process translates into a school setting through a case study.

The National Professional Development Center on Autism Spectrum Disorders is a multiuniversity research and implementation program that began in 2007. The program is funded by the U.S. Department of Education, Office of Special Education Programs. The primary goal of the center is to provide resources, professional development, and technical assistance to states in order to increase the number of highly qualified personnel serving children and youth with ASD and their families. The center also works with states to promote evidence-based practices for early identification, intervention, and education through professional development activities and ongoing technical assistance. Included in these professional development trainings are a series of tools and steps to facilitate the process of linking student goals to specific evidence-based practices. In addition, the NPDC on ASD has developed a coaching manual and training package to help technical assistance providers and school teams work effectively together during the implementation process.

STEP 1: EVALUATE AND STRENGTHEN OVERALL PROGRAM QUALITY

The program for the child or youth with ASD serves as the architecture within which evidence-based practices are implemented. Implementing evidence-based practices effectively is challenging when the existing program is not supportive of this work. To assist educators in developing and sustaining supportive programs for the implementation of evidence-based practices, the NPDC on ASD has developed a rating scale to assess and provide feedback on quality features of inclusive and self-contained education programs. The psychometric properties of this tool, the Autism Program Environment Rating Scale (APERS), have not yet been tested, and thus the instrument is not currently available for wide distribution.

The NPDC on ASD developed two versions of the APERS to assess the developmental quality of programs for learners with ASD. The preschool and elementary version and the middle and high school version provide a summary assessment of program quality for learners with ASD, which teachers, school teams, technical assistance providers, and supervisors can use to gather detailed information about features of programs that may be of high or low quality. The APERS is a formative instrument intended to provide useful information to the team of educators and parents to support their own improvement plan.

Although the APERS is currently not widely available, the components upon which it is based should be familiar to all educators as important elements of program quality:

- Safety and organization of the learning environment
- Learning environment structure and schedule
- Positive learning climate
- Assessment and individualized education program (IEP) development process
- Foundations of curriculum and instruction
- Communication-rich environment and processes supportive of communication
- Social competence
- Personal independence and competence
- Functional behavior development and support
- Family involvement
- Collaborative and productive teaming
- Well-planned transitions (for middle school and high school only)

Educators should consider the quality of their programs based on each of these areas and consider how the quality could be improved or ways in which program strengths could be further emphasized.

Strengthening the quality of an education program strengthens the foundation upon which evidence-based practices are implemented. For example, implementing any of the evidence-based practices effectively is nearly impossible without a strong collaborative culture among team members. Team members who are comfortable collaborating are more likely to provide good feedback to each other, to share their challenges in implementing evidence-based practices, and to follow through on decisions about which practices are to be implemented in what ways. Educators are encouraged to reflect on their program's quality and prioritize areas for improvement.

The following case study, alluded to throughout the chapter, illustrates how educators in one school reflected on their special education program and then continued to work through the steps of the NPDC on ASD process in their classrooms.

Lincoln Intermediate is a school that houses 420 third- through fifth-grade students, most of whom are attending their neighborhood school. Two special education teachers, Mary Harris and Michael Johnson, share a cross-categorical caseload. Many students with special needs, including those with ASD, receive much of their education in the general education setting. The special education team decided to look closely at their program for students on the autism spectrum to identify relative strengths and areas for growth, because they knew that these program attributes were contributing to their students' outcomes. Ms. Harris and Mr. Johnson met with general education staff, related service providers, paraprofessionals, administrators, and families to discuss different aspects of the special education program. Together the team discovered that they were particularly strong in the areas of social competence, IEP development, and collaborative teaming. However, they all agreed that improvements could be made in the areas of learning environment and structure and schedule (especially in general education settings, which lacked the visual supports students used in the special education room) and personal independence (all staff reported an overreliance on paraprofessional staff to shepherd students with ASD across their day).

STEP 2: USE IEPS TO DEVELOP GOAL ATTAINMENT SCALING

The NPDC on ASD posits that improvements in overall program quality positively influence student outcomes. In working with schools, the NPDC on ASD encourages the teams of educators and parents to look closely at the goals that have been developed for each student through his or her IEP. When outcomes are clearly defined and functional in nature, teachers and other team members have an easier time identifying EBPs that may be helpful in targeting the expected outcome, designing data collection systems for ongoing assessment, and communicating with team members. In some cases, teams, including parents, have used their time with the NPDC on ASD to rework their IEP goals. Identification of a clear and measurable outcome has then allowed these teams to move forward in the process with a common goal, which is understood and agreed upon by all team members.

Teams are also encouraged to develop goal attainment scaling (GAS) on priority goals. GAS is a process that allows teams to collect information about a student's progress on individual goals by prioritizing targeted goals. Teams ask results-oriented questions, such as "What would make the biggest change for this student this year?" or "Given the goals we want to work on this year, which ones do we need to monitor closely?" Teams are then coached to ensure that the goals are discrete and measurable, and these goals become the focus of the teams' work with the NPDC on ASD in the coming year.

Once these priority goals have been identified, teams are taught how to scale the goals on a five-point continuum. The five points on the scale progress from "much less than expected" to "much more than expected." Baseline data, typically taken from the student's "present level of performance" statement on his or her IEP, inform the "much less than expected" level, and the "expected" level is typically the outcome as reflected on the student's IEP (that is, the level that the student is expected to reach within one academic year). A sample goal attainment scaling form is included in Table 6.1.

Overall, school personnel have responded positively to the GAS process. Reasons for this include the following:

- The opportunity to examine priority goals more closely
- The encouragement to think beyond expected outcomes and imagine what it might look like if a student exceeded expectations
- The opportunity to plan specifically for generalization of skills to other people, environments, and activities
- The acknowledgment that progress might be made even if a student does not meet expectations (that is, the "somewhat less than expected" outcome, as opposed to the typical "goal met" versus "goal not met" language on many IEPs)

TABLE 6.1 Sample Goal Attainment Scaling Form

Much less than expected	When he enters the classroom, Jon does not greet his peers or professionals.
Somewhat less than expected	When entering the classroom in the morning and with a verbal prompt and picture cue, Jon will greet at least one peer by saying "hi" or waving, for 4 out of 5 mornings for a week.
Expected level of outcome	When entering the classroom in the morning and with a visual prompt, Jon will greet at least one peer by saying "hi" or waving, for 4 out of 5 mornings for two consecutive weeks.
Somewhat more than expected	When entering the classroom in the morning and without a prompt, Jon will greet at least one peer by saying "hi" or waving, for 4 out of 5 mornings for two consecutive weeks.
Much more than expected	When entering school in the morning and without a prompt, Jon will greet at least one peer and one nonclassroom professional by saying "hi" or waving, for 4 out of 5 mornings for two consecutive weeks.

Some school teams have incorporated the GAS process into their regular IEP development, and others have reported that writing IEP goals with the GAS levels as benchmarks, or objectives, has been useful. In addition, development of GAS provides a clear way of communicating progress to team members, including families, on the targeted goals.

In general, although developing GAS is initially time consuming, teams have become skilled at the process and it has become more streamlined. For students on the autism spectrum, the identification of discrete and measurable goals can be challenging, especially when dealing with skills as nuanced and abstract as social interactions and nonverbal behaviors. The GAS process provides teams with a structure in which to have conversations about desired outcomes and methods for monitoring progress.

Ms. Harris had a fifth-grade student named Ricky, who had a diagnosis of autism and was included in general education for much of his day. He received daily reading support in a resource room and was involved in a social skills class twice per week. His general education teacher, Miss Murphy, reported that Ricky was quiet in class and rarely participated in the small-group work that was especially important during science lessons. When asked for more detail, Miss Murphy reported that Ricky sat silently during group work while the other students "talked around him." The team decided to add a goal to his IEP about participation in small groups and used goal attainment scaling to develop the goal along a continuum. Using information from his present level of performance, they identified his baseline level: he independently participated when he was in the resource room. The team decided it would be reasonable for Ricky to initiate comments in general education, especially with some visual prompts to remind him to do so. They came up with the following continuum to help Ricky generalize these skills to his general education classroom. The goal attainment scaling form developed for this goal is shown in Table 6.2.

TABLE 6.2 Completed Goal Attainment Scaling Form for Ricky

Much less than expected	Ricky independently initiates two comments per fifteen-minute session during a social skills group session in the resource room.
Somewhat less than expected	When given a visual and verbal prompt, Ricky will make one comment per fifteen-minute small-group session in the general education classroom, across three consecutive data collections.
Expected level of outcome	When given a visual prompt, Ricky will initiate one comment per fifteen-minute small-group session in the general education classroom, across three consecutive data collections.
Somewhat more than expected	When given a visual prompt, Ricky will initiate one comment per fifteen-minute small-group session in two different general education environments (for example, art and social studies, P.E. and science), across three consecutive data collections.
Much more than expected	Ricky will independently initiate one comment per fifteen-minute small-group session in two different general education environments (for example, art and social studies, P.E. and science), across three consecutive data collections.

STEP 3: SELECT EVIDENCE-BASED PRACTICES

Following the program quality review, the selection of targeted IEP outcomes, and the development of GAS, the next phase of the process is to identify evidence-based practices that will facilitate learning and progress for the specified student goals. As mentioned in this chapter's introduction, the NPDC on ASD identified twenty-four focused intervention practices that have demonstrated effectiveness in meeting academic, social, and behavioral outcomes for students with ASD. For a practice for individuals with ASD to be considered as evidence based, efficacy must be established through peer-reviewed research that uses one of the following:

- Two high-quality experimental or quasi-experimental group design studies
- Five high-quality single-subject design studies, conducted by three different investigators or research groups
- One high-quality randomized or quasi-experimental group design study and three high-quality single-subject design studies conducted by at least three different investigators or research groups (across the group and single-subject design studies)

High-quality studies do not have critical design flaws that confound, and they include features that allow readers to rule out competing hypotheses for study findings. These criteria are based on previous research in the field.[3]

Deciding which EBP to implement with a particular student is a collaborative process involving input from the student's family members; teachers; technical assistance providers (for example, district autism specialists or mentors); instructional assistants; and other service providers. Part of this process should include direct observation of the student in the classroom. In addition, the history of what services the student has previously received or is currently receiving ought to be taken into account. Educators working directly with the student

Fidelity of implementation (that is, ensuring that the actual teaching looks as much like it did in the supporting research as possible) is an important aspect to using an EBP; without fidelity, the teaching practice is, in fact, not evidence based at all.

should feel supported in their use of the practice and should have the resources available to implement the EBP with fidelity.

Online training modules have been developed for all twenty-four EBPs. These modules were created in partnership with the Ohio Center for Autism and Low Incidence (OCALI) and are available on the Autism Internet Modules (AIM) Web site, www.autisminternetmodules.org. The modules contain several key components necessary for learning each practice. A description of each component of these EBP printable modules is listed here:

- *Overview of the practice.* This provides basic information, including a general definition of the practice and information about with whom it might be best used.
- *Evidence base.* This lists the research articles that the NPDC on ASD used to classify the practice as being an EBP. These articles may be interesting for educators and families to review.
- *Steps for implementation.* Each of the stages necessary to implement the practice with fidelity are outlined. These step-by-step directions walk school personnel through the processes involved in the EBP, providing examples and clear directions as they attempt to use the practice in their own classroom.
- *Sample data collection sheets.* These have been developed for many of the practices and provide examples of how teams can collect data on a targeted behavior or skill to monitor progress. Gathering accurate baseline data as well as ongoing data guides the decision-making processes necessary for effective teaching.
- *Implementation checklist.* This parallels the step-by-step directions for how to use the EBP. Each checklist is divided into three phases: the planning stage, direct intervention, and progress monitoring. The checklist is designed to be used across the school year at multiple points in time. Each phase of implementing the practice can be tracked as not having been implemented, having been partially implemented, or having been fully implemented. These documents are located in the resource section of the module, which can be located by using the module menu. Teams of educators and parents can work together throughout the year to complete the implementation checklists for EBPs that have been selected and to monitor the steps that have been taken. A checklist can be used as a self-monitoring device or as an observation tool to determine if the steps for implementation have been completed. A sample implementation checklist is included in Form 6.1.

Form 6.1   Implementation Checklist for Visual Supports[4]

Instructions: The implementation checklist includes steps for the development and implementation of visual supports. Please complete all of the requested information, including the site and state, the individual being observed or interviewed, and the learner's initials. To ensure that a practice is being implemented as intended, an observation is *always* preferable. This may not always be possible. Thus items may be scored based on observations with the implementer, discussions, and record review as appropriate. Within the table, record a 2 (implemented), 1 (partially implemented), 0 (did not implement), or NA (not applicable) next to each step observed to indicate to what extent the step was implemented and addressed during your observation. Use the last page of the checklist to record the targeted skill, your comments, whether others were present, and plans for next steps for each observation.

Site: _____ State: _____

Individual observed: _____ Learner's initials: _____

The skills in this chart can be implemented by a practitioner, parent, or other team member.

Observation	1	2	3	4	5	6	7	8
Date								
Observer's Initials								
Planning (Steps 1 – 2)								
Step 1. Developing Visual Supports for Individual Learners				Score*				
1. Determine WHAT information should be presented visually for the learner (e.g., upcoming events, location of specific materials, an academic concept). *Note: Look for activities/events across environments that are causing frustration/ anxiety for learners, that require a great deal of adult support, and/or that learners' comprehension of expectations may be compromised.*								
Observation	1	2	3	4	5	6	7	8
Date								
Observer's Initials								
Step 1. Developing Visual Supports for Individual Learners (Cont.)				Score*				
2. After selecting the information to be presented visually, conduct individualized assessments of the learner's comprehension levels to select one of the following **forms of representation**: a. object (e.g., furniture provides the most meaningful visual boundary, a piece of an activity such as a peg or puzzle piece attached to the outside of a container is the most meaningful label); b. photograph (e.g., photo of the speech therapist lets the learner identify days for therapy, photo of learner's shirt is on outside of drawer so learner can get appropriate clothing); c. drawing or picture symbol (e.g., stop sign used in classroom areas to designate boundaries, calendar with icons that represent upcoming field trips); d. word (e.g., learner's desk and chair labeled with learner's name, graphic organizer used when writing a story with learner); e. phrase or sentence (e.g., learners read notes on PDA from teacher that describes who they will be working with that day, office area labeled with "Incoming mail goes here," "Attendance records go here"); or f. combination of the above formats.								

*Scoring Key: 2 = implemented; 1 = partially implemented; 0 = did not implement; NA = not applicable

Observation	1	2	3	4	5	6	7	8
Date								
Observer's Initials								
Step 2. Organizing Visual Supports for Individual Learners				Score*				
1. Ensure that all visual supports are gathered and arranged prior to activity/event (e.g., classroom locators/labels properly positioned, curriculum supports paired with academic materials).								
Intervention & Monitoring (Step 3)								
Step 3. Implementing Visual Supports for Individual Learners								
1. Show the learner the visual support (e.g., locator, label, technology support).								
2. Teachers/practitioners teach the learner how to use the visual support by:								
a. showing the learner the visual support (e.g., a graphic organizer, locator, label);								
b. standing behind the learner when prompting use of visual support (to ensure learner is looking at visual information, not the staff member);								
c. using only relevant language while teaching use of visual support (e.g., "Today you have speech" rather than "Today is Thursday, Liz, and this picture of the speech therapist means you have speech today");								
d. assisting the learner in participating in activity/event with visual support (e.g., staying in location with visual boundaries, putting items away in labeled containers); and								
e. fading prompts as quickly as possible.								
3. Once the learner has learned how to use the visual support, prompts are minimal during support use.								
4. Use visual support consistently throughout the day.								
5. Teachers/practitioners prepare the learner for changes in activity/event that requires use of visual support (e.g., speech therapy or field trip is cancelled, technology is not working correctly).								
6. Visual supports move with the learner across settings, OR visual supports are located across settings.								
7. Teachers/practitioners use a data collection system to record how learners use visual supports.								

*Scoring Key: 2 = implemented; 1 = partially implemented; 0 = did not implement; NA = not applicable

Date	Observer Initials	Targeted Skill/Behavior, Comments, and Plans for Next Steps
Date	Observer Initials	Targeted Skill/Behavior, Comments, and Plans for Next Steps
Date	Observer Initials	Targeted Skill/Behavior, Comments, and Plans for Next Steps

In addition to the printable aspects described previously, the online modules include more in-depth training information about implementing each practice and monitoring student progress. Each module contains background information about the practice, a description of the ages of children with which the EBP is most effective, and how to use the practice in educational settings. Case study examples from different age ranges are included to illustrate the use of the practice in a variety of settings. The modules also include discussion questions and activities that are appropriate for a range of professional development settings. For example, a school team could work together to learn the practice and use the discussion questions and activities to facilitate this process. The modules also include video examples that show different phases of the practice being used with students.

Finally, pre- and postassessments help individuals monitor their knowledge levels before and after reviewing the materials (see Figure 6.1). The information available in the online modules provides educators with a variety of resources to help both during the selection of EBPs and during the implementation phase. Once EBPs have been selected, technical assistance providers, teachers, and other team members can review the content and implementation steps outlined in the selected module and begin the process of implementation.

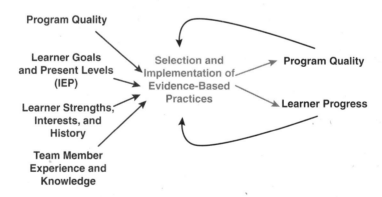

Assessment → Implementation → Outcomes

FIGURE 6.1 Process of Assessment, Selection of Evidence-Based Practices, and Monitoring of Outcomes

After the team had developed goal attainment scaling, they began to discuss how to best encourage Ricky to participate in small groups. Ms. Harris was able to explain to Ricky's general education teacher, Miss Murphy, how she had supported Ricky and his friends in the resource room, beginning by having the students respond to questions in a group session and then by using sentence starter cards (which contained such prompts as "I see . . . " and "I wonder if . . . "). Miss Murphy appreciated these suggestions and asked if Ms. Harris could help her develop these tools for her classroom. The team, including classroom staff and related service providers, decided to look at the online training modules for visual supports and prompting to help them in their teaching. The team also realized that incorporating more visual supports and having less reliance on adult prompting would help them with the aspects of their overall program quality that they had identified as areas for growth. As the team reviewed the practices step-by-step, they became more aware of their teaching methods, and they were confident that they would be able to bring their own teaching more in line with the original research.

STEP 4: COACH TEACHERS AND PARAPROFESSIONALS IN IMPLEMENTING EVIDENCE-BASED PRACTICES

Implementing evidence-based practices can be challenging work, particularly when these practices are novel skills for teachers and paraprofessionals to implement in the classroom. As with learning any new skill, finding supports is critically important. The NPDC on ASD strongly encourages coaching as a process that is supportive of educators' learning and conducive to effective implementation of evidence-based practices.

Coaching can come in the form of a formal relationship between an autism specialist or other subject matter expert hired by the district and a teacher, a peer coaching relationship between two teachers working in the same building or across a district, and the ongoing coaching that a teacher provides to her or his paraprofessionals on a daily basis. Coaching is also a process embedded in the work of teams whose members see their role as one of supporting each other's learning and implementation of evidence-based practices.

The NPDC on ASD based the development of its coaching model for K–12 schools on the work of Mary Ross Moran, Brenda Smith Myles, Joyce Anderson Downing, Chris Ormsbee, and Phoebe Rinkel.[5] The NPDC on ASD encourages the use of materials developed by Rush and Shelden[6] and Hanft, Rush, and Shelden[7] in early intervention settings.

These coaching approaches for early intervention and work with school-age children encourage the creation of a mutually developed plan for support through observation, learning, modeling, and feedback. This cyclical process of support—observation, learning, modeling, and feedback—is well documented by both the coach and the person being coached and can be renegotiated if a need arises. Coaching assumes that both partners share a willingness to teach and learn from each other. Because time is a universal concern when using coaching as a process for support, educators should make efforts to share the value of and need for coaching with school and district administrators to garner their support in scheduling coaching conversations and observations.

To coach and be coached productively, both partners need to decide what tools will be used throughout the process. Overwhelming feedback from technical assistance providers working with model sites has been that the NPDC on ASD resources (for example, the AIM Web site, brief packages, implementation checklists, and steps for implementation) are very helpful in providing nonjudgmental feedback about an educator's practice. Educators also share that the materials were helpful in prioritizing first steps for focusing and planning their work. Further, coaches are encouraged to use these materials to build a common language around evidence-based practices and the steps required for fidelity of their implementation.

Coaching provides the process through which the NPDC on ASD tools and resources can be used to further each team member's implementation of the evidence-based practices. Here are specific examples of how coaching can be used in conjunction with the previously described resources and tools to support a partner in implementing evidence-based practices with fidelity:

- A district-level coach models least-to-most prompting procedures while the teacher watches and rates implementation on the implementation checklist.

In doing so, the teacher further incorporates her knowledge of the specific steps of implementation and how they look when implemented. The teacher provides the coach with feedback on the implementation, further deepening their learning.

- A middle school special education teacher asks her team of eight paraprofessionals to rotate for a week between reviewing the module on reinforcement and bus monitoring. The next week, she brings all the paraprofessionals together with the reinforcement implementation checklist to discuss questions they have related to specific students. During the third week, she meets with each team member to design a plan for reinforcement for the child for whom the paraprofessional has primary responsibility during the school day.
- A team in an elementary school uses the functional behavior assessment materials to make decisions about how to perform a functional behavior assessment for a child.

The staff at Lincoln Intermediate did not have access to an autism specialist. However, because Ms. Harris had had success in getting Ricky to participate in her social skills group, she agreed to coach Miss Murphy in using some of the same techniques in her classroom. First, the team accessed the online training module on visual supports. This provided all of them with some basic information about why visual supports are helpful for students with ASD and what these supports might look like. Using the step-by-step directions and the implementation checklists, Ms. Harris and Miss Murphy worked to develop visual supports to help Ricky participate. These included the same sentence starters he used in the resource room, but also included visually represented directions for the small-group session and a visual timer to help Ricky know how long the session will last. However, when going through the implementation checklist, the team realized they did not have the visual supports available anywhere but the general education classroom. Once they made supports to be used in the art room and the gymnasium, they were confident that they had increased the fidelity of their implementation.

STEP 5: ASSESS AND EVALUATE DATA TO INFORM DECISION MAKING

As exemplary teachers know, lesson planning is a process that has no defined end in terms of evaluation. To design the next lesson, a teacher constantly evaluates not only the lessons he or she presents but also the student products and the feedback received from coaches and mentors. High-quality teaching requires self-evaluation and a desire for continued improvement, and the NPDC on ASD encourages teachers to evaluate and analyze their teaching through the data they collect.

The model emphasizes the importance of two kinds of data to help educators evaluate their teaching and determine next steps: *implementation data* and *intervention data.* Implementation data focus on the actual teaching practices and how they are being used in the classroom. Intervention data are specific to student outcomes and provide teachers with an answer to the question, "Is what I'm doing actually working?"

The NPDC on ASD has developed several tools to assist educators and coaching partners in collecting data to plan their use of evidence-based practices in classrooms. Implementation data are collected through the implementation checklists and used to track the sequence of steps necessary to implement a practice with fidelity. Checklists allow the teacher or paraprofessional and coach to keep a record of the progress they have made together learning about and using each EBP they select. In addition to tracking the use of EBPs through the checklist, coaching partners collect a record of their meetings through the use of the NPDC on ASD coaching logs (see Form 6.2).

These coaching logs are designed to record learning targets, observational data, and recommendations for next steps during each coaching meeting, while also providing a framework for the conversations inherent in the coaching process. NPDC on ASD partners have used coaching logs in many different ways. They are used to

- Document individual student IEPs
- Conduct self-assessment
- Provide coaching feedback to others
- Drive a team discussion about a particular EBP

Form 6.2   NPDC on ASD Coaching Log

COACHING LOG

Inviting Partner _____   Coach _____

EBP/GAS/Program Target _____   Lesson/Activity _____

PRE OBSERVATION CONFERENCE

Date: _____
Time: _____

During:
[ ]

Length: _____
Setting: _____

○ New Target
○ Revisited Target

FOCUS/CONCERN:

DATA COLLECTION METHOD:

OBSERVABLE BEHAVIOR:

ADULT:

STUDENT:

ADULT MASTERY CRITERION _____ %

MAINTENANCE CRITERION _____ TIMES

OBSERVATION

Date: _____
Time: _____

Length: _____
Setting: _____

FOCUS/CONCERN:

NOTES FOR DISCUSSION:

POST OBSERVATION CONFERENCE

Date: _____
Time: _____

During:
[ ]

Length: _____
Setting: _____

NOTES:

MASTERY ACHIEVED:
[ ] YES [ ] NO

MAINTENANCE ACHIEVED:
[ ] YES [ ] NO

NOTES:

FUTURE PLANS/NOTES:

COMMUNICATION SKILLS REMINDERS

* Reflects partner's words
* Uses open questions
* Clarifies words and feelings
* Takes turns; no interrupting
* Uses encouragement

By helping clarify where things are now and how best to proceed, the combination of checklists and coaching logs moves the coaching conversation forward toward the effective use of EBPs in classroom settings.

The NPDC on ASD trains coaching partners to collect intervention data to create a record of student outcomes. The teams are led through the goal attainment scaling process to give them a clear picture of desired outcomes for each student goal targeted by the team. Once outcomes have been set for each targeted goal, the NPDC on ASD offers sample data collection tools with each EBP to help teams decide how to gather empirical data on the desired student outcomes. Used in conjunction, the GAS outcomes and intervention data give coaching teams solid evidence of the relative effectiveness of the programming they have selected for each student. Frequent review of student data leads teams to adjust and improve programming to increase the desired outcomes for each goal.

Data collection tools allow participants to collect and record implementation data and intervention data to assess program improvements continually in the use of EBPs as well as student outcomes resulting from the implementation of EBPs. These tools complement the cyclical processes of support described earlier. As partners move through the coaching year and use the data collection materials, most find that the tools save time, give direction to the coaching process, and validate the effectiveness of certain EBPs for students with ASD.

Working together, Ms. Harris and Miss Murphy regularly reviewed the implementation checklists for visual supports and prompting. Because of the collaborative coaching relationship, Ms. Harris discovered that she could make small tweaks to her already successful program in order to bring it closer to fidelity, and Miss Murphy gained confidence in her ability to provide visual supports throughout the school day. They worked together to encourage paraprofessionals to use less restrictive prompting, and having visual prompts available helped the whole team follow through on this recommendation. Meanwhile, they collected data on Ricky's commenting during small-group sessions and were pleased to see that he made significant gains in the general education classroom and was beginning to comment during art class. Over the course of their conversations, both Ms. Harris and Miss Murphy realized that a self-management system could help Ricky monitor his own participation, further decreasing the need for adult support and increasing Ricky's independence. They then went to the self-management training module, and started the process again. Both teachers reported increased confidence in their teaching and stronger feelings of support from their team members.

TO SUM UP

This chapter provides an overview of some of the processes and related resources that have been developed by the National Professional Development Center on Autism Spectrum Disorders in its work with schools and educators across the United States. Although school teams unaffiliated with the NPDC on ASD might not have access to *all* of the tools described in this chapter, most of the materials are currently available on the NPDC on ASD (http://autismpdc.fpg.unc.edu) and AIM (www.autisminternetmodules.org)Web sites. Using the steps outlined here can help school personnel and families better serve students with ASD. The NPDC on ASD promotes the following:

- Start the process by looking at aspects of overall program quality, because improvements to the greater program can result in both increased collaboration among school teams and positive student outcomes.
- Prioritize and target IEP goals that will make the biggest difference for individual students. The process of goal attainment scaling is a way for teams to track student progress over a set period of time.
- Select evidence-based practices that best suit individual students and their goals, choosing from the list of twenty-four focused intervention practices that the NPDC on ASD has identified as having a solid research base.
- Use NPDC on ASD materials within the supportive relationship of a coaching partnership to help school personnel implement evidence-based practices with fidelity in their school and community settings.

- Collect data continually to help school teams monitor how well the practices are being implemented in classrooms and the extent of student success on identified goals.

> Materials on evidence-based practices, including online training modules and printable resources, can be found on the AIM Web site, www
> .autisminternetmodules.org. Additional information on the NPDC on
> ASD can be found at http://autismpdc.fpg.unc.edu.

Technology for Staff Training, Collaboration, and Supervision in School-Based Programs for Children with Autism

Robyn M. Catagnus, Jamie Pagliaro, and
Bridget A. Taylor

With the growing prevalence of autism spectrum disorders (ASD), educators are challenged with an exploding demand for services. This challenge is further compounded by the current economic climate, requiring public school districts to serve students with autism within local public schools rather than specialized out-of-district private placements. Given that the demand for effective services far exceeds the availability of well-trained teachers and clinicians, school personnel will have to create efficient and economically feasible systems of staff training and ongoing support.

Every year more children are diagnosed with autism than with AIDS, diabetes, and cancer combined, making autism the fastest-growing serious developmental disability in the United States. If special education systems are to keep pace with the growing number of students with autism, innovative practices in cultivating well-trained and supervised treatment staff are essential.

Technology-based innovations are potential solutions to these issues and can help more children with autism receive the interventions they need. Although technology cannot possibly replace real-life clinicians, it does afford school districts palpable options in developing and enhancing intervention programs for children with autism.

This chapter will propose promising applications of current technology to enhance training and supervision of staff as well as collaboration among clinicians to provide state-of-the-art educational services for children with autism.

This chapter highlights the following specific technologies:

- Web-based systems to train professional educators in the design and implementation of individualized, behavior-based intervention programs for students with autism
- Live streaming videoconferencing and video-sharing formats that can be used to facilitate supervision and consultation
- Online collaboration tools to enhance communication and problem solving across teachers, clinicians, and settings

We also provide an overview of impediments to technology use, research outcomes, suggested areas for future research, and other considerations surrounding the use of these technologies.

WEB-BASED TRAINING AND PROFESSIONAL DEVELOPMENT

Training occurs when new school staff members are oriented to their job responsibilities (pre-service training) and when experienced staff members are provided with information on how to improve or broaden job skills (in-service training). The topics of training, also referred to as professional development, can include general student support strategies, specific intervention techniques, school policies and procedures, and other job requirements. Schools typically provide training to groups of staff at designated times, and the format is usually passive in nature (for example, lecture-based workshops).

The challenge is that the cost, the availability of trainers, the limited number of training days, and such coordination issues as classroom coverage and ongoing staff turnover make it difficult to ensure consistency in staff training programs. Insufficient resources or staff expertise to provide specialized training on working with specific populations of students can also be problematic. As a result, teachers and paraprofessional staff may not be adequately prepared to address the needs of more complex students, such as those on the autism spectrum.

Web-based training, also called e-learning, allows trainees to access content anywhere and at any time over the Internet. This alternative format offers an innovative means to deliver training in schools, and multiple types of media, such as video, can be incorporated. Because content can be accessed at the trainees' discretion, many of the time and coordination issues previously mentioned can be overcome. Schools and individual teachers can create their own training content, upload training materials to a content-sharing Web site, and modify the content at will. If an outside consultant or district-level specialist is presenting specialized content, it is possible to broadcast the live training session via webcam or webinar across multiple sites, thus allowing for interactivity with the presenter, or to record the presentation and make it available online for those who could not participate in the live session. There are currently a number of free and commercially available autism-specific training products, and it is likely that more will emerge due to the growing population of individuals with autism. Some of these products offer a static library of text or video content, whereas others incorporate dynamic learning systems that guide trainees through a predefined sequence with online competency testing and automated feedback on performance.

> Teachers and schools should critically evaluate any outside training content, including the credibility of the source and its underlying research, before incorporating it into a formal staff training program.

Case Study: Moodle and Podcasts

The Bucks County Intermediate Unit (BCIU) in Pennsylvania is part of the state structure of public education, positioned between the state education agency and local school districts. Intermediate Units offer specialized services to children in local schools on a regional basis. The BCIU serves children in multiple districts that are widely dispersed over a large geographical area. The BCIU staff includes itinerant teachers, classroom teachers, speech therapists, occupational therapists, physical therapists, and behavior specialists, including Board Certified Behavior Analysts. Many of the students served by the BCIU are diagnosed as having autism spectrum disorders, and several classrooms are specially designed to serve these children. Although there are well-developed programs for autism treatment, and although the BCIU has Board Certified Behavior Analysts on staff, they needed a solution for continued and improved training systemwide.

With such a large and dispersed staff, the BCIU required an affordably standardized and replicable training method for induction and ongoing professional development. For topics of autism education and behavior analytic teaching, in particular, they needed a streamlined and powerful way to educate many people in an efficient manner. They chose Moodle, a software package for creating online learning environments and Internet-based courses, and podcasts, audio or video files that can be e-mailed to or downloaded by staff to help address some of their training needs.

Using Moodle to create a Web site with training curricula, lesson plans, and collaboration tools like assignments and discussion forums, the BCIU organized materials and made them readily available across staff and settings. To improve information dissemination they also used podcasts to share important new topics with all team members. Thanks to the availability of these technologies, staff members do not travel to all trainings. Classes can be held online, and information and quizzes can be sent and collected via the Web. The behavior analysts on staff save time on trainings by sending information to all participants at one time. When material sent online is likely to generate many staff questions, the BCIU organizes a webinar with chat capabilities so staff can attend virtually, ask questions, and share ideas. Special education supervisors at the BCIU anecdotally report that this process has saved money, increased consistency among staff, increased staff skills in behavior analytic teaching, and freed staff and autism experts from having to conduct repeated trainings for induction so they can focus on student-specific issues.

Moodle is an open-source course management system used by educators to create dynamic Web sites for students. Moodle is free to download, and registration is voluntary. For more information, see http://moodle.org.

Case Study: Email, Video, and Cell Phone Instruction for Professional Development

As of 2009, Bristol Township School District (BTSD) served approximately 6,300 students in a suburb in Pennsylvania. At least 50 students in BTSD were identified as having an autism spectrum disorder at the time of publication. According to a special education supervisor at the district, 28 percent of BTSD students had support services through a behavioral health program due to learning disabilities; increased identification by teachers; and barriers to learning common in districts with high cultural diversity, low income, and many English language learners.

In addition to having special education instructors, psychologists, guidance counselors, and social workers, BTSD provided additional training in behavioral health issues for general education teachers, paraprofessionals, assistant principals, and principals. However, BTSD faced a problem with increased challenging behaviors in kindergarten inclusion classrooms and sought a fully replicable training solution to teach behavior management skills to staff and social skills to students.

Hired as a consultant, the first author of this chapter created a one-year Web-based program of training and staff development for three kindergarten classes. Written lesson plans and training videos were collected or created to explain methods of reinforcement and behavior management. The consultant integrated both published training materials and material created based on the needs of the students in each room. Student training materials were focused on a curriculum for teaching social skills, anger management, empathy, coping, and self-control.

Because teachers and paraprofessionals were at different schools and had very little time to meet, all materials were e-mailed. Twenty short lessons were sent to staff over twenty-two weeks. Each module introduced a classroom management topic and instructed teachers explicitly on how to change their strategies of responding to behavior and how to teach specific social skills lessons to the students. Teachers accessed these trainings via computer or cell phone at their convenience. They also recorded student behavior with a small, portable digital video camera. The consultant reviewed the tapes and sent feedback by phone or e-mail. Short site visits were conducted as needed, but the majority of training and feedback was Web based. In addition, the school Web site was used to share information, updates, and strategies with the students' families. Survey results of teacher feedback on this system of delivery were positive.

Outcomes for teacher behavior included an increase in positive teacher language, a decrease in negative teacher language, and 74 to 94 percent treatment fidelity for targeted classroom management skills. Student outcomes included decreased absences, reduced rates of behavior-related incidents, and increased learning (as measured by changes in rates of acquisition for early literacy fluency measures).

Tool Overview: Rethink Autism

Two of this chapter's authors have been involved with the development of Rethink Autism, a Web-based applied behavior analysis treatment platform designed for use by professionals, paraprofessionals, and family members who are delivering services to individuals with autism. The platform allows users to create and manage an individual child profile, which can be accessed online by team members working with the child across settings. It includes a brief skills checklist that determines individualized program recommendations, a comprehensive video-based skills curriculum, video-based training modules, and data tracking and automated progress reporting tools. Rethink Autism attempts to translate existing research on autism interventions into easy-to-follow video content, contained within a user-friendly interface that can be accessed online anywhere and at any time.

The core feature of Rethink Autism is a comprehensive, state-of-the-art curriculum spanning eight categories (pre-academic, academic, social-emotional, daily living, motor, play and leisure, expressive language, and receptive language) and consisting of more than 1,200 video-based exercises. The exercises are linked together as teaching step progressions, which make up skill acquisition programs or "lessons." Each lesson video is approximately five to seven minutes long, and is intended to function as a model for staff and parent training purposes.[1] All of the teaching strategies depicted in the lesson videos are research based, including errorless teaching, incidental teaching, and peer-mediated interventions.[2] The lesson videos are planned, executed, and carefully edited with voiceover by a team of special educators and Board Certified Behavior Analysts to ensure clinical integrity. The team also develops a written description for each of the lesson videos, which details the teaching strategy and contains additional information, such as generalization steps, alternate prompting and error correction procedures, and troubleshooting tips. Data tracking tools allow for ongoing analysis of skill acquisition, and new lessons are automatically recommended as the child masters lessons.

Although Rethink Autism offers an innovative approach to addressing some of the training and intervention needs of the autism population, more research is needed to determine whether it truly leads to meaningful changes in the behavior of teachers, paraprofessionals, family members, and children. To date, there is no published research on the utility or efficacy of this product, despite its being developed around evidence-based intervention strategies. Because Web-based products are easily modified, it is likely that any new research could influence the content of Rethink Autism in a timely manner.

Disclosure: The authors of this chapter have a financial interest in Rethink Autism. For more information on Rethink Autism, see www.rethinkautism .com.

ONLINE STAFF COLLABORATION

In special education, collaboration amongst individualized education program (IEP) team members is mandated by law and by practice, offering opportunities to identify problems, develop interventions, and monitor outcomes.[3] Despite the clear need and potential benefits, collaboration among school staff can be difficult to accomplish. The most common barriers to collaboration are distance, which prevents travel to a shared meeting location, and lack of time, which may be due to difficulty with scheduling, overwhelming job duties, or the unavailability of shared planning periods. Finding ways to overcome these barriers is particularly important for teams serving students with autism, as input from multiple staff and family members is often necessary to make effective programmatic decisions on an ongoing basis.

Web-based asynchronous collaboration, such as through message boards, live chat, e-mail, and online discussion groups, offers a viable option for schools to foster structured and informal collaboration. These forums offer the flexibility to chat live across locations, thus removing the distance barrier, or to post messages with delayed feedback to eliminate schedule coordination as well as distance issues. For example, geographically dispersed support teams can set up confidential chat sessions or discussion groups to solicit input and share updates about a specific student, or groups of teachers may come together to share materials, experiences, and best practices using an open message board. Increasingly, schools are moving to Web-based forums to educate and encourage collaboration among educators in a more efficient manner.

Researchers note that social distance and anonymity in regard to race, gender, and social status make online discussions more equitable,[4] and that Web-based collaboration fosters reflection, conflict resolution, and discussion. It is recommended that teachers and schools develop formal communication guidelines, establish policies to ensure confidentiality of student information, and verify the security of any Web-based forum they use.

Case Study: Online Collaboration to Develop Intervention Plans

Catagnus and Hantula[5] describe the use of computer-mediated collaboration by an IEP team. The setting was a large private school serving more than five hundred students, many of whom were diagnosed with autism. The study investigated the use and outcomes of online threaded discussion boards and file sharing by a teacher, speech therapist, and occupational therapist. Members of the team used an online platform to develop a behavioral intervention plan for a teen male with autism who engaged in inappropriate conversational initiation and responses. Online collaboration was explored as a solution because of scheduling and time constraints common to special educators.

The addition of online collaboration to typical daily staff interactions was found to speed up the development of a behavioral intervention plan, shortening the time required from three to six weeks on average at the school to nine days in this case. An effective plan was produced, and the student's problem behavior was reduced as the teacher's behavior management skills related to inappropriate conversation improved. Although the online discussion was not viewed as a suitable replacement for meeting in person, team members were fairly satisfied with the process and viewed it as a useful augmentation to their face-to-face interaction. Interestingly, participants reported an increase in face-to-face dialogue at work as a result of their online involvement. Members of the team also reported improved interpersonal relationships.

Tool Overview: Video Annotation for Self-Reflection by Practicing Teachers

Rich and Hannafin[6] describe the use of video annotation tools to enhance educator self-reflection and collaboration. It is quite common for examples of teaching to be provided (or for teachers to share samples of instruction) through video. Video case studies, video uploads, and real-time videoconferencing have been explored in the literature as means of sharing the instructional experiences of educators. However, tools designed to annotate video may extend the medium's use for self-analysis and coordinating service delivery teams. After capturing real examples of teaching, teachers can review and analyze their performance through a process of reflection in which they describe what they observe, analyze their own performance, and develop a plan of action for improvement. In some cases they engage peers or supervisors to collaborate about their performance. Some of these programs are stand-alone applications, whereas others are Web based.

To provide an example of how video annotation might look and work, Rich and Hannafin[7] describe a process by which teachers videotape segments of their work in the classroom and upload them into a Web-based software program. The program then takes them through a sequence of "guided noticing" analysis activities designed to scaffold the reflection process. Writing panes, open simultaneously on the screen, prompt teachers ("What do you notice?"), and cue them to write evidence for what they notice, to interpret their findings, and to generate questions about what they observed. Teachers can use a space on the screen to write a transcript of the video and to view uploaded related documents, work samples, and artifacts related to the instruction. The screen has a video review panel in which they can watch, pause, and note the time of teaching or interaction events.

A number of video annotation products have similar characteristics. Each of the video annotation products reviewed allowed teachers to share their annotated video segments with others. However, some of the products better facilitated collaboration than others through more complex features. Although most of these applications were used by student teachers, a natural extension of their functionality would be for academic and behavioral collaboration around programs for students with autism.

> Reischl and Oberleitner[8] describe BI-Capture (recently renamed "Behavior Capture" at the time of publication), and BI-CARE (recently renamed "Behavior Connect" at the time of publication), technologies marketed to the autism community for the purposes of capturing and sharing videos to document and analyze challenging behavior. The Web site for the products, www.behaviorimaging.com, describes an online portal for collaboration that allows people to share videos of behavioral incidents, annotate and organize the videos, and collaborate with team members. The video capture software is a digital video tool that records continuously while on, yet allows users to save and mark a specific behavioral event's video data and to digitally save a specified period of time *before* the event occurred.

Tool Overview: Online Communities for Collaboration

Teachers use the Internet to engage in socializing, professional networking, and informal collaboration. Tapped In is an example of an online teacher community. Barab, Kling, and Gray[9] envision Tapped In as instrumental in developing and growing systemic online communities more locally at the district or state levels. The site is used for professional development and to create regional collaborative infrastructures, and they report that thousands of people log in each month and actively engage in creating and taking courses or workshops and participate in group discussions. Online communities like this one benefit pre-service and in-service professionals and offer the autism specialist unique opportunities to garner wider support and gather ideas from more colleagues. A search of Tapped In results in several discussion threads related to autism specifically.

Information at www.tappedin.org includes such communication features as live chat, messaging, and discussion boards. Users are able to share information through file storage, directories, and group rooms. Additional features include calendars, a job bank, and event rooms for registration and online sessions. The site authors suggest that participants can engage in collaborative learning projects and discussions, mentor others, and create and attend online courses. The online community consists of international educators, K–12 teachers, paraprofessionals, researchers, students, administrators, and others.

TECHNOLOGY-BASED SUPERVISION AND COACHING

Supervision, coaching, consultation, or mentoring is an ongoing process that occurs when feedback is provided to an individual to maintain or improve his or her job performance. Feedback is typically delivered by a more experienced staff member. In schools, supervision can take a variety of formats, including a review of written plans and teaching materials, direct classroom observation, and the monitoring of student outcome data. Supervision is particularly important in special education classrooms, where staff members are implementing multiple-component plans that vary across students and require frequent modifications.

Real-time supervision involves observing someone and then providing immediate performance feedback. Time-delayed supervision differs in that feedback is provided by phone or in writing sometime after the observation has occurred. The challenge in both cases is scheduling time for observations and feedback. In classrooms serving students with autism, supervision may be provided by district-level specialists or outside consultants. The limited on-site availability of these types of supervisors creates another coordination challenge.

Web-based videoconferencing and video sharing present opportunities for supervision to occur more regularly, and can also help educators overcome some time and availability barriers. For example, live videoconferencing allows a supervisor to observe interactions between teachers and their students in real time using a webcam. Although this format still requires coordination of schedules, it can enable a supervisor to observe from a different location and still provide immediate feedback on teacher performance. This option means the specialist travels less between locations and can thus observe more often or for longer. Video sharing presents another alternative to enable delayed observation and feedback, thus eliminating the need to coordinate schedules. Using this format, the teacher videotapes a portion of his or her teaching session and uploads the video to a secure video-sharing site, and the supervisor reviews the video to evaluate performance at a convenient time. This format eliminates some of the coordination issues encountered in live videoconferencing, but it does create a delay in feedback and therefore requires follow-up observations.

Data reviews are another important element of supervising programs for students with autism. Specifically, data on skill acquisition and the occurrence of problem behavior can help inform intervention decisions. Supervision should include ensuring that data are reliably recorded, correctly displayed, and used to make program modifications. Traditional pencil-and-paper data collection and graphing procedures may limit access to data for supervisors who are not always on-site.

Many smart phone and Web-based applications are available to streamline the process of data collection for teachers and paraprofessionals. Examples include software to collect information about the rate, intensity, duration, and other measures of challenging behavior. Some programs also provide for the collection of information about antecedents, behaviors, and consequences. These types of measures can be used to conduct functional assessments and develop behavioral intervention plans. Applications also exist for collecting academic data during discrete trial teaching. Most applications automatically graph and upload data to a Web site, thus allowing for real-time sharing and analysis.

Video-based supervision formats and online data reviews offer a way for school programs and districts with limited supervisor availability to become more efficient in providing ongoing supervision. They also present opportunities to engage district-level specialists or outside consultants while minimizing travel costs.

Case Study: Desktop Videoconferencing

Rule, Salzberg, Higbee, Menlove, and Smith[10] conducted a pilot study to evaluate the use of videoconferencing for implementing programs in a rural area for a student with autism. For this study an autism specialist worked directly with classroom staff as a consultant. Prior to using videoconferencing, the consultant made four visits to the child's location and also held a full-day training workshop for the teacher and classroom professionals. The consultant demonstrated intervention and teaching procedures, and trained staff members on their implementation. Subsequent consultations were made through scheduled thirty- to sixty-minute videoconferencing sessions, during which the consultant observed classroom staff members teaching the student in real time.

However, although the consultant planned to give immediate verbal feedback and coaching, the equipment often malfunctioned and the educators could not hear the instructions. Over two months, five such video consultations were conducted in which the consultant watched the instruction but could not always be heard by classroom staff. When necessary, the consultant would watch and then call the staff person or send e-mail feedback. Classroom staff collected data about student responding and shared them over the phone and via e-mail. Despite the technical difficulties encountered, the child made significant progress during this process.

Skype is a free and readily accessible Web-based communication tool that allows users to make phone calls or videoconference over the Internet. For more information, see www.skype.com.

Case Study: Headsets and Ear "Bugs"

Scheeler, Congdon, and Stansbery[11] sought to understand whether a method involving immediate and corrective feedback through "bug-in-ear" (BIE) technology could change teacher behavior in a way that was both socially acceptable and practical in a real teaching situation.

Using a personal FM system made up of a portable audio transmitter and receiver, teachers were trained to give each other verbal feedback across the room as far as 150 feet. The person wearing the transmitter had a small microphone, and the person receiving wore a small and unobtrusive "bug" in his or her ear.

After practicing the use of the personal FM system, the teachers developed some short feedback phrases to communicate with each other. The goal of their interaction was to increase the use of effective behavior contingencies during instruction. Over fifteen- to thirty-minute sessions, coteaching dyads used a BIE system to coach each other on completing more three-term contingencies to increase specific, positive, and corrective feedback to students. Three dyads participated in the study. While one member of the dyad instructed a student, the other was observing and reminding him or her with such phrases as "Complete the trial," "Reinforce the student," "Good praise," or "Stick with him."

The BIE method of coaching worked to increase the teachers' percentage of three-term contingency trials to an established criterion of 90 percent for three consecutive sessions. Postintervention, the teachers maintained the behavior of completing trials and generalized the behavior to other settings without the coteacher providing feedback. Social acceptance of the BIE method was high, and participants found it to be efficient and practical for coaching unobtrusively in real time.

The use of BIE technology, or a Bluetooth headset, seems readily applicable as an extension of video-based consultation. Perhaps Web-based forms of consultation, such as those in the previous examples, could be enhanced even further with an element of private and immediate coaching.

HELPFUL ONLINE TOOLS AND RESOURCES

Training

ASD Video Library www .autismspeaks.org/video /glossary.php

This Web-based glossary contains over a hundred video clips illustrating the subtle differences between typical and delayed development in young children and ways to spot the early red flags for ASD.

Autism Internet Modules (AIM) www.autisminternetmodules .org	This series of online learning modules includes information on assessment and identification of autism spectrum disorders, recognizing and understanding behaviors and characteristics of individuals with ASD, transition to adulthood, employment, and numerous evidence-based practices and interventions.
GoToMeeting www.gotomeeting.com	Web conferencing, desktop-sharing, and other online meeting tools, which can be used for live broadcasts or to record sessions, are found here. There is also a webinar option for larger groups.
Interactive Collaborative Autism Network (ICAN) www .autismnetwork.org	This Web site disseminates information about characteristics and assessment of children and youth with ASD, along with evidence-based interventions and services for this population.
Moodle www.moodle.com	This is a course management system designed to help educators who want to create quality online courses. It is open-source and completely free to use.
Rethink Autism www.rethinkautism.com	This Web-based autism treatment platform includes a comprehensive curriculum with over 1,200 video-based applied behavior analysis exercises, staff and parent training modules, and automated data tracking tools.
USTREAM www.ustream.com	This site offers a space for free live video streaming, which can be used to create webcasts, to video chat, and to watch videos on the Internet.

Collaboration

Autism4Teachers www.autism4teachers.com	This free Web site, created by teachers, has printable materials, data sheets, lesson ideas, and much more.

Boardmaker Share www.boardmakershare .com	This is an online community for finding and sharing visual activity schedules, and finding the groups who are using them along with you. (*Note:* To use this site you must have Boardmaker communication software, which can be purchased at www.mayer-johnson.com/products/boardmaker.)
Doodle www.doodle.com	This online scheduling service helps groups of people find the right date and time to meet. The basic service is free and requires neither registration nor a software download.
Google www.google.com/apps/intl/ en/edu/collaboration .html	Google offers a variety of free online collaboration tools, including live video chat, document sharing, and blogs.
Tapped In www.tappedin.org	This is a free, membership-based online community that gathers education professionals to learn, collaborate, share, and support one another.
TeacherTube www.teachertube.com	This is an online community for sharing instructional videos. It is a site to provide anytime, anywhere professional development, and a place where teachers can post videos designed for students to view in order to learn a concept or skill.
Vizzle www.monarchteachtech .com	This is interactive Web-based software for creating and sharing visual lessons for children with autism.
Wiki www.wiki.com	This is a database of pages that visitors can edit live. You can edit a page in real time, search content, and view updates since your last visit. In a "moderated wiki," wiki owners review comments before they are added to the main body of a discussion on a topic.

Supervision

ABC Data for iPhone http://itunes.apple.com/us/ app/abc-data-pro/ id349426906?mt=8	ABC Data is an unobtrusive data collection tool for counting the incidence of behaviors and recording session durations. Further, ABC Data is also a general-purpose stopwatch and tally counter. There is also a "pro" version with advanced features.
Behavior Imaging Solutions www.behaviorimaging.com	This site enables collaboration and consultation between patients and professionals through video capture and a secure health record application that allows users to store, share, and annotate video files.
Behavior Tracker Pro www.behaviortrackerpro .com	This behavior data collection application for personal digital assistants (PDAs) allows educators, behavioral therapists, aides, teachers, and parents to track and graph behaviors.
DDTrac Special Education Progress Monitoring www.developingmindssoftware .com	This online progress monitoring system allows customized data collection and analysis to meet the individual needs of special education students.
Kid's Zone, National Center for Education Statistics, U.S. Department of Education www.nces.ed.gov/nceskids	This is a free Web site that offers a variety of online tools, including a Web-based graphing application that allows users to create and save custom graphs.
Skype www.skype.com	This software application allows users to make voice calls over the Internet. Calls to other users within the Skype service are free, and users can videoconference using a webcam.

Case Study: Web- and Video-Based Field Experiences

Field experiences for educators can also be conducted via the Web or be enhanced by Web-based technology. For example, autism specialists who are attempting to become board certified in behavior analysis are required to have a supervised field experience. After candidates begin coursework in behavior analysis, they accrue hours of fieldwork applying the principles of behavior analysis under the supervision of a Board Certified Behavior Analyst (BCBA). Supervision requires that the BCBA *see* the candidate working in the field every other week and interact one-on-one to provide feedback. Group supervisory meetings are allowed to account for half of the supervision in any two-week period.

For candidates in remote areas, for those who don't work directly under the supervision of a BCBA at their job, or for those whose schedules are very restricted, an online experience via a distance supervision program may be a good fit. During Web-based supervision, videos of the candidate's work are shared so the supervisor can offer feedback. Alternatively, real-time observation via webcam is an option. Group meetings can also be held using Web-conferencing systems. In this way, a candidate for board certification can be seen in his or her work environment, get coaching and feedback, and develop a cohort of collaborators for sharing information during group meetings.

He, Means, and Lin[12] describe the use of a Web-based system for tracking and managing instructional field experiences. They noted that field experience programs generate many records about visits, paperwork for documentation, and student written responses. These data are typically stored as paper, as opposed to digital formats. The authors sought to design and evaluate a system to store, aggregate, and manage documents and records created throughout the supervision process. The system they developed has modules for administrators, host teachers, field experience students, and course instructors to track classroom field time, record written information about a given experience, collect student reflections or permanent products, and increase communication and collaboration among participants.

Field experiences for teachers in distance learning programs raise special challenges. Simpson[13] describes international field experiences in which the instructor was not able to observe the student in the field due to distance or availability. She describes a New Zealand pre-service teacher education program in which costly and infrequent instructor site visits were augmented by print, video, phone, and computer-mediated communication to bridge the gap for these pre-service teachers and help make their field experience meaningful.

IMPEDIMENTS TO TECHNOLOGY USE

Technology is very new for some people,[14] and some more experienced teachers are less comfortable with Internet technology than are their younger, more tech-savvy counterparts.[15] However, with access and exposure to technology, independent learning and experience, professional development, and peer support, people can become much more comfortable with technology.

Technical difficulties inherent in using machines and virtual systems may inhibit participation,[16] but these can be overcome. Educators need an established method for accessing support if they encounter technical difficulties. This may be complicated if educators are using multiple products or online services. Users of products or services need to know whether they can contact the company directly, or whether they should contact an information technology person within the school or district for assistance.

Other barriers inherent in using technology in the classroom include time and work pressures, as well as the necessity of functioning simultaneously in two different behavior settings: the classroom and online. To overcome this barrier, the use of a work-related online community must be approved by the school or district, and users must be supported in their participation.

Our own biology may present another kind of technological barrier.[17] Communicating via technology may be difficult due to our inability to decipher and read the social cues typically available in face-to-face interactions. Simply put, face-to-face communication is the natural and preferred method for most people. Researchers have also found that participants in their studies have experienced confusion over missing the social context cues in a virtual environment.[18] Such variables as tone of voice, facial expressions, and gestures may be "lost in translation" in online communication. However, organizations and groups might be more motivated to rely on an "unnatural" medium if it is easy, is cost-effective, and becomes part of the culture's norm. In addition, these difficulties may lessen as people adapt to the new environment. One suggestion is for groups of educators to meet in person first before starting to work together online.

Time is also cited as a major requirement of online collaboration in regard to planning and implementation.[19] Online processes may save time by making scheduling easier or shortening the overall time needed to collaborate and solve a problem, but the communication medium, such as typing, may be more time consuming than meeting face-to-face. Researchers have noted the extended time required to complete an online discussion,[20] and online groups may take more time to come to overall consensus in a decision-making process.[21] The increased effort involved in reading and typing[22] or the inability to type have also been cited as problematic.[23] Each of these variables has been linked in the literature to participant dissatisfaction with online communication methods.

Technology has not found a stronghold in education the way it has in other businesses. Educators and the education system have not yet consistently incorporated technology into teaching, and they did not do so even when technology was simply defined and no special electronics or tools were required.[24] However, everyday use of computers, the Internet, and data stored online may be changing all of this, opening up educators to the idea of training, collaborating, and delivering supervision online. It is worth the effort involved because education—especially the education of students with autism—now requires professionals to collaborate across boundaries and share specialized knowledge.

TO SUM UP

From including Web-based training programs and collaboration tools to incorporating video-based supervision programs and online data reviews, school districts can create cohesive systems of training, can provide avenues for educators to collaborate, and may improve the frequency and quality of supervision. To summarize the key points discussed in this chapter:

> As technology becomes more integrated into systems of education, applied research on the impact of technology on teachers—and, more important, on technology's influence on the outcomes of students with autism—is clearly needed. To date, most research examining the effectiveness of computer- or Web-based technology as a tool for learning has been in the areas of business and medicine.[25] There are numerous studies, however, addressing the

online communication and education of adult participants in distance learning programs.[26] There have also been a few studies on pre-service educators or teacher-students earning a degree online.[27] In addition, research about computer-based communication or collaboration by education professionals includes analyses of online teacher communities,[28] with most studies focused on the reflective practices of pre-service teachers, and a only a few focused on support communities of working professionals.[29] Nonetheless, taken together the emerging research indicates that technology-mediated modes of learning and collaboration can be viable learning tools for enhancing teachers' skills and knowledge. What is less known is the impact of this technology on practices to improve supervision and on the educational outcomes of students, particularly those with autism. Perhaps, as applied research begins to support these practices, more school systems will be willing to import these tools into systems of education for students with autism. Alternatively, as more schools begin to use technology, applied research is likely to follow.

- Web-based systems can be used to train educators in the design and implementation of behavior-based intervention programs for students with autism.
- Live streaming videoconferencing and file-sharing formats can be used to facilitate coaching and collaboration efforts among educators.
- Online collaboration tools can be used to enhance communication and problem solving among teachers, clinicians, and administrators.
- Although some impediments to technology use do exist, it seems reasonable to expect that technology will continue to grow in importance as a tool for educating children with autism.

PART TWO

Summary and Synthesis

It is currently evident that the population of students diagnosed with autism is larger and more diverse than previously thought. Perhaps more significant, many of these children are now clearly visible in regular education environments. With increasing efforts to promote inclusion, the regular education classroom provides an optimal environment for students with autism to interact with typically developing peers, who can serve as mentors and mediators of interventions. The regular education environment provides a context for students to develop positive self-efficacy, increases self-esteem, and offers models for appropriate and expected classroom behavior. The chapters in Part Two are specific in their aim of describing, improving, translating, and facilitating best practices for children with autism with a focus on evidence-based practices in classrooms. In the overview of educational interventions in Chapter Three, these evidence-based practices are described with the caveat that as children with autism sequentially progress through grade levels with increasing academic achievement expectations, social difficulties are more likely to manifest and to interfere with both academic performance and social interactions. For some children with autism these manifestations include the following: difficulty initiating and maintaining relationships with peers; an inability to consistently engage in reciprocal social exchanges; limited ability to understand the perspectives of others, and a lack of or limited awareness of nonverbal communication or social norms. Although social manifestations vary among children with autism, as these children reach middle school age—and as social demands and expectations increase—they are often vulnerable to social exclusion, ridicule, and bullying, which can not only compound their sense of isolation but also have a direct impact on their academic classroom experience overall.

Several comprehensive treatment models are described in Part Two that are designed to incorporate classroom interventions, including such specific instructional strategies as positive behavior supports, pivotal response treatment (see Chapter Five for a description of the development of classroom pivotal response teaching), and social skills training. Given that helping students with autism develop social relationships is critical, effective social interventions should incorporate opportunities for them to work with typically developing students in small peer groups, include such programs as Circle of Friends or the Big Buddy Program, and embed socialization scripts. Chapter Four describes specific and detailed strategies to use in the classroom, including socialization scripts; cooperative arrangements; and antecedent interventions, such as priming and contingent escape and instructional fading. The National Professional Development Center on Autism Spectrum Disorders, as described in Chapter Six, completed comprehensive reviews of established evidence-based interventions for use in classroom contexts, including differential reinforcement, peer-mediated intervention, and parent-implemented intervention, among others. This chapter also provides an exemplar of a specific implementation checklist, as well as steps for coaching professionals implementing the practices. This includes developing goal attainment scaling to track student progress over a set period of time and prioritizing and targeting IEP goals that are linked to the evidence-based interventions.

In order to effectively use these interventions, both teachers and classroom staff—including paraprofessionals—should be trained in multiple intervention strategies and have specific training in autism spectrum disorders. The intervention programs should be individualized, include specific and measurable goals, and have a documented system of progress. The classroom environment should be flexible while including both structured and naturalistic contexts for instructional opportunities and promoting generalization and maintenance of skills. Although these evidence-based interventions are designed for use in the classroom, they also include the critical component of parent involvement. This involvement is necessary for the generalization of skills to other contexts; further, evidence suggests that integrating goals and objectives across classroom and home contexts, as well as providing support and training to parents, helps foster collaboration and partnership among school personnel, teachers, and parents.

Access to appropriate training and guidance for the implementation of evidence-based practices is critical in order to translate these practices into classroom settings and activities. Adequate training of staff and consistent programmatic implementation that is coordinated and intensive enhance positive experiences for both teachers and students, and provide the context for children with autism to make important developmental and academic gains. Using technology for staff training, collaboration, and supervision is one mechanism for providing effective, efficient, and feasible ongoing support. Also, emerging research indicates that technology mediates modes of learning and collaboration that appear be viable tools for enhancing skills and knowledge. Chapter Seven describes Web-based training, podcasts, and asynchronous communication through message boards, live chat, and online discussion groups for classroom staff. These tools allow teachers and staff to collaboratively develop intervention plans; annotate videos to share samples of instruction for the purpose of self-reflection among teachers that promotes teaming; and discuss instructional practices, successes, and challenges.

Systematic implementation of evidence-based interventions lays the groundwork for children with autism to have successful classroom experiences in both academic and social domains. Clearly documented in these chapters is that using evidence-based interventions improves the quality of educational programming and has implications for long-term positive outcomes for children with autism.

The Roles of School Staff, Administrators, and Families

The Role of School Administrators in Working with Children and Families Affected by Autism Spectrum Disorders

Cynthia M. Herr

Today's administrators must lead their schools in the face of challenges unimagined by their predecessors fifteen years ago—among them, the unprecedented national increase in the number of children with autism in elementary and secondary school. Currently, the Centers for Disease Control and Prevention has reported the prevalence of children with ASD to be at about 1 in 110.[1]

School administrators face significant difficulties in providing appropriate services to students identified as having an autism spectrum disorder (ASD). They must learn about special education law as it relates to ASD and, in particular, about all of the required procedures for identifying students with autism, developing meaningful and legal individualized education programs (IEPs), and providing appropriate special education services, as well as staying current with any changes to the law. In addition, school administrators must

- Know the federal and state laws that govern the provision of services to students with disabilities, and students with ASD in particular
- Have basic knowledge of autism spectrum disorders in their many forms
- Be familiar with research-based interventions for students with ASD, and know what gaps exist in the research
- Provide ASD training and related resources for instructional staff, and training in ASD as appropriate for support staff
- Have skills for working effectively with parents of students with ASD

The required procedures for students with autism are no different from the required procedures for all students with disabilities. Yet being aware of these procedures is no easy task, especially when one considers that school administrators have many other responsibilities and many other laws pertaining to education of which they must also be aware.[2] There is evidence, however, that "[administrators] who focus on instructional issues, demonstrate administrative support for special education, and provide high-quality professional development for teachers produce enhanced outcomes for students with disabilities and for others at risk for school failure."[3]

This chapter addresses the five challenges just listed and provides recommendations for steps that school administrators can take to address each challenge. For each of these five challenges, a brief scenario illustrates the problems administrators might encounter in working with children with ASD and their families. Each scenario is based on an actual situation, although the names and identities of all individuals have been changed. Following each scenario, the particular challenges such a problem creates for administrators are discussed, along with recommendations that administrators might follow in overcoming the challenges.

KNOWING THE PERTINENT LAWS

It is late September, and Emily, a fourth grader with Asperger syndrome, has been attending her new school for a month. At the beginning of the school year, Emily's mother, Mrs. Wilson, had requested an IEP meeting to review and revise Emily's IEP from third grade. According to the school principal, Mrs. Jones, this last week in September was the earliest date that a meeting could be arranged. Emily's records from her previous school had already been forwarded to her new school, but Mrs. Wilson brought a copy of Emily's third-grade IEP with her to the meeting. When Mrs. Wilson entered the conference room for the meeting, the school team members were already assembled. Emily's teacher, Mr. Tanaka, and Mrs. Jones were there. Mrs. Wilson was introduced to Ms. Dominguez, the itinerant special education teacher assigned to the school, and to Mr. Leed, a district behavior specialist.

After introducing everyone, Mrs. Jones announced that the meeting would be a short one because there wasn't much to discuss. When Mrs. Wilson asked for clarification, Mrs. Jones stated that the team had already discussed Emily's progress in the first month of fourth grade, and because Emily was doing well in school and didn't have any academic issues, there was no reason for Emily to continue to receive special education services. Mrs. Jones further explained that the only reason for the meeting was to inform Mrs. Wilson that Emily would not be receiving special education services. When Mrs. Wilson protested that Emily continued to need social skills instruction, which she had received the previous year, Mr. Tanaka responded that Emily was very polite in class, and he didn't see any need for her to have social skills lessons. In addition, Mr. Leed explained that there were no other students in the school who needed social skills instruction, and that the district couldn't provide social skills instruction for an individual child. Again, Mrs. Wilson protested that although Emily was indeed very polite with adults, she had no friends and did have significant difficulty interacting with her peers. Again, Mr. Tanaka replied that he had not observed Emily having problems with her classmates. He said Emily was very quiet in class and never caused problems on the playground, keeping to herself. Mrs. Wilson also explained that Emily had always had several accommodations as part of her IEP. Mr. Tanaka replied that because Emily was doing well academically, she clearly did not need any accommodations. Ms. Dominguez, the itinerant special education teacher, said nothing during the meeting other than to state, in response to Mrs. Wilson's inquiry, that she had neither met nor observed Emily.

Mrs. Wilson, clearly very upset at the direction the meeting had taken, burst into tears. Without responding to Mrs. Wilson's obvious distress or offering tissues, Mrs. Jones asked the other team members, one by one, if they were in agreement that Emily did not need an IEP. Each member other

Although the names of all participants have been changed, this scenario reflects a real IEP meeting for a child with ASD. The unfortunately brusque and hurried nature of this meeting is not necessarily characteristic of IEP meetings. The dilemma of the difference between appearance and need, however, is often all too real for school-age children and families affected by autism.

It is clear from the opening scenario that Mrs. Jones, the principal, was unaware of the requirements of the Individuals with Disabilities Education Act (IDEA) of 2004 in regard to numerous issues. Among the errors Mrs. Jones and the other members of the school team made were the following:

- Failure to notify Mrs. Wilson in writing of the team's intention to discontinue Emily's special education services
- Failure to gather and provide recent evaluation information to document that Emily was no longer eligible for special education services
- Failure to include an IEP team member knowledgeable about ASD, and one who had interacted with and observed Emily
- Failure to consider Mrs. Wilson's input about Emily's need for accommodations and social skills instruction

STATE AND FEDERAL LAWS

Public school administrators must be aware of the federal laws that govern the provision of special education services to students with disabilities. The most critical federal laws related to special education are IDEA of 2004, Section 504 of the Vocational Rehabilitation Act of 1973, and the No Child Left Behind Act of 2001. Administrators must also be aware of any state laws that govern the provision of special education services. Although states must provide all of the rights guaranteed by federal law to parents of students with disabilities, an individual state may choose to provide *additional* rights, and therefore public school administrators must be familiar with their own state laws in addition to the relevant federal laws.

Challenge: Litigation

As the number of students with ASD has increased in the United States,[4] so too has the number of disputes between parents and schools concerning the provision of special education and related services.[5] Litigation involving children with autism falls into two broad categories: procedural or substantive. *Procedural* errors occur when school personnel fail to follow the procedural requirements of IDEA as demonstrated in the preceding scenario. School administrators need to be knowledgeable about the procedural requirements of IDEA and Section 504 in the areas of child evaluation, IEP development, child placement, and inclusion of qualified personnel at IEP meetings.[6] *Substantive* errors occur when school personnel do not provide appropriate special education services to children with autism. There is much controversy about what constitutes an "appropriate" program for a child with autism, and this has resulted in numerous due process hearings or court cases in which parents have challenged the programs that school personnel offered to children with autism.

Litigation, whether it be a due process hearing or a suit filed in a state or federal court, is expensive. For example, districts in Minnesota spent an average of $12,300 on due process hearings during 2009.[7] Other states have put the cost of due process hearings in the range of $13,000 to $61,000.[8] Due process cases, which eventually end up in a state or federal court, are even more expensive. Avoiding litigation is a powerful reason for school administrators to be knowledgeable about special education law.

What You Can Do

- Access the IDEA, Section 504, and No Child Left Behind statutes and regulations, either online (see the third bulleted item) or through a local library.

- Take a class on special education law from a local university, if such a class was not required in one's own licensing program.
- Access one of several Web sites that provide up-to-date information on IDEA, Section 504, and No Child Left Behind. Reliable information is available on the Web site of the U.S. Department of Education's Office of Special Education Programs (www2.ed.gov/about/offices/list/osers/osep/index.html?src=mr) and the Wrightslaw Web site (http://wrightslaw.com).
- Access your state's Department of Education Web site to find information about state laws and regulations governing the provision of special education services, as well as information about resources available to school personnel charged with monitoring the provision of special education services in their district.
- Seek the advice and expertise of the special education director and special education teachers in the district who should have received training in special education law in their licensing program.

UNDERSTANDING ASD IN ITS MANY FORMS

School administrators need to be familiar with basic information about ASD, and because children with ASD are so diverse, administrators must be open to learning about a child's specific ASD characteristics from those who know the student the best: the parents. Autism is known as a "spectrum of disorders that vary in severity of symptoms, age of onset, and associations with other disorders."[9] In the *Diagnostic and Statistical Manual of Psychiatric Disorders* (DSM-IV),[10] the autism spectrum includes five major diagnoses:

- Autistic Disorder
- Asperger's Disorder (or syndrome)
- Pervasive Developmental Disorder-Not Otherwise Specified
- Rhett's Disorder
- Childhood Disintegrative Disorder

The last two diagnoses may be less common, and administrators may seldom work with children with either of these diagnoses; however, the first three diagnoses have become increasingly common, and administrators need to understand how these disorders affect children educationally.

One car after another pulls into the busy school parking lot, alongside buses and vans. Other students quickly find their waiting vehicles, while Natalya, a fourth grader with ASD, anxiously searches for her bus. She cannot tell which bus is hers, and she begins to cry. Mr. Stephens, the principal, sees Natalya and tells her that her bus has already left. Natalya cries, flaps her hands, and refuses to talk to Mr. Stephens. Natalya is unable to explain what she is feeling. Mr. Stephens takes Natalya into his office and becomes irritated when his efforts to talk with her are rebuffed.

Mr. Stephens telephones Mrs. Fedorov, Natalya's mother, to tell her that Natalya has missed her bus for the third time this term, and that she is acting spoiled and rude. When Mrs. Fedorov asks if an adult was helping Natalya find her bus, Mr. Stephens replies that any student who reads at the eighth-grade level as Natalya does is certainly capable of finding her own school bus. He adds that Natalya clearly manipulates her mother, so that her mother will sympathize with her and Natalya can avoid taking responsibility.

The problem presented in this scenario is that the principal, Mr. Stephens, didn't know enough about ASD and about Natalya's particular difficulties related to her ASD. Mr. Stephens assumed that because Natalya could read well above grade level that she would be able to read the signs on the buses to figure out which bus to board. What Mr. Stephens didn't understand is that Natalya, like many children with ASD, was overwhelmed by the sensory input in this situation. The noise and confusion of all of the children rushing to find their buses or their parents' cars, and the smells of the exhaust from vehicles, made it impossible for Natalya, who was actually a very good reader in class, to concentrate well enough on reading the bus identification numbers to find her own bus.

Mr. Stephens also assumed that Natalya was deliberately being rude and uncooperative when he tried to talk with her and she ignored him. Natalya, normally very polite and respectful of adults, was unable to use her social skills in this situation because she was very upset at having missed her bus and was overwhelmed by the sensory overload caused by the buses, cars, and other children. This, too, is typical of children with ASD. "One distinctive characteristic of all children with ASD that many educators and parents attempt, often unsuccessfully, to understand is their sensitivity and abnormal reactions to various stimuli within their environment."[11] Instead of recognizing Natalya's reaction as typical of children with ASD, Mr. Stephens assumed that Natalya was spoiled and that Mrs. Fedorov overprotected Natalya by coming to pick her up instead of insisting that Natalya take responsibility for getting on the correct bus.

Challenge: Each Child's Unique Characteristics

By definition, all children with ASD have deficits in regard to social interaction; impairments in communication; and restricted, repetitive, and stereotyped patterns of behavior, interests, and activities. It is important, however, for administrators to realize that no two children with ASD present with identical characteristics. A huge challenge for school administrators is "the reality that ASDs encompass an extraordinary range of symptoms and degrees of impairment that vary from child to child, and that may manifest differently in one child over time."[12]

EACH CHILD IS UNIQUE

Knowing and understanding one child with ASD does not ensure that an administrator knows anything about the next child who has ASD.

One child with ASD may have social deficits that cause her to be oblivious to all others. She may have no desire to interact with peers or to follow the directions of adults. Such a child may not find peer or adult interactions at all reinforcing and may much prefer to spend all of her time in isolated activities. Another child may seem to interact with peers; but upon close observation, one may realize that he always plays or works on the fringes of the activities other children are involved in without ever actually interacting with those children.

One child with ASD may have no verbal language and may communicate through sign language or through a system of picture cards, if she communicates at all. Another child may discuss in great detail how pianos work and the many different models of pianos, but that same child may not be able to answer simple inferential questions about a short story the teacher reads to the class. A youth with ASD may seem to have very good communication skills and may have learned to greet others by asking how they are, but that same youth may not answer others when they ask how he is.

One child with ASD may look like he is playing with the toy cars in the kindergarten classroom, but in fact all he ever does is line up all of the red cars, followed by all of the blue cars. His play never varies. Another child may insist on always following the same routine when it's time to go home, first carefully lining up all of her papers to put them in her backpack, then putting on her knit cap (even if it's warm outside), then putting on her coat and her backpack, and only then saying goodbye to the teacher. An older youth might write pages about his favorite topic, but when his teacher assigns an essay on some other topic he may write only five lines.

All of these children have ASD, but their social and communication abilities and their interests differ.

In addition to the defining characteristics of autism, many other traits are shared by children with ASD:

- Challenging behavior problems can stem from their frustrations around social and communication deficits.
- Sensory sensitivities to visual, auditory, olfactory, tactile, or gustatory stimuli can result in a child's being hypersensitive or hyposensitive, and the child may have mixed sensitivity depending on which senses are involved.
- Motor coordination problems can cause a child to appear awkward and clumsy in gym class (gross motor activities), or the child may have illegible handwriting (fine motor activity).
- Significant executive functioning problems among academically gifted children diagnosed with ASD can make it difficult for them to organize themselves and their materials and to break large tasks, such as writing a term paper, into small, manageable steps.
- The child may have uneven development in the area of adaptive behavior skills, such as toileting, eating, dressing, and grooming. For example, a child who already knows how to read when she comes to kindergarten might not

yet be able to dress herself independently. A youth in high school might not bathe, wash his hair, or dress appropriately without prompting from an adult.

Challenge: Differentiating Comorbid Disorders

An additional challenge for school administrators is learning to distinguish autism from other disorders that share common characteristics with ASD and learning about disorders that can be present along with ASD (that is, comorbid disorders). Many children with ASD are first diagnosed with a different disorder, sometimes more than one, before finally being diagnosed with ASD. Some disorders that frequently occur along with ASD or that may be confused with ASD are anxiety and depression, attention deficit hyperactivity disorder, bipolar disorder, obsessive-compulsive disorder, social anxiety disorder, and oppositional defiant disorder. It is absolutely essential that an experienced autism consultant or a school psychologist who has experience assessing children for ASD be included on the evaluation team for a child who is suspected of having ASD.

Challenge: Creating Programs Across Grade Levels

A further challenge for school administrators involves creating programs across all grade levels to serve children with ASD. Although children who are identified as having ASD early in life and who receive effective early intervention services may make great strides in their social and communication abilities, they do not outgrow autism,[13] and young children with ASD will grow into youth and then adults with ASD. They will require ongoing education programs to help them become as self-sufficient as possible and ready to join their community as productive young adults when they leave school.[14] Their needs will change over time, and this may be confusing to school administrators who may expect a child's characteristics to remain static. That National Autism Center's *Evidence-Based Practice and Autism in the Schools* manual has a very clear table[15] that illustrates the developmental changes that may occur in children with ASD throughout their school years. School administrators who examine this table carefully may find it quite informative.

With all of these variations among children with ASD, how are school administrators to know what issues an individual child has that could have an impact on his or her education?

What You Can Do

- Listen to parents. A parent typically knows his or her child with ASD better than anyone else. Most parents of a child with ASD are very willing to share what they know about their child's ASD. Parents can provide valuable information about the difficulties their child may encounter at school, and often they are able to offer suggestions for accommodating their child's social, communication, sensory, or motor issues.

- Read articles and books about ASD such as those listed in the reference list for this chapter. In the last ten years a great deal has been written about ASD. Large chain bookstores, such as Barnes & Noble, and online stores, such as Amazon.com, now carry numerous books that provide clear, basic information about ASD.

- Seek out the advice of autism consultants, who are often hired by school districts. They should be able to answer questions about ASD and provide suggestions for working with children with ASD and their parents.

- Explore the Internet. The Autism Society Web site (www.autism-society.org) has a plethora of information about ASD and is a reliable source of information. There are many other Web sites dedicated to ASD. As when using any Internet source, the user must be cautious about the credibility of the information.

UNDERSTANDING RESEARCH-BASED INTERVENTIONS

IDEA regulations require that public schools provide each child with a disability with a "free, appropriate public education that emphasizes special education and related services designed to meet their unique needs." In 2004 Congress added the requirement that schools use research-based methodology "whenever practicable" in the provision of an appropriate education.

As a young child, Takumi, a fifth-grade student with Asperger syndrome and extreme anxiety, had shown no interest in drawing. But when Mrs. Holbein, his fifth-grade teacher, began teaching her students the basics of pen-and-ink drawing during the winter term, Takumi immediately took a liking to it and quickly showed promise. Within a few months he was drawing surprisingly accurate renderings of regional wildflowers and deciduous trees, two of his favorite subjects. At school he had little time to draw, and when the class did have an art session he was assigned drawing themes, which displeased him. But at home he spent many hours drawing flowers and trees. His mother, Mrs. Saito, sent an e-mail to the principal, Ms. Alioto, requesting an IEP meeting very soon to discuss an addition to Takumi's services and schedule for his first year of middle school.

At the meeting, Mrs. Saito enthusiastically reported impressive positive changes in Takumi's Asperger syndrome–related, anxiety-driven behaviors. While drawing, she said, Takumi's anxiety was noticeably reduced, and he seemed calm and focused. Mrs. Saito had read about the benefits of art for children with autism, and she could now attest to benefits in her own son. Therefore, Mr. and Mrs. Saito wanted Takumi to have at least one hour of art class every day in middle school. Principal Alioto explained that although she certainly agreed that art instruction was valuable for all students, in the middle school schedule art class was an elective that took place twice a week for forty minutes for one term during the year. The school did not have the scheduling time or qualified staff to provide more. Ms. Saito asserted that because art, or art therapy as she called it, had helped many children with Asperger syndrome and was clearly helping her son as well, Takumi must be in art class daily as part of his special education services under IDEA.

The main problem that arises in the scenario is whether Takumi's IEP team must agree to provide art therapy as part of Takumi's special education services. Currently, no research supports the effectiveness of art therapy for students with autism. This does not mean that art therapy could not be helpful to Takumi, nor does it mean that the district should not provide art therapy if it is available. What it does mean, however, is that Ms. Alioto's district is not likely to be faulted by a hearing officer or a court for not providing the service, unless the IEP team chooses to include it on Takumi's IEP—which means, of course, that it must then be provided.

Challenge: Determining and Providing "Appropriate" Education

How are school administrators to know what an "appropriate" education is for a child with ASD?

In the 1982 case *Board of Education of Hendrick Hudson Central School District v. Rowley*,[16] the U.S. Supreme Court answered this question. The standard the court set in the *Rowley* case was that an appropriate program must provide "some educational benefit." The court declined to rule that an appropriate program must maximize a child's educational progress. The Supreme Court has not changed its definition of "appropriate education" since 1982.

THE CHALLENGE OF UNDERSTANDING AUTISM

"ASD, which manifests in children's minds as well as in their bodies, is unlike any other disability . . . [it is] complex."[17] The ASD learning curve is steep and ongoing, and it cannot be mastered alone. Administrators will be most successful in leading the way to providing effective services for their students with ASD when they recognize with humility their need for greater understanding of ASD as it relates to special education law, students' individual profiles, intervention research, staff training, and families; seek reliable sources through which to increase their knowledge; and listen to the concerns and embrace the insights and support of staff, specialists, and parents.

Although the definition of "appropriate" has not changed, however, researchers have strongly demonstrated that intensive early intervention for young children with ASD provides positive changes in their language, social, or cognitive outcomes.[18] This has led to many hearings and court cases in which parents have requested that school districts be required to provide or pay for intensive, often one-to-one interventions for children with ASD. "In such cases, parents frequently argue that the district's various (or 'eclectic') methodologies are not reasonably calculated to provide the student with educational benefit."[19]

The Supreme Court in *Rowley* also addressed this issue of methodology and declared that methodological disputes between parents and school personnel are best left to educational authorities rather than to judicial officials in due process hearings or court cases.[20] This means that unless a parent can show that school personnel did not provide an appropriate education for his or her child with ASD, a due process hearing officer or a judge is unlikely to overrule an education program provided by the district.

However, this doesn't mean that a hearing office or a court will find just any program appropriate. School administrators must pay attention to the more recent requirement of IDEA in 2004 that special education services be based on "peer-reviewed research to the extent practicable." How can school administrators know if their programs for children with ASD are based on peer-reviewed research?

This has become such a major issue for school personnel and parents that the National Autism Center[21] recently developed a manual to encourage schools to adopt evidence-based practices for children with autism. The authors of this manual note, "Evidence-based practice is complex and requires both ongoing communication and respectful interactions among all stakeholders. Even when a list of effective treatments is identified, collaboration is the key to achieving the best outcomes."[22]

The National Autism Center labeled eleven interventions as "Established Treatments" that have sufficient research support to be considered effective. Another twenty-two interventions were labeled "Emerging Treatments" because there was some evidence of their effectiveness, and other interventions were labeled "Unestablished Treatments" because there was no sound evidence of their effectiveness.[23] The following eleven Established Treatments are described in detail in the National Autism Center's *Evidence-Based Practice and Autism in the Schools* manual:[24]

- Antecedent Package
- Behavioral Package
- Comprehensive Behavioral Treatment for Young Children (based on applied behavior analysis)
- Joint Attention Intervention
- Modeling

- Naturalistic Teaching Strategies
- Peer Training Package
- Pivotal Response Treatment
- Schedules
- Self-management
- Story-based Intervention Package

What You Can Do

- Engage in strategic planning that involves all stakeholders: parents; general education and special education teachers; related service personnel, such as school psychologists, speech therapists, and others; building administrators; and district-level administrators.
- Follow the guidelines for building and maintaining comprehensive autism programs provided by Schillinger[25] and by the National Autism Center.[26]
- Develop districtwide comprehensive programs of research-based interventions for students with ASD.

TRAINING EDUCATORS AND SUPPORT STAFF

General education teachers have various levels of knowledge and experience working with students with ASD. Unfortunately, many special education teachers will have learned very little about ASD in their training programs, and thus might not be effective in helping general education teachers learn about appropriate ways to support students with ASD in their classes.

School administrators must ensure that all of their instructional staff learn some basic skills in working with students with ASD and learn what their responsibilities are to implement education programs for children with ASD or to provide accommodations that are included on students' IEPs. Further, school administrators should ensure that noninstructional staff, including bus drivers, custodians, and cafeteria personnel, also receive some training to acquaint them with ASD and techniques for interacting appropriately with students with ASD. School administrators set the tone in their building, and "administrative attitudes and support are critical in improving schools, as are explicit strategies for keeping skilled personnel within the field."[27]

As Aiesha walked through the front door after school, she exclaimed loudly, "Well, he did it again today!" Her mother's heart sank, as she wondered why Aiesha's eleventh-grade geography teacher was not open to learning more about her daughter's ASD and was not more patient with her. Aiesha went on to describe yet another discouraging incident in which the geography teacher, Mr. Cappelli, had corrected her in front of the class for talking back to him and being distracted. Even though this was her daughter's third year in high school, Mrs. Cummings knew that some teachers still did not realize that some of Aiesha's difficulties, such as appearing to talk back or being easily distracted, were directly related to the neurological differences behind her ASD. They were not because she was intentionally being rude or purposely not focusing in class. Mrs. Cummings always made sure that Aiesha had her preferred "fidget" in her backpack, a small object used by some individuals with ASD, which she could manipulate in her hand to help her concentrate. Mr. Cappelli, however, refused to allow fidgets, or "toys" as he called them, in his classroom, saying they were disruptive to learning. Mrs. Cummings had also offered Mr. Cappelli a brief handout on ASD so that he might better understand Aiesha's challenges and needs, but he was not interested.

Mrs. Cummings thought back to the previous week, when Mrs. Jennings, the biology teacher, had complimented Aiesha on her work in front of her peers. After learning that Aiesha had ASD, Mrs. Jennings had told Mrs. Cummings that although she knew very little about ASD, she was eager to learn more and do what she could to help Aiesha have a positive year in her class. Mrs. Cummings made some suggestions about how to support Aiesha in the biology lab, where Mrs. Cummings knew that her daughter would have sensory issues with the sights, smells, tactile sensations, and safety rules she would encounter. Mrs. Jennings asked if Mrs. Cummings could recommend something she could read about the sensory challenges of ASD.

In this scenario, we see two teachers and their different responses to Aiesha, a youth with ASD. Mr. Cappelli seems uninterested in learning about Aiesha and how he can help her succeed in his class, whereas Mrs. Jennings is eager to learn more about ASD so that she can support Aiesha. School administrators are likely to encounter both kinds of teachers.

Challenge: Funding and Implementing Effective Training

Five types of training are beneficial for school personnel. Although it can be challenging for administrators to fund and schedule such preparation, well-trained school personnel make administrators' jobs easier in the long run.

Type 1, which is the most basic level of training that all teachers and staff should receive, focuses on common characteristics of students with ASD.

> Children with autism spectrum disorders (ASD) are truly unique and special people. ASD, which manifests in children's minds as well as in their bodies, is unlike any other disability; it results in a combination of many disabling conditions, which is why it is such a complex disability. It is difficult initially to understand what ASD is and thus why children who have it behave as they do.[28]

School administrators should arrange one or more workshops or training sessions in which this initial level of information can be shared with all school personnel. There may be district personnel, such as autism consultants, who can provide this level of training, or a school administrator may need to contract with an independent agent to provide it. All school personnel should attend such training sessions, even those who have some experience working with students with autism. This will ensure that everyone shares a common set of information.

Type 2 training should be provided to all noninstructional staff who interact with children in a school. This level of training should build on the information presented in Type 1 training sessions but should focus on strategies that secretaries, bus drivers, playground assistants, custodial staff, cafeteria personnel, and other school staff can use to interact successfully with children with ASD. This would be an ideal forum for allowing these staff members to brainstorm ways they can support children with ASD during noninstructional and often less structured times of the school day. A critical element of Type 2 training should be the introduction of a standard set of procedures that noninstructional staff should follow if they experience difficulty dealing with a particular child with ASD. Staff should know what to do in the event that a child with ASD has a "meltdown"—that is, becomes overwhelmed in a situation and has difficulty controlling his or her behavior. Staff should know what the appropriate reporting procedures are in such a situation, and should have easy access to autism "experts" to help answer any questions they have as a result of interacting with children with ASD.

Type 3 training focuses on general education teachers and teaching them how to appropriately support students with ASD in their content classes. General education teachers need access to students' IEPs and need to be trained in any behavioral interventions that are designed for a specific student. They also need to be informed about accommodations written into the IEP that are to be provided for a student with ASD in his or her general education classes. General education teachers should be trained in techniques for modifying the general curriculum to enable students with ASD to successfully participate in their classes. Whenever an IEP team modifies a child's IEP, all of the child's general education teachers should be informed of those modifications if they affect the child's education in the general education classroom. General education teachers should have access to autism experts who can provide ongoing support as these teachers implement their training with actual students.

Type 4 training is aimed at the specialists (for example, special education teachers, speech-language pathologists, and autism consultants) who provide specialized interventions to children with ASD. These specialists, if they are not already trained in the specific research-based interventions delineated in the district's strategic plan (described in the previous section), must receive appropriate training in how to correctly implement the chosen interventions. Generally such training can be provided in one of two ways: school administrators can either hire outside consultants to come into a district and train those specialists who need the training, or administrators can arrange for those personnel to attend workshops or classes to obtain the training. Another possibility is to arrange for a specialist in the district who already knows about and can implement a particular intervention to obtain the necessary training and perhaps certification to become a trainer in the intervention. That specialist can then provide training to others in the district who need it. This is one way to build sustainability into the strategic plan. "Homegrown" trainers give the district the ongoing capability to train new personnel as they are hired.

Type 4 training cannot be accomplished in one or even several training sessions. Just providing information or a single workshop is not an effective method of training.[29] Schillinger[30] notes,

It is the follow up support that makes the change in teacher behavior. Follow up can, and should, take several forms: in-class consultation and modeling by . . . specialists; teacher observation in a model classroom; a model classroom teacher doing demonstration lessons in the teacher's classroom; . . . specialists doing model lessons in the teacher's classroom; supportive feedback from site administrators, etc.

Type 5 training involves the teams responsible for conducting individual, comprehensive assessments of children with ASD. An assessment team typically includes an autism consultant, a school psychologist, a special education teacher, a speech-language therapist, and possibly an occupational or physical therapist. School administrators must ensure that all of these individuals have the specialized training they need to administer the variety of tools and procedures required for a comprehensive ASD assessment.

The challenge for school administrators is determining how each of these types of training will be provided and which staff members require which types of training, scheduling all of the training, and finding a way to pay for the training.

What You Can Do

- Be sure the issue of training is addressed in the strategic plan.
- Take advantage of any ASD experts already employed by the district who can assist with training.
- Look for ASD specialists in the local community. If there is a teacher training university in the area with a special education department, contact that department to find out whether the department has faculty with expertise in ASD or whether the department offers any course work in ASD.
- Contact administrators in other districts to find out if their districts have a comprehensive program of services for students with ASD. Find out how they obtained training.
- Contact your state's Department of Education and find out if the department offers any ASD training or has ASD experts who could provide training or consultation.

WORKING EFFECTIVELY WITH PARENTS

The increasing number of due process hearings and court cases that involve parents of children with ASD[31] is a testament to the difficulties school administrators and parents often have in communicating effectively.

In this scenario, and in the opening scenario of this chapter, there are clearly problems with communication between the parents and the school administrators. The increasing number of due process hearings and court cases that involve parents of children with ASD is a testament to the difficulties school administrators and parents often have in communicating effectively.[32]

It was Friday morning, and the middle school principal, Mrs. Delgado, was looking forward to the upcoming weekend. Suddenly her office door opened, and Ms. Johansen, the English teacher, entered, flushed and angry, with Peter, a seventh-grade boy with ASD, in tow. Ms. Johansen explained that she was bringing Peter to see Mrs. Delgado because Peter kicked her when she asked him to finish his essay assignment and then threw his pencil across the room. Principal Delgado told Ms. Johansen that she would contact Peter's father, Mr. Langley, and asked Ms. Johansen to return to her class.

Mrs. Delgado told Peter that he was going to be expelled for kicking a teacher. She directed him to sit down and wait while she called his father. Peter started spinning in place as Mrs. Delgado called Mr. Langley to tell him that Peter was being expelled from school for violence and must be picked up immediately. By the time Mr. Langley arrived from his office twenty minutes later, Peter was spinning rapidly and making clicking noises with his tongue. Principal Delgado again told Mr. Langley that Peter was going to be expelled for kicking his teacher.

Mr. Langley asked to speak to Ms. Johansen or to read the incident report, but Mrs. Delgado told him that there was no report, and that she had already told Mr. Langley what he needed to know. She added that Peter was clearly out of control and needed to leave the building. Mr. Langley left with Peter after threatening to sue Principal Delgado and the school.

Challenge: Providing Guidance to Meet Individual Student Needs

Several researchers[33] have explored the reasons behind such communication challenges. Lake and Billingsley[34] found that often parents and administrators have inconsistent views of the child's needs:

> The language used in special education has been deficit laden, and parents are often offended by language that describes only the difficulties children experience. Attention needs to be paid to the whole child, and his or her abilities, strengths, aspirations, and needs. Educators also need to provide opportunities for parents to describe their children and their dreams for their children, and to include parents' perceptions in educational planning. This sharing of parent and school perspectives and viewing the child as a whole person provides a firm foundation for good parent-school partnerships.

Lake and Billingsley[35] also found that parents were often frustrated by their lack of knowledge about special education procedures, especially if their child had just recently been found eligible for services. Too often administrators didn't provide the guidance parents needed to understand the special education system. This imbalance of knowledge, perceived by parents as an imbalance of power, was an escalating factor in parent-administrator conflicts. Stoner et al.[36] interviewed parents of children with ASD and found that parents reported that "entering the special education system was traumatic, initial IEP meetings were confusing, and obtaining services was complicated." In the Stoner et al. study, parents whose children initially received early intervention services reported that the change from an individualized family services plan (IFSP) for preschool children to an IEP for school-age children was also confusing. An IFSP is focused on the needs of the entire family, whereas an IEP is focused just on the child. This change in focus often was not carefully explained to parents, resulting in parents' feeling "abandoned" by the system.

Stoner et al.[37] found additional elements that influenced parent-administrator communication. Many parents reported that their struggle to obtain a diagnosis for their child had resulted in a distrust of medical professionals. This distrust carried over into parents' interactions with education professionals. Further, once parents received an ASD diagnosis for their child, they typically responded to the diagnosis by searching for as much information as they could find about ASD. As a result of this search for knowledge, parents often were much better educated about ASD than the school administrators they eventually communicated with about their child's needs and services. Some school administrators find knowledgeable parents intimidating,[38] and, as Yell et al.[39] noted, "Parents of children with autism are prone to exercise their rights under IDEA." However, Stoner et al.[40] reported that "administrators who were accessible, were supportive, and addressed parental concerns were perceived more positively by parents than those who failed to demonstrate these fundamental behaviors." So, what can administrators do to foster positive communication with parents?

What You Can Do

- Trust is a critical factor in building a positive relationship with parents, and trust is built through open and honest communication.[41]
- Although it is necessary to discuss a child's deficits with his or her parents, always begin and end conversations with parents, including IEP meetings, with positive statements about the child. Recognize that parents want school administrators to view the whole child as a unique individual with many strengths, not just deficits.
- Communicate frequently with parents, and don't just send home negative information about a child. Let parents know what is going on at school. If there will be a delay in providing some service to a child, let the parents know and provide a reason. Informed parents tend to be much more reasonable to deal with than parents who find out after the fact that a service hasn't been provided.
- Always seek parents' input in meetings about their child. Actively listen to parents and let them know that you hear their concerns for their child.

TO SUM UP

In the scenarios presented in this chapter, Principals Jones, Stephens, Alioto, and Delgado, and their staffs, faced situations involving students with autism and their parents that are now typical of those occurring daily in schools across the United States. But these leaders had something else in common—they were alarmingly unprepared for the sophisticated understanding of the legal, intervention, training, family, and ASD issues needed today to establish and maintain an appropriate context in which to serve students with ASD.

As stated at the beginning of the chapter, today's school administrators must do the following:

- Know the federal and state laws that govern the provision of services to students with disabilities, and students with ASD in particular. This requires reading the laws pertaining to special education, seeking workshops and specialists who can increase their knowledge and understanding, and staying abreast of current changes to the laws through Web sites and publications.
- Develop basic knowledge of ASD in its many forms by attending trainings, consulting with district specialists, and seeking online and media updates on this multilayered, constantly evolving disability.
- Become familiar with research-based interventions for students with ASD, about which they can learn by consulting the National Autism Center's *Evidence-Based Practice and Autism in the Schools* manual[42] and other current publications.
- Engage all stakeholders in designing their district- and schoolwide approach to serving their students with ASD, paying particular attention to the gaps that exist in services and working together to close those gaps.
- Recognize that both their instructional and their support staffs need ASD training and access to appropriate, up-to-date ASD resources. Further, due to the complexity of ASD, this instruction cannot be squeezed into the last twenty minutes of a staff meeting; it must be thorough, focusing on specific, practical information and strategies over multiple training sessions.
- Access their most valuable resource in understanding their students with ASD: parents. Administrators must develop the skills necessary to build effective working partnerships with parents of students with ASD. Trust is far more likely to flourish with parents when administrators communicate regularly with them, sharing both positive as well as negative information about their children, and when administrators actively seek out parents' opinions and knowledge about their children; learn how to share honestly and diplomatically with parents; and treat parents as vital, meaningful members of the IEP team.

Incorporating Parent Training into School Curricula for Children with Autism Spectrum Disorders

Brooke Ingersoll and Allison Wainer

The importance of parents' direct involvement in interventions for and education of children with autism spectrum disorders (ASD) has been widely recognized in the autism literature. Therefore, the National Research Council[1] has suggested that parent and family participation is a critical and necessary component of effective autism intervention. Parents can become active participants in their child's intervention program in a variety of ways, including via parent training, which provides parents with direct instruction in evidence-based intervention strategies to manage their child's behavior and support their child's development.[2]

The evidence base for the effectiveness of parent training in ASD, either as a sole intervention or as a component of a more comprehensive intervention, is growing.[3] The literature suggests that parent training has benefits for both the child and the parent. Parents of children with ASD can been taught to implement evidence-based intervention techniques to do the following:

- Improve the quality of parent-child interactions[4]
- Produce gains in language and communication skills[5]
- Produce gains in imitation,[6] joint attention, engagement,[7] and appropriate play skills[8]
- Decrease problem behavior[9]

Training parents in such techniques is generally considered an efficient and cost-effective way to increase the amount and intensity of intervention a child receives.[10]

Training parents to implement intervention also leads to the following:

- Better maintenance and generalization of the child's skills[11]
- Reduced parent stress[12]
- Increased family leisure time[13]

Although early demonstrations of the efficacy of parent training for children with ASD involved school-age children,[14] current research on parent training in autism has focused almost exclusively on toddlers and preschool-age children. Only a handful of empirical studies, reviewed later in this chapter, have examined parent training interventions for school-age children with ASD. These studies suggest that parent training services should also be made available to families of children with ASD well beyond the preschool years.

Despite the benefits associated with parent training, the availability of parent training programs is often limited, especially for families of school-age children with ASD. For example, in an Indiana survey, only 21 percent of parents of children with ASD up to age eight reported receiving parent training, despite the fact that, among those who did, parent training was rated as the most important service for promoting their child's development.[15]

Given the increasing rate of ASD diagnoses, as well as the growing number of children in need of specialized services in primary and secondary school settings,[16] it is critical to explore ways to augment access to parent training for families of school-age children with ASD.[17] One possible approach for expanding access to parent training is to incorporate it into school curricula for school-age children with ASD.

This chapter summarizes the current literature on training parents of school-age children with ASD to implement specific types of interventions, discusses programs that have integrated parent training into school curricula, and provides suggestions for the future development and implementation of such programs.

BEHAVIOR MANAGEMENT TRAINING

Behavior management is an important element of intervention, given the profound impact disruptive behavior can have at home and in the classroom.[18] Four randomized controlled trials, discussed in the following paragraphs, demonstrated that parent-implemented behavior management interventions are effective for reducing behavior problems in school-age children with ASD.

In one study, Sofronoff and colleagues[19] assessed a parent management training intervention aimed at increasing parents' ability to control and regulate problem behaviors in school-age children with Asperger syndrome. Parents were randomly assigned to one of three intervention groups: group workshop, individual sessions, or waitlist control. Individuals assigned to the group workshop met for a one-day workshop, whereas the individuals who received individual sessions received one hour of training a week for six weeks. Individuals assigned to the waitlist control did not receive services until the completion of the study. As compared to the children of participants in the waitlist control condition, children whose parents received training (group format or individual sessions) experienced significant decreases in the overall number and intensity of problem behaviors as indicated by changes in parent ratings on the Eyberg Child Behavior Inventory (ECBI) from pre- to postintervention. In addition, children in the two intervention conditions displayed significantly higher scores on parent ratings of social skills on the Social Skills Questionnaire from pre- to postintervention. Improvements in these areas were maintained from postintervention to a three-month follow-up. Parents in both intervention conditions reported that the training was useful and expressed satisfaction with the program, although many parents in the individual training indicated a preference for the group format because of the convenience associated with attending just one training session.

In another study, Whittingham and colleagues[20] examined the effect of training parents of school-age children with ASD in Stepping Stones Triple P, a program that integrates general adaptive parenting strategies with more specific behavior management techniques. Parents of fifty-nine children with ASD between two and nine years old were randomly assigned to a treatment or waitlist control group. Parents in the treatment group attended group instructional sessions and received individualized coaching and feedback during one-on-one sessions with a therapist trained in the intervention protocol. In comparison with the parents in the waitlist control group, parents in the treatment group reported significant reductions in dysfunctional parenting styles and decreases in child behavior problems. Such gains were maintained at the follow-up six months later.

In a third study, Solomon and colleagues[21] used a waitlist control design to examine the efficacy of a social learning–based behavioral intervention, Parent-Child Interaction Therapy (PCIT), in five- to twelve-year-old high-functioning children with ASD. Child participants were matched by age, cognitive level, and symptom severity, and then randomly assigned to the treatment or control group. Parents in the treatment group were provided with twelve individual sessions using the standard PCIT curriculum. Treatment had no effect on parent reporting of the intensity of child behavior problems on the ECBI, and no effect on parent stress. However, parents of children in the treatment group perceived their child's behavior to be less problematic than did parents in the control group after treatment. Further, treatment had positive effects on parent reporting of child adaptability and atypicality and of improvements in shared positive affect during parent-child interactions.

In a large-scale randomized controlled trial, Aman and colleagues[22] examined the benefits of adding parent training to pharmacological intervention for the treatment of severe behavior problems in children with ASD. Researchers assigned 124 children with ASD between the ages of four and thirteen (with an average age of seven years) to the parent training plus medication group (COMB) or the medication-only group (MED). Children in both groups received treatment with risperidone. Parents of children in the COMB group also received an average of eleven individual parent training sessions in behavior management strategies based on the principles of applied behavior analysis (for example, visual schedules, effective use of positive reinforcement, teaching compliance, functional communication skills, and specific adaptive skills). After twenty-four weeks of treatment, participants in the COMB group showed a significantly greater improvement on the Home Situations Questionnaire, a parent reporting measure of noncompliant behavior during everyday activities, as well as on the Irritability scale of the Aberrant Behavior Checklist, a parent reporting measure used to assess significant behavior problems in children with developmental disabilities. Further, children in the COMB group were maintained on a lower dose of risperidone than the children in the MED group. The added benefit of parent training was evident above the large improvement due to medication,[23] providing strong evidence for the effectiveness of behavior-based parent training for reducing severe behavior problems in children with ASD with a range of functioning levels.

All of these studies are limited by the reliance on parent reporting to assess changes in child behavior from pre- to postintervention. The efficacy of such programs would be better supported by the use of observational measures and other standardized assessments. In addition, none of these studies assessed generalization of child skills, making it difficult to know if children were able to transfer improvements to settings outside the home with adults other than the trained parents.

SOCIAL SKILLS TRAINING

School-age children with ASD often struggle with social skills and the development of friendships, particularly with peers. Although most social skills interventions typically involve peers rather than parents, parents can be integral in teaching, supervising, and supporting their child's development of friendships.[24] Thus several social skills interventions used with school-age children with ASD have included a parent training component in conjunction with direct group instruction.

Laugeson and colleagues[25] used a randomized controlled trial to examine the efficacy of a parent-assisted social skills intervention for high-functioning adolescents with ASD. This program was not directly focused on parent training, but rather incorporated parent education as one component of the protocol.

The adolescents attended group social skills training sessions while their parents attended separate concurrent training sessions. Parents received instruction in techniques aimed at developing their child's social skills. They were also taught approaches to help their child face and overcome obstacles around socialization, so that parents could support and extend their child's training outside of the immediate social skills group. When compared to a waitlist control group, adolescent participants reported improvements in the quality of friendships, reported hosting significantly more social gatherings, and displayed greater knowledge about social rules and standards related to making and keeping friends. Moreover, parents of adolescents in the treatment condition reported significant improvements in their child's social abilities.

Using a similar curriculum, Frankel and colleagues[26] evaluated the efficacy of a parent-assisted children's friendship training program with 68 high-functioning elementary school children with ASD using a randomized controlled design. Children in the treatment group received group instruction in friendship skills in twelve weekly, one-hour sessions. Parents concurrently received instruction in how to support their child's social interaction with peers. When compared to the waitlist control group, children in the immediate treatment group made greater gains—child-reported feelings of loneliness were reduced, child-reported feelings of popularity increased, and parents reported a greater number and quality of playdates. These gains were maintained at a three-month follow-up. However, differences were not evident between groups on teacher-reported measures of withdrawal and aggression, suggesting that outcomes did not generalize to the school environment.

In another study, Solomon, Goodlin-Jones, and Anders[27] examined the effect of a social adjustment enhancement intervention for eight- to twelve-year-old high-functioning children with ASD using a waitlist control design. The intervention involved twenty weekly child group sessions that focused on developing social skills. Parent group sessions ran concurrently with the child group sessions, during which parents were taught to support the skills their child was learning outside of the group and to appropriately handle child behavior problems. Mothers in the treatment group reported fewer problem behaviors in their children and greater satisfaction in how they handled these problems over time. Further, compared to the waitlist control group, children in the immediate treatment group made greater gains in identification of facial expressions of emotion and in social problem solving. However, an analysis of individual responses to treatment suggested that the younger, higher-functioning children improved their performance on the assessment of social problem solving, whereas the older, lower-functioning children did not. These findings suggest that this approach may only be effective for high-functioning children with ASD.

Beaumont and Sofronoff[28] used a randomized controlled trial to examine the effect of a multiple-component social skills intervention, the Junior Detective Training Program, on forty-nine elementary-age children with high-functioning ASD. Children in the treatment group received a combination of computer-assisted instruction on social problem solving and small-group instruction focused on helping them generalize social problem-solving skills learned on the computer, while parents participated in a concurrent group focused on teaching them to support their child's social skills in home and community contexts. In addition, teachers were provided with handouts outlining program content so that they could support learned skills in the classroom setting. Results of this study indicated that children in the treatment condition, but not the control condition, improved significantly on the parent-reported Social Skills Questionnaire and Emotion Regulation and Social Skills Questionnaire. These gains were maintained at six-week and five-month follow-ups. Results also indicated that children in the treatment condition improved in their knowledge of emotion coping strategies more than did children in the control condition. On measures of emotion recognition, results indicated that participants in both groups improved over time, making it difficult to attribute gains in emotion recognition to the intervention.

Overall, these data suggest that teaching parents to support their children's peer interactions is a promising approach for promoting social skills and friendships in high-functioning children and adolescents with ASD. However, with the exception of data gathered in the Solomon et al. study,[29] the majority of the data collected in these studies were child and parent reported; given that individuals with ASD often struggle to understand their own social behavior, a more accurate way to measure improvements in social skills might have been with peer or teacher reports or direct observational measures. The only study to collect data from the children's teachers did not indicate improvements in child behavior, despite improvements reported by the children and their parents.[30] Further, only two of the studies collected follow-up data after the intervention ended. Information about the maintenance of skills developed in these programs is therefore limited.

Also important, due to the comprehensive nature of the programs it is difficult to ascertain the direct impact of the parent training component on the children's social skills. Further, although a parent training component was included in each of these programs with the specific goal of enhancing skill generalization, none of the studies measured the generalization of targeted skills to real-life social contexts; this type of evaluation is critical to supporting the effectiveness of a social skills training program. Additional research is necessary to better understand how parent training can help support the development of children's social skills in real-world contexts.

Finally, because all of these social skills interventions were aimed at higher-functioning school-age children with ASD, it is unclear whether parent-supported social skills instruction can be used to improve social functioning in children with significant cognitive or language delays. Indeed, Solomon et al.[31] found that children with lower language abilities did not make improvements in social problem solving. Thus further research is needed on effective parent training approaches for supporting social development in school-age children with ASD with a range of functioning levels.

LANGUAGE DEVELOPMENT TRAINING

Many school-age children with ASD, particularly those with cognitive delays, also display deficits in language. In response to this need, a limited number of studies have examined training parents of school-age children with ASD in techniques targeting the development of verbal language. Unlike the studies reviewed earlier, these studies have used mainly single-subject research designs, in which a small number of subjects are studied intensively before and during intervention.

In one of the earliest studies of parent training for children with autism that was focused on language development, Laski et al.[32] used a single-subject, multiple-baseline design with eight children with autism, five of whom were school age, to examine the efficacy of training parents to use the Natural Language Paradigm, a naturalistic behavioral intervention, to promote their child's spontaneous speech. All children in the study were nonverbal or echolalic and exhibited significant cognitive delays. The results indicated that all parents increased their use of eliciting language (that is, presenting a clear direction to which the child could respond), and all children increased their rate of vocalizations. Parents and children generalized their use of language to a break room setting in the training clinic and the home, suggesting that parents were able to transfer their newly learned skills to other environments. Despite evidence for generalization, this study did not examine the maintenance of parent or child skills; thus it is unclear whether parents were able to maintain their use of the intervention strategies over time.

Charlop-Christy and Carpenter[33] used an alternating treatments design to explore the effect of parents' use of discrete trial, incidental teaching, and modified incidental teaching procedures on the development of spontaneous speech in three boys, ages six to nine, with ASD. The training included direct instruction, modeling, and coaching by an expert until initial fidelity of implementation was achieved. All of the children experienced gains in language when parents implemented the modified incidental teaching techniques. Two children increased their language when parents used discrete trial procedures, and the third child displayed language gains when his parents used traditional incidental teaching techniques. Fidelity ratings indicated that parents were able to consistently implement all three intervention procedures with few errors throughout the treatment. Although these initial results are promising, our ability to generalize the results of this study to other children is limited given that only three families participated in this study.

Seung and colleagues[34] also examined the impact of parent training on the development of verbal language in children with ASD. Eight fathers of children between the ages of four and seven were trained to wait expectantly and to imitate their child in an exaggerated manner during parent-child interactions. Fathers participated in ongoing instructional sessions, which involved viewing videos of their own implementation of the intervention techniques. Posttraining, fathers increased their use of intervention strategies, particularly imitation. In addition, the ratio of father-to-child language utterances decreased from pre- to postintervention, suggesting that after training, fathers were talking less, using more expectant waiting, and allowing time for the child to process and respond to the interaction. Increases in children's verbal communication, specifically in the number of single-word utterances and the variety of words produced, were observed as well. It is important to note that six out of the eight children in the study were receiving speech therapy and schooling concurrent with the parent training intervention. It is therefore difficult to separate the effects of the parent training from the effects of the other interventions on child outcomes.

The small number of participants across these three studies limits the generalizability of the findings to a wide range of families, necessitating additional controlled research with larger samples. However, these data along with parent training research for preschool-age children with ASD provide growing support for the idea that parents can be taught to accurately implement language interventions for school-age children with ASD and that, as a result, their children will improve their rate of spoken language. It should be noted that all of the children in these studies are elementary school age. Thus it is not clear whether these strategies are effective for older children with limited language who are likely to exhibit significantly greater impairment. Further, these studies have focused exclusively on teaching parents strategies to promote spoken language. Given that many school-age children with ASD remain nonverbal or minimally verbal, it is important to investigate the benefit of teaching parents to support their children's use of evidence-based augmentative and alternative communication systems for children with ASD, such as the picture exchange communication system.

These studies suggest that parents of school-age children with ASD can learn strategies to support their children's social and language development and to manage their behavior. Many of these interventions are similar to those for younger children with ASD, suggesting that interventions found to be effective for young children with ASD may be able to be extended upward with success. With the exception of the Laugeson[35] study, all of the parent training interventions were targeted at preschool-, elementary-, and middle-school-age children with ASD. Individuals with ASD continue to need intervention and support throughout their adolescent and adult years, although the specific focus of intervention is likely to change. In addition, a number of new needs arise with respect to sexuality, self-care, and increased independence skills, among other issues. Given that the majority of individuals with ASD continue to reside with their family as adults,[36] there is a specific need for intervention programs that assist parents in addressing these needs in their adolescent and young adult children with ASD. In addition, the majority of these programs targeted parents of mid-range to high socioeconomic status; it is unknown whether the high program satisfaction and parent and child gains would translate to other groups. To this end, examining the characteristics of program participants is also critical for understanding which individuals will respond best to a given parent training intervention.

INTEGRATING PARENT TRAINING INTO SCHOOL CURRICULA

Despite the clear benefits of parent training, it is rarely included in publicly funded school programs for children with ASD.[37] However, over the past decade a small body of literature has developed that describes programs that have attempted to make parent training an integral component within school curricula for children with ASD.[38] These programs, discussed in the subsections that follow, have thus far been limited to preschool settings.

Project ImPACT

Ingersoll and Dvortcsak[39] describe a pilot investigation of a parent training program, Project ImPACT, for preschool-age children with ASD. Project ImPACT is designed to be implemented by classroom teachers and easily adapted to a public school system. The training curriculum involves introducing parents of children in publicly funded early childhood special education programs to techniques aimed at increasing their child's communication and social skills during daily activities and routines.

The parent training program is designed such that parents attend six group training sessions for one-and-a-half hours and three individual coaching sessions for forty-five minutes over a nine-week period. Special educators attended preliminary didactic and hands-on training workshops that provided an overview of the rationale for teaching parents to use the intervention techniques.

Because this was a pilot program, the teachers ran the parent training program in conjunction with the program developers. However, teachers planned on continuing with Project ImPACT over the following school year, without the direct involvement of the program developers. Participation in this program required roughly an eleven-hour time commitment from parents extended across multiple weeks; however, the program, including the initial training, required approximately fifty hours of the teachers' time, with as many as twenty of those hours taking place outside of the normal school day.

In an evaluation of this pilot program, parents demonstrated increases in the understanding of the Project ImPACT intervention techniques on a knowledge quiz from pre- to postintervention. Parents also reported high satisfaction with the training and reported feeling as though their child improved his or her social engagement and communication as a result of this program. In addition, teachers reported high levels of satisfaction with their training and with the content and format of the program, and strongly believed the curriculum was both beneficial and sustainable in the classroom.[40] This suggests that teachers can be trained to implement parent training programs within a structure and format that is compatible with that of their established classroom and curriculum. Although asking teachers to work an additional twenty hours outside of the classroom has the potential to limit the acceptability of the program, teachers in this study felt comfortable taking on the role of parent trainer. Although there is initial evidence for the feasibility of this program, further research is necessary in order to assess the effectiveness of Project ImPACT. The empirical evaluation of this program, using standardized assessments and observational measures assessing parents' use of strategies and children's communication and social outcomes in school and home settings, is currently under way.

Scottish Centre for Autism

Parent training has also been used in conjunction with direct therapist-implemented intervention in educational settings. For example, the Scottish Centre for Autism (SCA) preschool treatment program[41] developed a model whereby intensive services and parent training are blended into school programming without placing extreme time demands on all involved parties. Although not implemented directly in schools, the SCA preschool treatment program is funded by the National Health Service in the United Kingdom and was designed as a complement to local special education services such that it could easily be formatted to work with area classrooms. The goal of this program is to improve children's social communication and social interaction skills through a combination of direct intervention by service providers and a regular schedule of parent training.[42]

The program was implemented for eight hours every two weeks, over an eleven-month period. Initially parents attended educational workshops focusing on the diagnosis of autism and its impact on the family, the rationale for the particular treatment approaches, and information about specific intervention techniques. Subsequently parents met with trainers and had the opportunity to observe and then implement intervention strategies with the child while receiving direct feedback. In addition, every two weeks parents met in a group format to discuss the training, parents' experiences as "cotherapists," treatment gains, and other pertinent issues.

Results of a controlled trial of the SCA preschool treatment program indicated that when compared to children in a control group, children who participated in the preschool treatment program had greater improvements in adaptive behavior, socialization, imitation, motor skills, joint attention, and daily living skills.[43] A program like this, with eight hours of training every other week, is highly adaptable and appropriate for modification into a preschool setting. However, further empirical research using random participant group assignment and larger sample sizes across a range of school districts is necessary for the purpose of drawing conclusions about program effectiveness. Further, the current study lacks information about parents' continued use of intervention techniques and long-term child outcomes.

Project DATA

Parent training has also been incorporated into comprehensive school-based intervention programs. One such program, Project DATA (Developmentally Appropriate Treatment for Autism),[44] is aimed at providing effective, inclusive, developmentally appropriate, and socially valid school-based services to preschoolers with ASD and their families. Although the initial classrooms were housed in a university-based early childhood program, the developers of this program focused on ways to make the program exportable, sustainable, and capable of fitting within the context and structure of early childhood special education programs. The core components of Project DATA are high-quality inclusive classrooms, extended instruction time, collaboration and coordination of services, transition support, and technical and social support for families. The specifics of this last component are adjusted depending on the needs of each child and family; however, at the very minimum parents receive monthly training in strategies for decreasing problem behaviors as well as increasing child independence and child participation in family life.[45]

In an examination of Project DATA, Schwartz and colleagues[46] found that the percentage of children who reached mastery in the use of functional skills—such as using speech to communicate, following complex directions, motor imitation, toilet training during daytime hours, symbolic play, and cooperative play with peers—increased from pre- to postparticipation. Participating families reported a high degree of satisfaction with the content and format of the program and with the progress the children made. The Project DATA model was quickly replicated in classrooms of neighboring school districts, and school district administrators reported similarly high levels of program satisfaction.[47] Positive child outcomes and consumer satisfaction (particularly from parents), as well as the rapid replication and extension of the program to other districts, suggest that a service delivery model like this has the potential to be a successful way of incorporating parent education into school curricula. However, given that parent training is just one component of this comprehensive program, it is difficult to distinguish the effects of the parent training from the larger intervention protocol. A more detailed program evaluation and further empirical research are therefore required before drawing conclusions about the efficacy and effectiveness of this parent education and support model.

The Children's Toddler School

A similar program model, the Children's Toddler School, involves an inclusive classroom-based intervention program for toddlers with autism.[48] Although this program is housed in a hospital setting, it receives local, Part C funding, making it compatible with publicly funded early intervention programs. The core components of the Children's Toddler School are a half-day inclusive classroom four days per week, special skills instruction in a 1:2 setting, and family education and support. The family education and support are provided via two-hour weekly home visits conducted by a classroom teacher that are focused on teaching parents to use behavioral strategies to promote their child's communication, social, and adaptive skills and to manage the child's behavior. Parents also attend a weekly group meeting run by the lead classroom teacher, which provided additional training and social support. An evaluation of this program indicated substantial child gains in functional skills as well as in performance on standardized measures of cognitive and adaptive functioning.[49] As with the previous program descriptions, it is unclear how much the parent training component contributed to child outcomes given that it was only one piece of a more comprehensive program. However, this program does provide a model for how parent training can be provided as part of a classroom-based intervention model.

A number of methodological limitations exist across these studies. Most of these studies were descriptive in nature and lacked empirical evaluation of child outcomes. In the studies in which changes in child behavior were reported, investigators were not able to separate the effects of parent training from other possible treatment effects. In addition, none of the studies examined parents' fidelity of implementation of the intervention techniques, further complicating the process of drawing accurate conclusions about the relationship between parent training and child outcomes.[50] Thus the empirical data supporting the effectiveness of such programs is limited. Future research that can isolate the effects of including parent training in more comprehensive, school-based preschool programs is needed. Despite these limitations, however, these studies provide preliminary evidence for the potential of parent training protocols to be successfully integrated into school curricula for preschool-age children.

HOW TO IMPLEMENT SCHOOL-BASED PARENT TRAINING PROGRAMS

The literature thus far presents a number of empirically supported parent training programs for school-age children with ASD conducted in nonschool settings, and describes several models for including parent training into school curricula for preschool-age children with ASD. Taken together, these studies indicate that including such parent training programs into school curricula could be beneficial for school-age children with ASD. However, the adoption of evidence-based parent training programs into school settings is likely to be hampered by a lack of fit between current parent training models and classroom structures for school-age students with ASD.[51]

Perhaps the best way forward is to modify existing curricula and to develop new parent training curricula in collaboration with the school personnel who will ultimately implement them. For example, treatment developers may begin by conducting focus groups with educators to identify perceived barriers to the implementation of existing models, and subsequently make modifications to the program structure accordingly. Then the modified program could be piloted by school personnel within the school setting to determine its feasibility. This approach is more likely to yield school-based parent training interventions that can be widely disseminated than developing the models in a lab setting.[52] In doing this, there are a number of issues to consider.

Identify the Training Format

Both the structure of the school program and the focus of the intervention may influence the selection of the training format to be used with parents. For example, one study suggested that both group and individual parent training models were equally effective for teaching behavior management strategies;[53] however, parents showed a preference for the group training due to its convenience (one day versus six days). Given the time limitations in public school settings, group models for training parents in behavior management (and social skills) might be preferred.

In contrast to parent training programs targeting behavior management, the parent training interventions that targeted language skills were all conducted individually. This individual format training model is by far the most common among parent training interventions focused on promoting communication and social skills in young children with ASD. There is some evidence to suggest that, unlike with behavior management strategies, parents require individual coaching and feedback in order to be able to use language teaching strategies with fidelity.[54] Therefore, parent training programs aimed at teaching language skills may need to provide opportunities for parents to practice with their child and receive feedback from the trainer.

One recently published study suggests that pivotal response treatment can be taught to parents of preschool-age children with ASD in a group format, with limited individual coaching sessions.[55] Given that a group training format is easier to integrate into school curricula,[56] educators should develop and evaluate group training models, which may or may not include some individual coaching, for teaching parents to promote their child's language skills.

Determine Who Will Provide Parent Training

There is evidence to suggest that special education teachers, itinerant staff (speech pathologists, autism consultants), school counselors, psychologists, and social workers can all be effectively taught to provide parent training in the schools.[57] Although having current school staff members provide training is ideal, it is not always possible given their existing responsibilities. For this reason, several alternative models of service delivery have been developed and evaluated for children with special needs other than autism, including the use of community mental health providers who coordinate with the school;[58] BA-level program consultants;[59] and parents who have already received training in the intervention techniques.[60] Research on the effectiveness and acceptability of these trainer models is needed. Further, because the skills involved in training parents are different from those involved in teaching students, additional research on effective models of personnel preparation would be beneficial.

Increase Parent Participation

A current limitation of school-based parent training programs is low rates of parent participation; this is particularly true in low-income areas.[61] A number of strategies have been identified to increase parent participation in parent training programs for children with conduct problems, particularly with low-income families.[62] These strategies include offering child care, assisting with transportation or providing training in the home, allowing flexible scheduling (for example, holding training sessions in the evenings), providing food, and offering incentives or rewards for attendance and progress in the program.[63]

Make the Programs Socially Valid to Parents, Teachers, and Other Consumers

Finally, it is important to consider the social validity of school-based parent training interventions if they are to be widely disseminated. Even highly effective programs are not likely to be adopted or sustained if relevant consumers do not consider the goals and outcomes of such programs to be important and the procedures to be acceptable. A number of factors may affect consumer ratings of social validity, including the target of the intervention, the intervention strategies used, the training model, the location of the training, and the time commitment required on the part of the families and staff.[64]

All of the school-based programs detailed here assessed parent satisfaction, which is an important first step in examining the feasibility and utility of an intervention.[65] However, a number of other important consumers should be considered when incorporating an intervention into a school curriculum. Future research should thus explore the satisfaction of other consumer groups, including additional family members, classroom teachers, and authorities at the school and district levels, to further assess the social acceptability of these programs and their outcomes.[66]

TO SUM UP

Incorporating parent training into school curricula for children with ASD is a promising strategy for increasing access to these services. Future development and evaluation of school-based parent training curricula should take the following into account:

- Explorations of intervention feasibility and effectiveness are essential to develop appropriate school-based delivery models for training parents of school-age children with ASD.
- The existing classroom and school structure, cost, time, content of training, and types of students and families targeted are necessary considerations when developing and implementing school-based parent training programs.
- Given the complexity of educational policies at the state, district, and school levels, as well as the variability of interventions and delivery formats, the integration of parent training into school programming is not without its own challenges.[67]
- Researchers should work with special educators and school administrators to develop accessible and adaptable parent training models that can be integrated into typical school programming.[68]

Summary and Synthesis

Understanding the roles of administrators, school staff, and parents in the context of working with children with autism and their families is a critical component of implementing effective interventions in the classroom environment. A school's culture, in regard to its adherence to special education laws and practices of inclusion, has a direct impact on the ways in which teachers and staff implement practices, communicate with parents, and develop cohesive plans for inclusive and individualized educational settings for children with autism. Chapter Eight highlights the numerous challenges school administrators face in light of the increasing numbers of children diagnosed with autism currently included in regular education classrooms. These challenges include understanding special education laws (especially the Individuals with Disabilities Education Act of 2004, Section 504 of the Vocational Rehabilitation Act of 1973, and the No Child Left Behind Act of 2001); knowing required procedures for identifying students with autism and recognizing the parameters for appropriate classroom placements; as well as understanding the legalities and specifics of individualized education programs. Further, administrators should have a basic knowledge of autism spectrum disorders and be familiar with evidence-based practices and interventions. In addition, establishing a culture of professional development and providing training in autism and other resources to teachers and staff are also warranted. Developing, facilitating, and maintaining partnerships and consistent communication with parents is necessary in order for parents to trust the intervention and inclusion process and to know that their beliefs, values, and goals and objectives are incorporated into their child's intervention plan.

Active parental involvement is an essential component in interventions for children with autism, and training parents in intervention techniques has been shown to result in significant and positive outcomes for children with autism spectrum disorders. The importance of this direct involvement has been widely disseminated in empirical studies, and has been recommended as a critical and necessary component by the National Research Council. Chapter Nine describes the overall benefits of parental involvement in interventions and details programs that have integrated parent training as part of the schoolwide plan for intervention implementation. Some of these programs include behavior management training, social skills training, and language development training. These domains are generally ones that have an impact on skills in children with autism. Therefore, providing parents with training enhances continuity and consistency in interventions across school and home contexts and facilitates partnerships among parents and professionals in both determining goals and substantiating adequate progress across interventions for their children. Designing a school-based parent training program necessitates steps to ensure cohesive implementation. This process should include identifying the training format, specifying who will provide the training, deciphering ways to increase parent participation in the program, and considering the factors that make these programs sustainable. Understanding such factors as the nature of a given targeted intervention, the intervention strategies used, the particular training model, and the location and time commitments required for parents—as well as their overall satisfaction with the training program—is important in assessing the feasibility, utility, and sustainability of parent training programs in classroom contexts.

APPENDIX: QUESTIONS FOR DISCUSSION

CHAPTER ONE: EFFECTS OF AUTISM ON SOCIAL LEARNING AND SOCIAL ATTENTION

1. How can you apply what you know about children on the spectrum to teaching *all* the students in your classroom, including high-functioning students?

2. How can you help parents of children with autism spectrum disorders (ASD) ready their children for school?

3. What are some ways you can engage the special interests of a child with ASD to help him or her achieve educational goals?

4. How might you integrate a student with autism's particular interests and passions into a lesson plan that can apply to the entire class?

5. What are some ways you can improve a student's understanding of reading materials by cueing?

CHAPTER TWO: EVIDENCE-BASED INSTRUCTIONAL INTERVENTIONS

1. Discuss the importance and effects of reinforcing appropriate behaviors for students with autism versus students without autism.

2. Computers have been used successfully in helping prompt students with autism to learn and complete tasks. What types of tasks can be taught using computer prompting? What types of prompts can be used to encourage students with these tasks?

229

3. If a computer is not available in the classroom, what are some other methods that can be used to prompt and encourage students with autism to learn and complete tasks?

4. Discuss some instructional strategies for integrating life skills, such as meal preparation and maintaining personal hygiene, into classroom teaching.

5. What types of antecedent prompts can help a student with ASD learn to behave appropriately in the classroom? Discuss several common scenarios and potential prompts that could be used.

6. If one-to-one instruction is not possible, what are some other instructional delivery methods that can be used to help a child with ASD improve his or her social skills in the classroom?

7. What is the role of leisure activities for older students with ASD? How can you help a student with ASD engage in appropriate leisure activities in the classroom?

8. Discuss ways you can track and evaluate the effectiveness of an intervention technique in the classroom.

CHAPTER THREE: EDUCATIONAL INTERVENTIONS FOR CHILDREN WITH AUTISM SPECTRUM DISORDERS

1. Discuss several methods for improving a family's involvement in the education of a child with ASD. What can a teacher do to help and encourage the family to support instructional goals?

2. What types of transitions must students with ASD undergo during the course of a day in school? How can you help students navigate through these transitions?

3. What types of positive behavioral strategies can be used to encourage students with ASD to participate in the classroom and discourage disruptive behaviors?

4. How important is it for teachers to embrace teaching models in designing procedures and programs to use in the classroom? Why?

5. Suppose your school has begun to use a particular teaching model that you have not found to be successful in your experience with students in the classroom. What can you do to improve or change the situation?

6. Discuss particular types of in-service training that would be of particular help to a new teacher dealing with children with autism in the classroom.

7. What types of support can an administrator offer teachers who face challenges in teaching students with severe ASD?

CHAPTER FOUR: IMPROVING EDUCATIONAL INTERVENTIONS FOR SCHOOL-AGE CHILDREN WITH AUTISM WITHOUT INTELLECTUAL DISABILITIES

1. Discuss the benefits of including students with autism in the regular classroom versus segregating them.
2. Students with autism are sometimes rejected by typically developing peers. Discuss some symptoms of autism that can make a student appear "different" from others. How can you prepare typical students to appreciate students with autism and accept them into classroom and social structures?
3. How can you teach typical students how to offer appropriate instructional and other types of assistance to students with ASD?
4. Discuss the differences and similarities between the concepts of *support* and *friendship* among peers and students. How can offering support encourage friendships between typical students and students with ASD?
5. Discuss opportunities in the classroom in which priming can be particularly effective.
6. What are some scenarios in which different types of antecedent interventions can be helpful for children with ASD? How do these interventions affect the particular scenarios discussed?
7. Discuss some scenarios and particular environmental fit therapies that could help students with ASD avoid disruptive behaviors. What would make these plans successful, and how would you gauge their success?
8. Discuss some scenarios in which a contingent escape and instructional fading intervention could prove successful.
9. How are symptoms of ASD similar to symptoms of other disorders, such as attention deficit hyperactivity disorder, anxiety, and depression? How can you determine whether a student is affected by a comorbid disorder?

CHAPTER FIVE: TRANSLATING EVIDENCE-BASED PRACTICES FROM THE LABORATORY TO SCHOOLS: CLASSROOM PIVOTAL RESPONSE TEACHING

1. Teachers often do not receive adequate training to meet the particular needs of students with disabilities. What resources can a teacher use to improve his or her ability to teach such students?

2. Discuss various scenarios and methods for directing a student's attention to improve his or her ability to participate in the class.

3. How can a teacher use a mixture of tasks to help a student master a new skill?

4. Students with ASD, like most of us, are motivated by interests. How can a teacher improve the learning environment and motivate a student with ASD by involving the student's particular interests?

5. Discuss the importance of cues in learning new skills for students with ASD.

6. What is the difference between direct reinforcement and indirect reinforcement? Why is direct reinforcement more successful for students with ASD?

7. What techniques can a teacher use to incorporate elements of classroom pivotal response teaching into group activities efficiently and successfully?

8. How can a teacher develop personal and student goals that are challenging yet realistic and reachable for a diverse student population?

CHAPTER SIX: FACILITATING THE USE OF EVIDENCE-BASED PRACTICES IN CLASSROOMS: THE NATIONAL PROFESSIONAL DEVELOPMENT CENTER MODEL

1. Discuss the difficulties of collaboration efforts among teachers with different experience levels and disparate views of methodologies and tools. How can collaboration efforts be improved in regard to teaching children with ASD?

2. Describe some of the difficulties in identifying goals and expectations for students with ASD. How can the use of goal attainment scaling improve that process?

3. What are the key components of online training models that help teachers understand and use evidence-based practices?

4. When professional training is not available, peer-to-peer training relationships can be developed to assist teachers. Discuss some important resources necessary for a successful peer-to-peer relationship.

5. Discuss the difference between implementation data and intervention data. How can teachers use each type of data to improve teaching practices?

CHAPTER SEVEN: TECHNOLOGY FOR STAFF TRAINING, COLLABORATION, AND SUPERVISION IN SCHOOL-BASED PROGRAMS FOR CHILDREN WITH AUTISM

1. What are the challenges of ensuring consistency in staff training programs?
2. The sharing of perspectives and information among teachers in special education is mandated by law and is a proven method for identifying, creating, and implementing best teaching practices. The most common barriers to this type of collaboration are distance and lack of time. Discuss some ways to overcome these barriers.
3. What are the benefits of Web-based collaboration and training?
4. How does video annotation work, and how can it be used in collaboration and training?
5. Discuss the role of online communities in teacher training and collaboration efforts.
6. Discuss the effectiveness of supervision via Web-based and video-based conferencing and sharing compared with real-time, in-person supervision. What are the benefits and problems associated with using these methods? What are the benefits and problems of in-person methods?
7. What are some impediments to using technology in the classroom? What are some ways to overcome these impediments?

CHAPTER EIGHT: THE ROLE OF SCHOOL ADMINISTRATORS IN WORKING WITH CHILDREN AND FAMILIES AFFECTED BY AUTISM SPECTRUM DISORDERS

1. How can school administrators and staff prepare to meet the challenges of federal laws concerning the provision of special education in public schools?
2. Discuss some specific challenges created by stereotypes among teaching staff, administrators, and parents in regard to students with ASD.
3. Discuss specific challenges in creating programs for students with ASD across grade levels with varying levels of abilities. Discuss some ways in which administrators and teachers can improve their ability to create successful programs.
4. Not all evidence-based practices are implemented successfully with every student with ASD. What are some things a teacher or administrator can do to ensure that interventions and treatments best serve individual students?

5. Discuss the challenges administrators face in implementing the five key steps for strategic planning developed by the National Autism Center:
   a. Establish the planning team.
   b. Clarify the problem and conduct a needs assessment.
   c. Develop a process for evaluating student outcomes.
   d. Develop a training plan for school personnel.
   e. Develop a plan for ensuring the sustainability of the strategic plan.
6. How can teachers and administrators create an atmosphere of collaboration and support throughout the school environment in regard to implementing programs for students with disabilities?
7. How can teachers and administrators provide opportunities for parents to discuss their children and their dreams for their children, and how can they include the parents' perceptions in educational planning?

CHAPTER NINE: INCORPORATING PARENT TRAINING INTO SCHOOL CURRICULA FOR CHILDREN WITH AUTISM SPECTRUM DISORDERS

1. How can parents become active participants in their child's educational intervention programs?
2. What barriers prevent administrators, teachers, and parents from collaborating and providing input regarding school curricula and programs? Discuss ways to overcome these barriers.
3. Discuss how parent-assisted social skills and friendship intervention training can affect a child's behavior and social skills in the classroom.
4. In low-income areas, parent participation is often at a lower level than desired. Discuss how a school can help overcome difficulties surrounding child care, scheduling, and other problems faced by parents who are struggling financially.
5. Discuss some ways in which parent training could be incorporated and integrated into typical school programming.

NOTES

CHAPTER ONE

1. World Health Organization, 1993, pp. 179–183.
2. Dingfelder & Mandell, 2011.
3. Hurley, Losh, Parlier, Reznick, & Piven, 2007.
4. Adapted from Hurley et al., 2007.
5. Seidel, 2011.
6. For example, Baron-Cohen, Leslie, & Frith, 1985.
7. For example, Ozonoff, Pennington, & Rogers, 1991.
8. For example, Frith, 1989.
9. Pelicano, 2010.
10. Wing & Gould, 1979.
11. Burnette et al., 2011.
12. Beglinger & Smith, 2005.
13. Sherer & Schreibman, 2005.
14. Institute of Education Sciences (IES), 2010.
15. Centers for Disease Control and Prevention (CDC), 2009.
16. IES, 2010.
17. CDC, 2009.
18. Ibid.
19. Machalicek et al., 2008.
20. Asperger, 1944; Kanner, 1943.
21. Sigman & Ungerer, 1984.
22. Dawson et al., 2004; McEvoy, Rogers, & Pennington, 1993.
23. Sigman & Ungerer, 1984.
24. Mundy, Sigman, Ungerer, & Sherman, 1986.

25. Dawson & McKissik, 1984.
26. Sigman & Mundy, 1989.
27. Mundy, Block et al., 2007.
28. Adapted from Ibid.
29. Rogers & Pennington, 1991.
30. For example, Klin, 1991.
31. Weeks & Hobson, 1987.
32. Kanner, 1943.
33. American Psychiatric Association (APA), 1980.
34. Wing & Gould, 1979.
35. Mundy & Sigman, 1989.
36. Rutter, 1978.
37. For example, Curcio, 1978; Dawson & Adams, 1984; Mundy & Sigman, 1989; Sigman & Mundy, 1989; Rutter, 1978.
38. APA, 1994, 2000.
39. APA, 2011.
40. Lord, Rutter, & Le Couteur, 1994.
41. Lord et al., 2000.
42. APA, 1994.
43. For example, Dawson, Meltzoff, Osterling, Rinalidi, & Brown, 1998; Klin, 1991; Mundy, Sullivan, & Mastergeorge, 2009; Schultz, 2005.
44. For example, Mundy & Newell, 2007; Tomasello, Carpenter, Call, Behne, & Moll, 2005.
45. Mundy & Jarrold, 2010.
46. Vaughan Van Hecke et al., 2011.
47. Mundy & Jarrold, 2010.
48. Ibid.
49. Brooks & Meltzoff, 2002, 2005; Mundy, Block et al., 2007.
50. Adapted from Baldwin, 1995.
51. Baldwin, 1995.
52. Tomasello et al., 2005; Mundy & Newell, 2007.
53. Tomasello & Farrar, 1986.
54. For example, Bayliss, Paul, Cannon, & Tipper, 2006.
55. Baldwin, 1995.
56. Mundy & Newell, 2007; Sullivan, Mundy, & Mastergeorge, 2011.
57. Dingfelder & Mandell, 2011, p. 601, citing National Research Council, 2001.
58. Siller & Sigman, 2002.

59. Cassel et al., 2007.
60. Siller & Sigman, 2002.
61. Bono, Daley, & Sigman, 2004.
62. See, for example, Courschesne & Pierce, 2005.
63. Mundy & Jarrold, 2010.
64. Dawson et al., 1998; Mundy, 1995; Tomasello et al., 2005.
65. Mundy & Sigman, 1989.
66. Nations & Penny, 2008.
67. Kasari, Sigman, Mundy, & Yirmiya, 1990.
68. Schilbach et al., 2010.
69. See, for example, Beglinger & Smith, 2005.
70. Dawson et al., 2009; Kasari, Freeman, & Paparella, 2006; Kasari et al., 2008; Koegel, Vernon, & Koegel, 2009.
71. Page, 2007.
72. Sinzig, Walter, & Doepfner, 2009.
73. Ibid.
74. Conners, 2004.
75. Ehlers, Gillberg, & Wing, 1999.
76. Skinner, 1957.
77. Panel A, adapted from Cohen, Amerine-Dickens, & Smith, 2006; Panel B, adapted from Dawson et al., 2009.
78. See Cohen et al., 2006.
79. Dawson et al., 2009.
80. Kasari et al., 2006; Kasari et al., 2008.
81. Kasari et al., 2006.
82. Adapted from Kasari et al., 2008.
83. Jones, Carr, & Feeley, 2006; Whalen, Schriebman, & Ingersoll, 2006.
84. Bono et al., 2004.
85. For example, Bruinsma et al., 2004; Koegel et al., 2009; Schertz & Odom, 2007.
86. National Autism Center, 2009.
87. Cowan & Allen, 2007; Wilczynski, Menousek, Hunter, & Mudgal, 2007.
88. Mundy & Crowson, 1997.
89. Blakemore, 2010; Blakemore & Choudhury, 2006.
90. Luna, Doll, Hegedus, Minshew, & Sweeney, 2007; O'Hearn, Schroer, Minshew, & Luna, 2010.
91. Luna et al., 2007.
92. For example, Koegel & Koegel, 1995.

93. Nation, Clarke, Wright, & Williams, 2006; Randi, Newman, & Grigorenko, 2010.

94. Huemer & Mann, 2010.

95. Mayes & Calhoun, 2008.

96. Nation et al., 2006.

97. Mar, 2011.

98. McKenzie, Evans, & Handley, 2010.

99. Jones et al., 2009.

100. Estes, Rivera, Bryan, Cali, & Dawson, 2011.

101. Randi et al., 2010.

102. Chiang & Lin, 2007; Huemer & Mann, 2010; Randi et al., 2010.

103. O'Conner & Klein, 2004.

104. Flores & Ganz, 2007.

105. Dingfelder & Mandell, 2011, p. 601, citing National Research Council, 2011.

CHAPTER TWO

1. Coleman-Martin, Heller, Cihak, & Irvine, 2005; Ledford, Gast, Luscre, & Ayres, 2008; Marcus & Wilder, 2009; Whalon & Hanline, 2008.

2. Delano, 2007.

3. Akmanoglu & Batu, 2004; Banda & Kubina, 2010; Cihak & Foust, 2008.

4. Banda & Kubina, 2010; Ferguson, Smith Myles, & Hagiwara, 2005; Reynhout & Carter, 2008; Soares, Vannest, & Harrison, 2009.

5. Songlee, Miller, Tincani, Sileo, & Perkins, 2008.

6. Soares et al., 2009.

7. Banda, Hart, & Liu-Gitz, 2010; Kohler, Greteman, Raschke, & Highnam, 2007; Lee, Odom, & Loftin, 2007; Licciardello, Harchik, & Luiselli, 2008; Wichnick, Vener, Pyrtek, & Poulson, 2010.

8. Davis, Boon, Cihak, & Fore III, 2010; Dotson, Leaf, Sheldon, & Sherman, 2010; Leaf, Dotson, Oppeneheim, Sheldon, & Sherman, 2010; Sansosti & Powell-Smith, 2006.

9. Reeve, Reeve, Buffington Townsend, & Poulson, 2007.

10. Charlop-Christy & Daneshvar, 2003.

11. Argott, Buffington Townsend, Sturmey, & Poulson, 2008; Leaf, Dotson, Oppeneheim, Sheldon, & Sherman, 2010.

12. Jones, 2009; Jones, Carr, & Feeley, 2006; Taylor & Hoch, 2008.

13. Esch, Carr, & Grow, 2009.

14. Harper, Symon, & Frea, 2008; Lund & Troha, 2008; Olive et al., 2007; Tincani, Crozier, & Alazetta, 2006.

15. Taylor & Harris, 1995.

16. Argott et al., 2008.

17. Ayres, Maguire, & McClimon, 2009; Bock, 1999; Cicero & Pfadt, 2002; Cihak & Grim, 2008; Cihak & Schrader, 2008; Copeland & Hughes, 2000; Gunby, Carr, & LeBlanc, 2010; Hagiwara & Smith Myles, 1999; LeBlanc, Carr, Crossett, Bennett, & Detweiler, 2005; Rosenberg, Schwartz, & Davis, 2010; Taylor, Hughes, Richard, Hoch, & Coello, 2004.

18. Cihak & Grim, 2008.

19. Rosenberg, Schwartz, & Davis, 2010.

20. Ayres, Maguire, & McClimon, 2009.

21. Cihak & Schrader, 2008.

22. Gunby, Carr, & LeBlanc, 2010.

23. Ayres et al., 2009.

24. Blair, Umbreit, Dunlap, & Jung, 2007; Blum-Dimaya, Reeve, Reeve, & Hoch, 2010; Ganz, Bourgeois, Flores, & Campos, 2008; Hine & Wolery, 2006; Hume & Odom, 2007; Kuhn Bodkin, Devlin, & Doggett, 2008; Kurt & Tekin-Iftar, 2008; Liber, Frea, & Symon, 2008; MacDonald, Sacramone, Mansfield, Wiltz, & Ahearn, 2009; Machalicek et al., 2009; Nelson, McDonnell, Johnston, Crompton, & Nelson, 2007; Paterson & Arco, 2007; Reagon, Higbee, & Endicott, 2006.

25. Barry & Burlew, 2004; Kuhn et al., 2008.

26. Blair et al., 2007; Blum-Dimaya et al., 2010; Boutot, Guenther, & Crozier, 2005; Ganz et al., 2008; Hume & Odom, 2007; Kuhn et al., 2008; Kurt & Tekin-Iftar, 2008; Machalicek et al., 2009.

27. Barry & Burlew, 2004; Ganz & Flores, 2008; MacDonald et al., 2009; Nelson et al., 2007.

28. Sansosti & Powell-Smith, 2006, 2008.

29. Machalicek et al., 2009.

30. Wang & Spillane, 2009.

31. Lang et al., 2009.

32. Westling & Fox, 2008.

33. National Institute of Child Health and Human Development, 2000.

34. That is, Coleman-Martin et al., 2005; Ledford et al., 2008; Marcus & Wilder, 2009; Whalon & Hanline, 2008.

35. National Council of Teachers of Mathematics, 2000.

36. Akmanoglu & Batu, 2004.

37. Banda & Kubina, 2010.

38. Cihak & Foust, 2008.

39. National Research Council (NRC), 1996.

40. Riesen, McDonnell, Johnson, Polychronis, & Jameson, 2003.

41. Courtade, Spooner, & Browder, 2007.

42. Loveland & Kelley, 1991; Volkmar et al., 1987.

43. Freeman, Del'Homme, Guthrie, & Zhang, 1999.

44. Jasmin et al., 2009.

45. Matson, Dempsey, & Fodstad, 2009.

46. Ibid.

47. For example, Kroeger & Sorensen, 2010; Murzynski & Bourret, 2007; Tekin-Iftar & Birkan, 2010.

48. Barry & Burlew, 2004; Bellini, Akullian, & Hopf, 2007; Blum-Dimaya et al., 2010; Chan & O'Reilly, 2008; Cihak & Schrader, 2008; Ganz & Flores, 2008; Hagiwara & Smith Myles, 1999; Krantz & McClannahan, 1998; MacDonald et al., 2009; Nikopoulos, Canavan, & Nikopoulou-Smyrni, 2009; Okada, Ohtake, & Yanagihara, 2008; Reynhout & Carter, 2008; Sansosti & Powell-Smith, 2006; Schneider & Goldstein, 2010.

49. Argott et al., 2008; Brown, Krantz, McClannahan, & Poulson, 2008; Ganz & Flores, 2008; Krantz & McClannahan, 1998; Wichnick, Vener, Pyrtek, & Poulson, 2010.

50. Betz, Higbee, & Reagon, 2008; Blum-Dimaya et al., 2010; Soares et al., 2009.

51. Copeland & Hughes, 2000; Ganz, Kaylor, Bourgeois, & Hadden, 2008.

52. Barry & Burlew, 2004; Chan & O'Reilly, 2008; Hagiwara & Smith Myles, 1999; Okada et al., 2008; Reynhout & Carter, 2008; Sansosti & Powell-Smith, 2006.

53. Schneider & Goldstein, 2010.

54. Davis et al., 2010.

55. Nelson et al., 2007.

56. Dyches, 1999; Schepis, Reid, Behrmann, & Sutton, 1998; Sigafoos, O'Reilly, Seely-York, & Edrisinha, 2004; West & Billingsley, 2005.

57. Jones et al., 2006.

58. Buffington, Krantz, McClannahan, & Poulson, 1998; Dyches, 1999; Ingvarsson & Hollobaugh, 2010; Jones et al., 2006; Kurt & Tekin-Iftar, 2008; Ledford et al., 2008; Liber et al., 2008; Riesen et al., 2003; Soluaga, Leaf, Taubman, McEachin, & Leaf, 2008.

59. Leaf, Sheldon, & Sherman, 2010.

60. Ingvarsson & Hollobaugh, 2010.

61. Cihak & Foust, 2008; Ganz & Flores, 2008.

62. Banda, Grimmett, & Hart, 2009; Boutot et al., 2005; Cihak, 2007; Jones, Feeley, & Takacs, 2007.

63. For example, Harper et al., 2008; Kravits, Kamps, Kemmerer, & Potucek, 2002; Schepis et al., 1998.
64. For a recent review of CBI, see Ramdoss et al., 2011; see also Coleman-Martin et al., 2005; Hetzroni & Shalem, 2005; Hetzroni & Tannous, 2004.
65. Ferguson et al., 2005.
66. For example, Marcus & Wilder, 2009.
67. Apple et al., 2002; Charlop-Christy & Daneshvar, 2003; Blum-Dimaya et al., 2010; D'Ateno et al., 2003; Hine & Wolery, 2006; MacDonald et al., 2009; MacDonald et al., 2005; Nikopoulos et al., 2009; Paterson & Arco, 2007; Reagon et al., 2006.
68. Bellini et al., 2007; Marcus & Wilder, 2009.
69. Cihak & Schrader, 2008.
70. Hetzroni & Shalem, 2005; Hetzroni & Tannous, 2004.
71. Coleman-Martin et al., 2005.
72. Ferguson et al., 2005.
73. Shabani et al., 2002.
74. Taylor et al., 2004.
75. Ramdoss et al., 2011.
76. Marcus & Wilder, 2009.
77. For example, Bellini et al., 2007; Blum-Dimaya et al., 2010; Cihak & Schrader, 2008; MacDonald et al., 2009; Nikopoulos et al., 2009.
78. Dotson et al., 2010; Garfinkle & Schwartz, 2002; Leaf, Sheldon, & Sherman, 2010; Ledford et al., 2008.
79. Leaf, Dotson, et al., 2010.
80. English, Goldstein, Shafer, & Kaczmarek, 1997; Kamps, Leonard, Vernon, & Dugan, 1992; Laushey, Heflin, Shippen, Alberto, & Fredrick, 2009; Laushey & Heflin, 2000.
81. Machalicek et al., 2008.
82. For example, Akmanoglu & Batu, 2004; Ferguson et al., 2005; Songlee et al., 2008.
83. Machalicek et al., 2009.
84. Ganz et al., 2008.
85. Blum-Dimaya et al., 2010.
86. Krantz & McClannahan, 1998; Thiemann & Goldstein, 2004.
87. Krantz & McClannahan, 1998.
88. Kroeger & Sorenson-Burnworth, 2009; Mastropieri, Bakken, & Scruggs, 1991; Xin, Grasso, Dipipi-Hoy, & Jitendra, 2005.
89. NRC, 2001.
90. Sherer & Schreibman, 2005.

CHAPTER THREE

1. Kanner, 1943.
2. Ibid.
3. Bettleheim, 1967.
4. Rimland, 1964.
5. DeMyer, Hingtgen, & Jackson, 1981.
6. Stevens et al., 2007.
7. For a review of this area, see Offit, 2008; Wing & Potter, 2009.
8. American Psychiatric Association, 1994.
9. Data Accountability Center, 2010.
10. Giangreco, 2009.
11. National Autism Center, 2009.
12. Edelson, 2006.
13. Boyd & Shaw, 2010.
14. Boutot & Dukes, 2011.
15. Leyfer et al., 2006.
16. Kenworthy, Black, Wallace, Ahluvalia, & Sirian, 2005.
17. Ashburner, Ziviani, & Rodger, 2008.
18. Odom, Collet-Klingenberg, Rogers, & Hatton, 2010, p. 276.
19. Odom et al., 2004; Odom, Collet-Klingenberg, et al., 2010; Rogers & Vismara, 2008.
20. Rogers & Vismara, 2008.
21. Rogers et al., 2006.
22. Hoyson, Jamieson, & Strain, 1984.
23. Cohen, Amerine-Dickens, & Smith, 2006.
24. Campbell et al., 1998.
25. Fenske, Zalenski, Krantz, & McClannahan, 1985.
26. Odom, Boyd, Hall, & Hume, 2010.
27. Rogers & Vismara, 2008.
28. Odom, Collet-Klingenberg, et al., 2010.
29. National Autism Center, 2009.
30. Mesibov & Shea, 2010.
31. See Mesibov & Shea, 2011, for a review.
32. Panerai et al., 2009.
33. National Autism Center, 2009.
34. Odom, Collet-Klingenberg, et al., 2010.
35. Boutot & Hume, 2010.

36. Dillenburger, 2011.

37. Lovaas, 1987; McEachin, Smith, & Lovaas, 1993.

38. See Gresham & MacMillan, 1997.

39. See for example Eldevick, Eikeseth, Jahr, & Smith, 2006; Sallows & Graupner, 2005.

40. Smith, Groen, & Wynn, 2000.

41. See Helt et al., 2008, for a review.

42. Steege, Mace, Perry, & Longenecker, 2007.

43. Lovaas, 1987.

44. Smith et al., 2000.

45. Eldevick, Eikeseth, Jahr, & Smith, 2006.

46. Sheinkopf & Siegel, 1998.

47. Reed, Osborne, & Corness, 2007.

48. See Olive, Boutot, & Tarbox, 2011.

49. National Autism Center, 2009; Odom, Collet-Klingenberg, et al., 2010.

50. Neitzel, 2010.

51. Hart & Risley, 1968.

52. Zagar & Shamow, 2005.

53. Koegel, O'Dell, & Koegel, 1987.

54. Koegel et al., 1989.

55. See Koegel & Koegel, 2006, Odom, Collet-Klingenberg, et al., 2010.

56. Delprato, 2001.

57. Greenspan & Weider, 1997.

58. Prizant, Wetherby, Rubin, Laurent, & Rydell, 2006.

59. Gutstein, Burgess, & Montfort, 2007.

60. Dawson, 2008.

61. See Prizant et al., 2006, for a review.

62. Greenspan & Weider, 1997.

63. Prizant et al., 2006.

64. Dawson et al., 2009.

65. Odom, Boyd, et al., 2010.

66. Eikeseth et al., 2007.

67. Shin, Stahmer, Marcus, & Mandell, 2010.

68. Ibid.

69. Stahmer, Reed, Shin, & Mandell, 2010.

70. Dingfelder, Shin, & Mandell, 2010.

71. Arick et al., 2003; Lerman, Tetreault, Hovanetz, Strobel, & Garro, 2008.

72. Boutot & Walberg, 2011.

73. Mandell, Listerud, Levy, & Pinto-Martin, 2002.

74. Boyd, 2002; Siklos & Kerns, 2007.

75. Stoner, 2005.

76. Fein & Dunn, 2007.

77. Boutot & Dukes, 2011; Scheuermann, Webber, Boutot, & Goodwin, 2003.

78. Schreibman & Winter, 2003.

79. Rogers & Vismara, 2008.

80. National Research Council, 2001.

CHAPTER FOUR

1. Howlin, 2000; Venter, Lord, & Schopler, 1992.

2. Howlin, 2000.

3. Bauminger & Shulman, 2003.

4. Bauminger, Solomon, Aviezer, Heung, Brown, & Rogers, 2008.

5. Bauminger, Solomon, Aviezer, Heung, Gazit, et al., 2008.

6. Koegel & LaZebnik, 2008; Volden, Coolican, Garon, White, & Bryson, 2009.

7. Koegel & LaZebnik, 2006.

8. Fisher & Meyer, 2002.

9. Stichter, Randolph, Gage, & Schmidt, 2007.

10. Ormrod, 2006.

11. Fisher & Meyer, 2002; Ormrod, 2006.

12. Cooper, Griffith, & Filer, 1999; Meyer et al., 1987.

13. Whitehurst & Howells, 2006.

14. Kamps et al., 1998.

15. Cooper et al., 1999.

16. Frederickson, Warren, & Turner, 2005; Greenway, 2000; Gus, 2000; Kalyva & Avramidis, 2005.

17. Greenway, 2000.

18. Newton, Taylor, & Wilson, 1996, as cited in Greenway, 2000.

19. Kalyva & Avramidis, 2005.

20. Morrison, Kamps, Garcia, & Parker, 2001.

21. Kalyva & Avramidis, 2005.

22. Gonzalez-Lopez & Kamps, 1997.

23. Koegel & LaZebnik, 2008.

24. Koegel, Werner, Vismara, & Koegel, 2005.

25. Zanolli, Daggett, & Adams, 1996.

26. Gengoux, 2009.

27. Koegel, Koegel, Frea, & Green-Hopkins, 2003.

28. Bevill, Gast, Maguire, & Vail, 2001.

29. Brookman et al., 2003.

30. For example, Cooper et al., 1999; Gus, 2000.

31. Koegel & LaZebnik, 2006.

32. Koegel, Dunlap, & Koegel, 1996.

33. Harrower & Dunlap, 2001.

34. Blakeley-Smith, Carr, Cale, & Owen-DeSchryver, 2009.

35. Durand & Crimmins, 1988.

36. Carr et al., 1999.

37. Frea, Koegel, & Koegel, 2004.

38. Kozlowski, Wood, Gilligan, & Luiselli, 2009.

39. Durand & Carr, 1991; Koegel et al., 2006.

40. Carr, Ladd, & Schulte, 2008.

41. Blakeley-Smith et al., 2009.

42. Butler & Luiselli, 2007.

43. Scattone, Wilczynski, Edwards, & Rabian, 2002.

44. Blakeley-Smith et al., 2009.

45. Ibid.

46. Butler & Luiselli, 2007.

47. Greenway, 2000; Rogers, 2000.

48. Rowe, 1999.

49. Spencer, Simpson, & Lynch, 2008.

50. Ozdemir, 2008.

51. Koegel, Koegel, & Parks,1995.

52. Harrower & Dunlap, 2001.

53. Wilkinson, 2005.

54. Ibid.

55. Koegel, Koegel, Hurley, & Frea, 1992.

56. Gardner, 2010.

57. Wood et al., 2009.

58. Gardner, 2010; Scahill & Pachler, 2007.

59. Santosh, Baird, Pirtaraststian, Tavare, & Gringas, 2006.

60. Ghaziuddin, Ghaziuddin, & Greden, 2002.

61. Reaven, 2009; Wood et al., 2009.

62. Howlin, 1998.

63. Reaven, 2009.

64. Velting, Setzer, & Albano, 2004.

65. Wood et al., 2009.

66. Ibid.

67. Ibid.

68. Myles & Adreon, 2002.

69. Koegel, Koegel, & Smith, 1997.

70. Adelman & Taylor, 1998.

71. Hewitt & O'Nell, 1998.

72. Carter, O'Rourke, Sisco, & Pelsue, 2009.

73. Test, Flowers, Hewitt, & Solow, 2004.

74. Carter et al., 2009.

75. Hewitt, 1998.

76. Hewitt & Larson, 1994.

77. Etscheidt, 2003.

78. Robinson, 2007.

79. Kohler, Anthony, Steighner, & Hoyson, 2001.

80. Ibid.

81. Robinson, 2007.

CHAPTER FIVE

1. National Research Council, 2001.

2. Sindelar, Brownell, & Billingsley, 2010.

3. Stahmer, Collings, & Palinkas, 2005.

4. Ibid.

5. Lovaas, 1987.

6. Nation Autism Center, 2009.

7. Koegel, Koegel, Harrower, & Carter, 1999.

8. Creedon, 1975.

9. Humphries, 2003.

10. Koegel, Camarata, Valdez-Menchaca, & Koegel, 1998; Laski, Charlop, & Schreibman, 1988.

11. Laski et al., 1988.

12. Koegel et al., 1998.

13. Sze, Koegel, Brookman, & Koegel, 2003.

14. Stahmer, 1995.

15. Thorp, Stahmer, & Schreibman, 1995.
16. Pierce & Schreibman, 1995.
17. Koegel, Carter, & Koegel, 2003.
18. Rocha, Schreibman, & Stahmer, 2007; Whalen & Schreibman, 2003.
19. Koegel, Tran, Mossman, & Koegel, 2006.
20. Humphries, 2003; Schreibman, Kaneko, & Koegel, 1991.
21. Delprato, 2001; Humphries, 2003.
22. Jones, Carr, & Feeley, 2006; Kuhn, Bodkin, Devlin, & Doggett, 2008.
23. Stahmer, 2007.
24. Ibid.
25. Stahmer, Suhrheinrich, Reed, Schreibman, & Vattuone, 2011.
26. Allen & Fuqua, 1985; Burke & Cerniglia, 1990; Dube & McIlvane, 1999; Gersten, 1983; Koegel & Schreibman, 1977.
27. Reed, Stahmer, Schreibman, & Suhrheinrich, 2011.
28. Stahmer, Suhrheinrich, Reed, Bolduc, & Schreibman, 2011.
29. Ibid.
30. R. L. Koegel, O'Dell, & Koegel, 1987.
31. Stahmer, Suhrheinrich, Reed, Bolduc, & Schreibman, 2011.

CHAPTER SIX

1. Williams, Fan, & Goodman, 2011.
2. Horner et al., 2005; Nathan & Gorman, 2002; Odom et al., 2004; Rogers & Vismara, 2008.
3. Ibid.
4. Adapted from Hume & Smith, 2009.
5. Moran, Myles, & Downing, 1990, 1993; Moran, Myles, Downing, & Ormsbee, 1996; Rinkel & Myles, 1997.
6. Rush & Shelden, 2011.
7. Hanft, Rush, & Shelden, 2004.

CHAPTER SEVEN

1. For an example of the use of video modeling to train staff, see Catania, Almeida, Liu-Constant, & Digennaro Reed, 2009.
2. Maurice, Green, & Fox, 2001.
3. Hobbs, Day, & Russo, 2002.

4. Im & Lee, 2003/2004.

5. Catagnus & Hantula, 2011.

6. Rich & Hannafin, 2009.

7. Ibid.

8. Reischl & Oberleitner, 2009.

9. Barab, Kling, & Gray, 2004.

10. Rule, Salzberg, Higbee, Menlove, & Smith, 2006.

11. Scheeler, Congdon, & Stansbery, 2010.

12. He, Means, & Lin, 2006.

13. Simpson, 2002.

14. Kochtanek & Hein, 2000.

15. Jones, 2001.

16. Kochtanek & Hein, 2000.

17. Hantula & Pawlowicz, 2004.

18. Winter & McGhie-Richmond, 2005; see also Ocker & Yaverbaum, 1999.

19. Anderson, Reinhart, & Slowinski, 2001.

20. Hawkes, 2000.

21. Fjermestad, 2004.

22. Ocker & Yaverbaum, 1999.

23. Hawkes, 2000.

24. Hantula & Pawlowicz, 2004.

25. For example, see Gasson, 2005; Kilo, 1999.

26. Blann & Hantula, 2004; Davis & Hantula, 2001; Lobel, Neubauer, & Swedburg, 2005.

27. Geer & Hamill, 2003; Holzer, 2004; McConnell, 2002.

28. Blanchard, 2004; DeWert, Babinski, & Jones, 2003; Selwyn, 2000.

29. Anderson, Reinhart, & Slowinski, 2001; Hawkes & Romiszowski, 2001; Järvelä & Häkkinen, 2002; Kurtts, Hibbard, & Levin, 2005.

CHAPTER EIGHT

1. Centers for Disease Control and Prevention (CDC), 2010.

2. DiPaola & Walther-Thomas, 2003.

3. Ibid, p. 9.

4. National Autism Center, 2009; Yell, Katsiyannis, Drasgow, & Herbst, 2003.

5. Tomsky, 2010; Yell et al., 2003.

6. Ibid.

7. Minnesota Department of Education, 2010.

8. Getty & Summy, 2004.

9. National Research Council, 2001, p. 11.

10. American Psychiatric Association, 2000.

11. de Boer, 2009, p. 22.

12. Tomsky, 2010, p. 23.

13. Zager & Alpern, 2010.

14. Roberts, 2010.

15. National Autism Center, 2009, pp. 1, 26.

16. *Board of Education of Hendrick Hudson Central School District v. Rowley,* 1982.

17. de Boer, 2009, p. 9.

18. National Research Council, 2001; Tomsky, 2010; Wilkinson, 2010.

19. Tomsky, 2010, p. 25.

20. *Board of Education of Hendrick Hudson Central School District v. Rowley,* 1982, at 206–207.

21. National Autism Center, 2009.

22. Ibid, p. 2.

23. Ibid, p. 38.

24. Ibid, pp. 39–68.

25. Schillinger, 2010.

26. National Autism Center, 2009.

27. National Research Council, 2001, p. 8.

28. de Boer, 2009, p. 9.

29. Hall, 2009.

30. Schillinger, 2010, p. 96.

31. Zirkel, 2002.

32. Ibid.

33. Lake & Billingsley, 2000; Stoner et al., 2005.

34. Lake & Billingsley, 2000, p. 249.

35. Lake & Billingsley, 2000.

36. Stoner et al., 2005, p. 43.

37. Stoner et al., 2005.

38. Hall, 2009.

39. Yell et al., 2003, p. 182.

40. Stoner et al., 2005, p. 46.

41. Boutot & Myles, 2011; Hall, 2009; Stoner et al., 2005.

42. National Autism Center, 2009.

CHAPTER NINE

1. National Research Council, 2001.
2. For example, Brookman-Frazee, Stahmer, Baker-Ericzén, & Tsai, 2006; Mahoney et al., 1999; McConachie & Diggle, 2007.
3. McConachie & Diggle, 2007.
4. Koegel, Bimbela, & Schriebman,1996; Symon, 2001; Mahoney & Perales, 2003.
5. Aldred, Green, & Adams, 2004; McConachie, Randle, Hammal, & Le Couteur, 2005; Charlop & Trasowech, 1991.
6. Ingersoll & Gergans, 2007.
7. Drew et al., 2002; Green et al., 2010; Kasari, Gulsrud, Wong, Kwon, & Locke, 2010.
8. Kasari et al., 2010.
9. For example, Aman et al., 2009; Moes & Frea, 2002.
10. For example, Brookman-Frazee, Vismara, Drahota, Stahmer, & Openden, 2009; Koegel, Schreibman, Britten, Burke, & O'Neill, 1982.
11. Koegel et al., 1982; Schreibman & Koegel, 2005.
12. Tonge et al., 2006.
13. Koegel, Schreibman, Johnson, O'Neill, & Dunlap, 1984.
14. For example, Laski, Charlop, & Schreibman, 1988.
15. Hume, Bellini, & Pratt, 2005.
16. Iovannone, Dunlap, Huber, & Kincaid, 2003.
17. Brookman-Frazee et al., 2006.
18. Summers, Houlding, & Reitzel, 2004.
19. Sofronoff, Leslie, & Brown 2004.
20. Whittingham, Sofronoff, Sheffield, & Sanders, 2009.
21. Solomon Ono, Timmer, & Goodlin-Jones, 2008.
22. Aman et al., 2009.
23. Arnold et al., 2003.
24. Laugeson, Frankel, Mogil, & Dillon, 2008.
25. Ibid.
26. Frankel et al., 2010.
27. Solomon, Goodlin-Jones, & Anders, 2004.
28. Beaumont & Sofronoff, 2008.
29. Solomon et al., 2004.
30. Frankel et al., 2010.
31. Solomon et al., 2004.
32. Laski et al., 1988.
33. Charlop-Christy & Carpenter, 2000.

34. Seung, Ashwell, Elder, & Valcante, 2006.

35. Laugeson et al., 2008.

36. Howlin, Goode, Hutton, & Rutter, 2004.

37. Mahoney et al., 1999.

38. Boulware, Schwartz, Sandall, & McBride, 2006; Ingersoll & Dvortcsak, 2006; Salt et al., 2001, 2002; Schwartz, Sandall, McBride, & Boulware, 2004; Stahmer & Ingersoll, 2004.

39. Ingersoll & Dvortcsak, 2006.

40. Ibid.

41. Salt et al., 2001.

42. Ibid.

43. Salt et al., 2002.

44. Schwartz et al., 2004.

45. Ibid.

46. Ibid.

47. Ibid.

48. Stahmer & Ingersoll, 2004.

49. Ibid.

50. Wheeler, Baggett, Fox, & Blevins, 2006.

51. Ingersoll & Dvortcsak, 2006.

52. Dingfelder & Mandell, 2011.

53. Sofronoff et al., 2004.

54. Kaiser, Hemmeter, Ostrosky, Alpert, & Hancock, 1995.

55. Minjarez, Williams, Mercier, & Harden, 2011.

56. Ingersoll & Dvortcsak, 2006.

57. For example, Ingersoll & Dvorcsak, 2006.

58. Kratochwill, McDonald, Levin, Scalia, & Coover, 2009.

59. Dishion, Kavanagh, Schneiger, Nelson, & Kaufman, 2002.

60. Neef, 1995.

61. For example, Reid, Webster-Stratton, & Hammond, 2007.

62. Forehand & Kotchick, 2002.

63. Ibid.

64. Dingfelder & Mandell, 2011.

65. Callahan, Henson, & Cowan, 2008.

66. Ibid.

67. Iovannone et al., 2003.

68. Dingfelder & Mandell, 2011.

REFERENCES

CHAPTER ONE

American Psychiatric Association (APA). (1980). *Diagnostic and statistical manual of mental disorders* (3rd ed.). Washington, DC: Author.

American Psychiatric Association (APA). (1994). *Diagnostic and statistical manual of mental disorders* (4th ed.). Washington, DC: Author.

American Psychiatric Association (APA). (2000). *Diagnostic and statistical manual of mental disorders* (4th ed., text rev.). Washington, DC: Author.

American Psychiatric Association (APA). (2011). *DSM-5 development: A 09 Autism Spectrum Disorder.* Available from www.dsm5.org/ProposedRevision/Pages/propose drevision.aspx?rid=94

Asperger, H. (1944). Die "Autistischen Psychopathen" im Kindesalter. *Archiv Für Psychiatrie und Nevenkrankheiten, 117*, 76–136.

Baldwin, D. (1995). Understanding the link between joint attention and language. In C. Moore & P. Dunham (Eds.), *Joint attention: Its origins and role in development* (pp. 131–158). Mahwah, NJ: Erlbaum.

Baron-Cohen, S., Leslie, A., & Frith, U. (1985). Does the autistic child have a theory of mind? *Cognition, 21*, 37–46.

Bayliss, A., Paul, M., Cannon, P., & Tipper, S. (2006). Gaze cuing and affective judgments of objects: I like what you look at. *Psychonomic Bulletin and Review, 13*, 1061–1066.

Beglinger, L., & Smith, T. (2005). Concurrent validity of social subtypes and IQ after early intensive behavioral intervention in children with autism. *Journal of Autism and Developmental Disorders, 35*, 295–303.

Blakemore, S.-J. (2010). The developing social brain: Implications for education. *Neuron, 65*, 744–747.

Blakemore, S.-J., & Choudhury, S. (2006). Development of the adolescent brain: Implications for executive function and social cognition. *Journal of Child Psychology and Psychiatry, 47,* 296–312.

Bono, M., Daley, T., & Sigman, M. (2004). Joint attention moderates the relation between intervention and language development in young children with autism. *Journal of Autism and Related Disorders, 34,* 495–505.

Brooks, R., & Meltzoff, A. (2002). The importance of eyes: How infants interpret adult looking behavior. *Developmental Psychology, 38,* 958–966.

Brooks, R., & Meltzoff, A. (2005). The development of gaze following and its relations to language. *Developmental Science, 8,* 535–543.

Burnette, C., Henderson, H. A., Sutton, S., Pradella Inge, A., Zahka, N., Schwartz, C., & Mundy, P. C. (2011). Brief report: EEG asymmetry, symptoms and the modifier model of autism. *Journal of Autism and Developmental Disorders, 41,* 1113–1124.

Cassel, T., Messinger, D., Ibanez, L., Haltigan, J., Acosta, S., & Buchman, A. (2007). Early social and emotional communication skills in the infant siblings of children with autism spectrum disorders: An examination of the broad phenotype. *Journal of Autism and Developmental Disorders, 37,* 122–132.

Centers for Disease Control and Prevention (CDC). (2009). Prevalence of autism spectrum disorders: Autism and developmental disabilities monitoring network 2006. *MMWR Surveillance Summaries, 58,* 1–20.

Chiang, H., & Lin, Y. (2007). Reading comprehension instruction for students with autism spectrum disorders: A review of the literature. *Focus on Autism and Other Developmental Disabilities, 22,* 259–267.

Cohen, H., Amerine-Dickens, M., & Smith, T. (2006). Early intensive behavioral treatment: Replication of the UCLA model in a community setting. *Journal of Developmental and Behavioral Pediatrics, 27,* 145–155.

Conners, K. (2004). *Conners 3rd Edition* [Assessment]. North Tonawanda, NY: Multi-Health Systems.

Courschesne, E., & Pierce, K. (2005). Why the frontal cortex in autism might be talking only to itself: Local over-connectivity but long-distance disconnection. *Current Opinion in Neurology, 15,* 225–230.

Cowan, R. J., & Allen, K. D. (2007). Using naturalistic procedures to enhance learning in individuals with autism: A focus on generalized teaching within the school setting. *Psychology in the Schools, 44,* 701–715.

F. (1978). Sensorimotor functioning and communication in mute autistic *Journal of Autism and Developmental Disorders, 8,* 281–292.

Dawson, G., & Adams, A. (1984). Imitation and social responsiveness in autistic children. *Journal of Abnormal Child Psychology, 12,* 209–225.

Dawson, G., & McKissick, F. C. (1984). Self-recognition in autistic children. *Journal of Autism and Developmental Disorders, 14,* 383–394.

Dawson, G., Meltzoff, A., Osterling, J., Rinaldi, J., & Brown, E. (1998). Children with autism fail to orient to naturally occurring social stimuli. *Journal of Autism and Developmental Disorders, 28,* 479–485.

Dawson, G., Rogers, S., Munson, J., Smith, M., Winter, J., Greenson, J., et al. (2009). Randomized, controlled trial of an intervention for toddlers with autism: The Early Start Denver Model. *Pediatrics, 125,* e17–e23.

Dawson, G., Toth, K., Abbott, R., Osterling, J., Munson, J., Estes, A., & Liaw, J. (2004). Early social attention impairments in autism: Social orienting, joint attention, and attention in autism. *Developmental Psychology, 40,* 271–283.

Dingfelder, H., & Mandell, D. (2011). Bridging the research-to-practice gap in autism intervention: An application of diffusion innovation theory. *Journal of Autism and Developmental Disorders, 41,* 597–609.

Ehlers, S., Gillberg, C., & Wing, L. (1999). A screening questionnaire for Asperger syndrome and other high-functioning autism spectrum disorders in school age children. *Journal of Autism and Developmental Disorders, 29,* 129–140.

Estes, A., Rivera, V., Bryan, M., Cali, P., & Dawson, G. (2011). Discrepancies between academic achievement and intellectual ability in higher functioning school aged children with autism spectrum disorder. *Journal of Autism and Developmental Disorders, 41,* 1044–1052.

Flores, M. M., & Ganz, J. B. (2007). Effectiveness of direct instruction for teaching statement inferences, use of facts, and analogies to students with developmental disabilities and reading delays. *Focus on Autism and Other Developmental Disabilities, 22,* 244–251.

Frith, U. (1989). *Autism: Explaining the enigma.* Oxford, England: Blackwell.

Huemer, S., & Mann, V. (2010). A comprehensive profile of decoding and comprehension in autism spectrum disorders. *Journal of Autism and Developmental Disorders, 40,* 485–493.

Hurley, R., Losh, M., Parlier, M., Reznick, J. S., & Piven, J. (2007). The Broad Autism Phenotype Questionnaire. *Journal of Autism and Developmental Disorders, 37,* 1679–1690.

Institute of Education Sciences. (2010). *The condition of education: Indicator 6: Children and youth with disabilities.* Alexandria, VA: National Center for Education Statistics, U.S. Department of Education.

Jones, C.R.G., Happé, F., Golden, H., Marsden, A.J.S., Tregay, J., Simonoff, E., et al. (2009). Reading and arithmetic in adolescents with autism spectrum disorders: Peaks and dips in attainment. *Neuropsychology, 23,* 718–728.

Jones, E., Carr, E., & Feeley, K. (2006). Multiple effects of joint attention intervention for children with autism. *Behavior Modification, 30,* 782–834.

Kanner, L. (1943). Autistic disturbances of affective contact. *Nervous Child, 2,* 217–250.

Kasari, C., Freeman, S., & Paparella, T. (2006). Joint attention and symbolic play in young children with autism: A randomized controlled intervention study. *Journal of Child Psychology and Psychiatry, 47,* 611–620.

Kasari, C., Paparella, T., Freeman, S., & Jahromi, L. B. (2008). Language outcome in autism: Randomized comparison of joint attention and play interventions. *Journal of Consulting and Clinical Psychology, 76,* 125–137.

Kasari, C., Sigman, M., Mundy, P., & Yirmiya, N. (1990). Affective sharing in the context of joint attention interactions of normal, autistic, and mentally retarded children. *Journal of Autism and Developmental Disorders, 20,* 87–100.

Klin, A. (1991). Young autistic children's listening preferences in regard to speech: A possible characterization of the symptom of social withdrawal. *Journal of Autism and Developmental Disorders, 21,* 29–42.

Koegel, R., & Koegel, L. K. (Eds.). (1995). *Teaching children with autism: Strategies for initiating positive interactions and improving learning opportunities.* Baltimore: Brookes.

Koegel, R. L., Vernon, T. W., & Koegel, L. K. (2009). Improving social initiations in young children with autism using reinforcers with embedded social interactions. *Journal of Autism and Developmental Disorders, 39,* 1240–1251.

Lord, C., Risi, S., Lambrecht, L., Cook, E. H., Leventhal, B. L., DiLavore, P. C., et al. (2000). The Autism Diagnostic Observation Schedule-Generic: A standard measure of social and communication deficits associated with the spectrum of autism. *Journal of Autism and Developmental Disorders, 30,* 205–223.

Lord, C., Rutter, M., & Le Couteur, A. (1994). Autism Diagnostic Interview-Revised: A revised version of a diagnostic interview for caregivers of individuals with possible pervasive developmental disorder. *Journal of Autism and Developmental Disorders, 24,* 659–685.

Luna, B., Doll, S., Hegedus, S., Minshew, N., & Sweeney, J. (2007). Maturation of executive functions in autism. *Biological Psychiatry, 61,* 474–481.

Machalicek, W., O'Reilly, M. F., Beretvas, N., Sigafoos, J., Lancioni, G., Sorrells, A., et al. (2008). A review of school-based instructional interventions for students with autism spectrum disorders. *Research in Autism Spectrum Disorders, 2,* 395–416.

Mar, R. (2011). The neural bases of social cognition and story comprehension. *Annual Review of Psychology, 62,* 103–134.

Mayes, S. D., & Calhoun, S. L. (2008). WISC-IV and WIAT-II profiles in children with high-functioning autism. *Journal of Autism and Developmental Disorders, 38,* 428–439.

McEvoy, R., Rogers, S., & Pennington, R. (1993). Executive function and social communication deficits in young autistic children. *Journal of Child Psychology and Psychiatry, 34,* 563–578.

McKenzie, R., Evans, J., & Handley, S. (2010). Conditional reasoning in autism: Activation and integration of knowledge and belief. *Developmental Psychology, 46,* 391–403.

Mundy, P. (1995). Joint attention and social-emotional approach behavior in children with autism. *Development and Psychopathology, 7,* 63–82.

Mundy, P., Block, J., Vaughan Van Hecke, A., Delgadoa, C., Venezia Parlade, M., & Pomares, Y. (2007). Individual differences and the development of infant joint attention. *Child Development, 78,* 938–954.

Mundy, P., & Crowson, M. (1997). Joint attention and early social communication: Implications for research on intervention with autism. *Journal of Autism and Developmental Disorders, 27,* 653–676.

Mundy, P., & Jarrold, W. (2010). Infant joint attention, neural networks and social-cognition. *Neural Networks* (Special issue: *Social-Cognition: From Babies to Robots*), *23,* 985–997.

Mundy, P., & Newell, L. (2007). Attention, joint attention and social cognition. *Current Directions in Psychological Science, 16,* 269–274.

Mundy, P., & Sigman, M. (1989). Specifying the nature of the social impairment in autism. In G. Dawson (Ed.), *Autism: New perspectives on diagnosis, nature, and treatment* (pp. 3–21). New York: Guilford Press.

Mundy, P., Sigman, M., Ungerer, J., & Sherman, T. (1986). Defining the social deficits of autism: The contribution of nonverbal communication measures. *Journal of Child Psychology and Psychiatry, 27,* 657–669.

Mundy, P., Sullivan, L., & Mastergeorge, A. (2009). A parallel and distributed processing model of joint attention and autism. *Autism Research, 2,* 2–21.

Nation, K., Clarke, P., Wright, B., & Williams, C. (2006). Patterns of reading ability in children with autism spectrum disorder. *Journal of Autism and Developmental Disorders, 36,* 911–919.

National Autism Center. (2009). *The National Standards Project—Addressing the need for evidence based practice guidelines for autism spectrum disorders.* Randolph, MA: Author.

National Research Council. (2001). Methodological issues in research on education interventions. In *Educating children with autism* (pp. 193–210). Washington, DC: National Academy Press.

Nations, K., & Penny, S. (2008). Sensitivity to eye gaze in autism: Is it normal? Is it automatic? Is it social? *Development and Psychopathology*, *20*, 79–97.

O'Connor, I., & Klein, P. (2004). Explorations of strategies for facilitating the reading comprehension of high-functioning students with autism spectrum disorders. *Journal of Autism and Developmental Disorders*, *34*, 115–127.

O'Hearn, K., Schroer, E., Minshew, N., & Luna, B. (2010). Lack of developmental improvement on a face memory task during adolescence in autism. *Neuropsychologia*, *48*, 3955–3960.

Ozonoff, S., Pennington, R., & Rogers, S. (1991). Executive function deficits in high-functioning autistic individuals: Relations to theory of mind. *Journal of Child Psychology and Psychiatry*, *32*, 1081–1105.

Page, T. (2007, August 20). Parallel play: A lifetime of restless isolation explained. *New Yorker*. Available from www.newyorker.com/reporting/2007/08/20/070820fa_fact_page

Pelicano, E. (2010). The development of core cognitive skills in autism: A 3-year prospective study. *Child Development*, *81*, 1400–1416.

Randi, J., Newman, T., & Grigorenko, E. (2010). Teaching children with autism to read for meaning: Challenges and possibilities. *Journal of Autism and Developmental Disorders*, *40*, 890–902.

Rogers, S., & Pennington, B. (1991). A theoretical approach to the deficits in infantile autism. *Developmental Psychopathology*, *6*, 635–652.

Rutter, M. (1978). Diagnosis and definition. In M. Rutter and E. Schopler (Eds.), *Autism: A reappraisal of concepts and treatments* (pp. 1–25). New York: Plenum.

Schertz, H. H., & Odom, S. L. (2007). Promoting joint attention in toddlers with autism: A parent-mediated developmental model. *Journal of Autism and Developmental Disorders*, *37*, 1562–1575.

Schilbach, L., Wilms, M., Eickhoff, S. B., Romanzetti, S., Tepest, R., Bente, G. B., et al. (2010). Minds made for sharing: Initiating joint attention recruits reward-related neurocircuitry. *Journal of Cognitive Neuroscience*, *22*, 2702–2715.

Schultz, R. (2005). Developmental deficits in social perception in autism: The role of the amygdala and fusiform face area. *International Journal of Developmental Neuroscience*, *23*, 125–141.

Seidel, K. (2011). Neurodiversity.com.

Sherer, M., & Schreibman, L. (2005). Individual behavioral profiles and predictors of treatment effectiveness for children with autism. *Journal of Consulting and Clinical Psychology*, *73*, 525–538.

Sigman, M., & Mundy, P. (1989). Social attachments in autistic children. *Journal of the American Academy of Child & Adolescent Psychiatry*, *28*, 74–81.

Sigman, M., & Ungerer, J. (1984). Attachment behaviors in autistic children. *Journal of Autism and Related Disabilities, 14,* 231–244.

Siller, M., & Sigman, M. (2002). The behaviors of parents of children with autism predict the subsequent development of their children's communication. *Journal of Autism and Developmental Disorders, 32,* 77–89.

Sinzig, J., Walter, D., & Doepfner, M. (2009). Attention deficit/hyperactivity disorder in children and adolescents with autism spectrum disorder: Symptom or syndrome? *Journal of Attention Disorders, 13,* 117–126.

Skinner, B. (1957). *Verbal behavior.* East Norwalk, CT: Appleton-Century-Crofts.

Sullivan, L., Mundy, P., & Mastergeorge, A. (2011). Joint attention, word learning and school readiness in preschool children. Manuscript in submission.

Tomasello, M., Carpenter, M., Call, J., Behne, T., & Moll, H. (2005). Understanding sharing intentions: The origins of cultural cognition. *Brain and Behavior Sciences, 28,* 675–690.

Tomasello, M., & Farrar, M. J. (1986). Joint attention and early language. *Child Development, 57,* 1454–1463.

Vaughan Van Hecke, A., Mundy, P., Block, J., Delgado, C., Parlade, M., Pomares, Y., & Hobson, J. (2011). Infant responding to joint attention, executive functions and self-regulation in preschool children. Manuscript in submission.

Weeks, S. J., & Hobson, R. P. (1987). The salience of facial expression for autistic children. *Journal of Child Psychology and Psychiatry, 28,* 137–152.

Whalen, C., Schreibman, L., & Ingersoll, B. (2006). The collateral effects of joint attention training on social initiations, positive affect, imitation and spontaneous speech for young children with autism. *Journal of Autism and Developmental Disorders, 36,* 655–664.

Wilczynski, S. M., Menousek, K., Hunter, M., & Mudgal, D. (2007). Individualized education programs for youth with autism spectrum disorders. *Psychology in the Schools, 44,* 653–666.

Wing, L., & Gould, J. (1979). Severe impairments of social interaction and associated abnormalities in children: Epidemiology and classification. *Journal of Autism and Developmental Disorders, 9,* 11–29.

World Health Organization. (1993). *The ICD-10 classification of mental and behavioral disorders: Diagnostic criteria for research.* Geneva: Author. Available from www.who.int/classifications/icd/en/GRNBOOK.pdf

CHAPTER TWO

The following asterisked entries indicate reviewed articles. Please see Machalicek et al. (2008) review for full references of reviewed articles published prior to 2005.

Akmanoglu, N., & Batu, S. (2004). Teaching pointing to numerals to individuals with autism using simultaneous prompting. *Education and Training in Developmental Disabilities, 39*, 326–336.

*Argott, P., Buffington Townsend, D., Sturmey, P., & Poulson, C. L. (2008). Increasing the use of empathic statements in the presence of a non-verbal affective stimulus in adolescents with autism. *Research in Autism Spectrum Disorders, 2*, 341–352.

*Ayres, K., Maguire, A., & McClimon, D. (2009). Acquisition and generalization of chained tasks taught with computer based video instruction to children with autism. *Education and Training in Developmental Disabilities, 44*, 493–508.

Banda, D. R., Grimmett, E., & Hart, S. L. (2009). Activity schedules: Helping students with autism spectrum disorders in general education classrooms manage transition issues. *TEACHING Exceptional Children, 41*(4), 16–21.

*Banda, D. R., Hart, S. L., & Liu-Gitz, L. (2010). Impact of training peers and children with autism on social skills during center time activities in inclusive classrooms. *Research in Autism Spectrum Disorders, 4*, 619–625.

*Banda, D. R., & Kubina, R. M. (2010). Increasing academic compliance with mathematics tasks using the high-preference strategy with a student with autism. *Preventing School Failure, 54*, 81–85.

Barry, L., & Burlew, S. (2004). Using social stories to teach choice and play skills to children with autism. *Focus on Autism and Other Developmental Disabilities, 19*, 45–51.

*Bellini, S., Akullian, J., & Hopf, A. (2007). Increasing social engagement in young children with autism spectrum disorders using video self-modeling. *School Psychology Review, 36*, 80–90.

*Blair, K. C., Umbreit, J., Dunlap, G., & Jung, G. (2007). Promoting inclusion and peer participation through assessment-based intervention. *Topics in Early Childhood Special Education, 27*, 134–147.

*Blum-Dimaya, A., Reeve, S. A., Reeve, K. F., & Hoch, H. (2010). Teaching children with autism to play a video game using activity schedules and game-embedded simultaneous video modeling. *Education and Treatment of Children, 33*, 351–370.

Bock, M. (1999). Sorting laundry: Categorization strategy application to an authentic learning activity by children with autism. *Focus on Autism and Other Developmental Disabilities, 14*, 220–230.

Boutot, E. A., Guenther, T., & Crozier, S. (2005). Let's play: Teaching play skills to young children with autism. *Education and Training in Developmental Disabilities, 40*, 285–292.

Buffington, D., Krantz, P., McClannahan, L., & Poulson, C. (1998). Procedures for teaching appropriate gestural communication skills to children with autism. *Journal of Autism and Developmental Disorders, 28*, 535–545.

*Chan, J. M., & O'Reilly, M. F. (2008). A social stories intervention package for students with autism in inclusive classroom settings. *Journal of Applied Behavior Analysis, 41,* 405–409.

Charlop-Christy, M., & Daneshvar, S. (2003). Using video modeling to teach perspective taking to children with autism. *Journal of Positive Behavior Interventions, 5,* 12–21.

Cicero, F., & Pfadt, A. (2002). Investigation of a reinforcement-based toilet training procedure for children with autism. *Research in Developmental Disabilities, 23,* 319–331.

*Cihak, D. F. (2007). Teaching students with autism to read pictures. *Research in Autism Spectrum Disorders, 1,* 318–329.

*Cihak, D. F., & Foust, J. L. (2008). Comparing number lines and touch points to teach addition facts to students with autism. *Focus on Autism and Other Developmental Disabilities, 23,* 131–137.

*Cihak, D. F., & Grim, J. (2008). Teaching students with autism spectrum disorder and moderate intellectual disabilities to use counting-on strategies to enhance independent purchasing skills. *Research in Autism Spectrum Disorders, 2,* 716–727.

*Cihak, D. F., & Schrader, L. (2008). Does the model matter? Comparing video self-modeling and video adult modeling for task acquisition and maintenance by adolescents with autism spectrum disorders. *Journal of Special Education Technology, 23*(3), 9–20.

Coleman-Martin, M. B., Heller, K. W., Cihak, D. F., & Irvine, K. L. (2005). Using computer-assisted instruction and the nonverbal reading approach to teach word identification. *Focus on Autism and Other Developmental Disabilities, 20,* 80–90.

Copeland, S., & Hughes, C. (2000). Acquisition of a picture prompt strategy to increase independent performance. *Education and Training in Developmental Disabilities, 35,* 294–305.

Courtade, G. R., Spooner, F., & Browder, D. M. (2007). Review of studies with students with significant cognitive disabilities which link to science standards. *Research and Practice for Persons with Severe Disabilities, 32,* 43–49.

*Davis, K. M., Boon, R. T., Cihak, D. F., & Fore, C., III, (2010). Power cards to improve conversational skills in adolescents with Asperger syndrome. *Focus on Autism and Other Developmental Disabilities, 25,* 12–22.

*Delano, M. E. (2007). Use of strategy instruction to improve the story writing skills of a student with Asperger syndrome. *Focus on Autism and Other Developmental Disabilities, 22,* 252–258.

*Dotson, W. H., Leaf, J. B., Sheldon, J. B., & Sherman, J. A. (2010). Group teaching of conversational skills to adolescents on the autism spectrum. *Research in Autism Spectrum Disorders, 4,* 199–209.

Dyches, T. (1999). Effects of switch training on the communication of children with autism and severe disabilities. *Focus on Autism and Other Developmental Disabilities, 13*, 151–162.

English, K., Goldstein, H., Shafer, K., & Kaczmarek, L. (1997). Promoting interactions among preschoolers with and without disabilities: Effects of a buddy skills-training program. *Exceptional Children, 63*, 229–243.

*Esch, B. E., Carr, J. E., & Grow, L. L. (2009). Evaluation of an enhanced stimulus-stimulus pairing procedure to increase early vocalizations of children with autism. *Journal of Applied Behavior Analysis, 42*, 225–241.

Ferguson, H., Smith Myles, B., & Hagiwara, T. (2005). Using a personal digital assistant to enhance the independence of an adolescent with Asperger syndrome. *Education and Training in Developmental Disabilities, 40*, 60–67.

Freeman, B. J., Del'Homme, M., Guthrie, D., & Zhang, F. (1999). Vineland adaptive behavior scale scores as a function of age and initial IQ in 210 autistic children. *Journal of Autism and Developmental Disorders, 29*, 379–384.

*Ganz, J. B., Bourgeois, B. C., Flores, M. M., & Campos, B. A. (2008). Implementing visually cued imitation training with children with autism spectrum disorders and developmental delays. *Journal of Positive Behavior Interventions, 10*, 56–66.

*Ganz, J. B., & Flores, M. M. (2008). Effects of the use of visual strategies in play groups for children with autism spectrum disorders and their peers. *Journal of Autism and Developmental Disorders, 38*, 926–940.

Garfinkle, A., & Schwartz, I. (2002). Peer imitation: Increasing social interactions in children with autism and other developmental disabilities in inclusive preschool classrooms. *Topics in Early Childhood Special Education, 22*, 26–38.

*Gunby, K. V., Carr, J. E., & LeBlanc, L. A. (2010). Teaching abduction-prevention skills to children with autism. *Journal of Applied Behavior Analysis, 43*, 107–112.

Hagiwara, T., & Smith Myles, B. (1999). A multimedia social story intervention: Teaching skills to children with autism. *Focus on Autism and Other Developmental Disabilities, 14*, 82–95.

*Harper, C. B., Symon, J. B., & Frea, W. D. (2008). Recess is time-in: Using peers to improve social skills of children with autism. *Journal of Autism and Developmental Disorders, 38*, 815–826.

Hetzroni, O., & Shalem, U. (2005). From logos to orthographic symbols: A multilevel fading computer program for teaching nonverbal children with autism. *Focus on Autism and Other Developmental Disabilities, 20*, 201–212.

Hetzroni, O., & Tannous, J. (2004). Effects of a computer-based intervention program on the communicative functions of children with autism. *Journal of Autism and Developmental Disorders, 34*, 95–113.

*Hine, J. F., & Wolery, M. (2006). Using point-of-view video modeling to teach play to preschoolers with autism. *Topics in Early Childhood Special Education*, *26*, 83–93.

*Hume, K., & Odom, S. (2007). Effects of an individual work system on the independent functioning of students with autism. *Journal of Autism and Developmental Disorders*, *37*, 1166–1180.

*Ingvarsson, E. T., & Hollobaugh, T. (2010). Acquisition of intraverbal behavior: Teaching children with autism to mand for answers to questions. *Journal of Applied Behavior Analysis*, *43*, 1–17.

Jasmin, E., Couture, M., McKinley, P., Reid, G., Fombonne, E., & Gisel, E. (2009). Sensori-motor and daily living skills of preschool children with autism spectrum disorders. *Journal of Autism and Developmental Disorders*, *39*, 231–241.

*Jones, E. A. (2009). Establishing response and stimulus classes for initiating joint attention in children with autism. *Research in Autism Spectrum Disorders*, *3*, 375–389.

*Jones, E. A., Carr, E. G., & Feeley, K. M. (2006). Multiple effects of joint attention intervention for children with autism. *Behavior Modification*, *30*, 782–834.

*Jones, E. A., Feeley, K. M., & Takacs, J. (2007). Teaching spontaneous responses to young children with autism. *Journal of Applied Behavior Analysis*, *40*, 565–570.

Kamps, D. M., Leonard, B. R., Vernon, S., & Dugan, E. P. (1992). Teaching social skills to students with autism to increase peer interactions in an integrated first-grade classroom. *Journal of Applied Behavior Analysis*, *25*, 281–288.

*Kohler, F. W., Greteman, C., Raschke, D., & Highnam, C. (2007). Using a buddy skills package to increase the social interactions between a preschooler with autism and her peers. *Topics in Early Childhood Special Education*, *27*, 155–163.

Krantz, P., & McClannahan, L. (1998). Social interaction skills for children with autism: A script-fading procedure for beginning readers. *Journal of Applied Behavior Analysis*, *31*, 191–202.

Kravits, T., Kamps, D., Kemmerer, K., & Potucek, J. (2002). Brief report: Increasing communication skills for an elementary-aged student with autism using the picture exchange communication system. *Journal of Autism and Developmental Disorders*, *32*, 225–230.

Kroeger, K., & Sorensen, R. (2010). A parent training model for toilet training children with autism. *Journal of Intellectual Disability Research*, *54*, 556–567.

Kroeger, K. A., & Sorenson-Burnworth, R. (2009). Toilet training individuals with autism and other developmental disabilities: A critical review. *Research in Autism Spectrum Disorders*, *3*, 607–618.

*Kuhn, L. R., Bodkin, A. E., Devlin, S. D., & Doggett, R. A. (2008). Using pivotal response training with peers in special education to facilitate play in two children with autism. *Education and Training in Developmental Disabilities*, *43*, 37–45.

*Kurt, O., & Tekin-Iftar, E. (2008). A comparison of constant time delay and simultaneous prompting within embedded instruction on teaching leisure skills to children with autism. *Topics in Early Childhood Special Education, 28*, 53–64.

Lang, R., Machalicek, W., O'Reilly, M. F., Sigafoos, J., Rispoli, M. J., Shogren, K., & Regester, A. (2009). Review of interventions to increase functional and symbolic play in children with autism. *Education and Training in Developmental Disabilities, 44*, 481–492.

Laushey, K., & Heflin, L. (2000). Enhancing social skills of kindergarten children with autism through the training of multiple peers as tutors. *Journal of Autism and Developmental Disorders, 30*, 183–193.

*Laushey, K. M., Heflin, L. J., Shippen, M., Alberto, P. A., & Fredrick, L. (2009). Concept mastery routines to teach social skills to elementary children with high functioning autism. *Journal of Autism and Developmental Disorders, 39*, 1435–1448.

*Leaf, J. B., Dotson, W. H., Oppeneheim, M. L., Sheldon, J. B., & Sherman, J. A. (2010). The effectiveness of a group teaching interaction procedure for teaching social skills to young children with a pervasive developmental disorder. *Research in Autism Spectrum Disorders, 4*, 186–198.

*Leaf, J. B., Sheldon, J. B., & Sherman, J. A. (2010). Comparison of simultaneous prompting and no-no prompting in two-choice discrimination learning with children with autism. *Journal of Applied Behavior Analysis, 43*, 215–228.

LeBlanc, L., Carr, J., Crossett, S., Bennett, C., & Detweiler, D. (2005). Intensive outpatient behavioral treatment of primary urinary incontinence of children with autism. *Focus on Autism and Other Developmental Disabilities, 20*, 98–105.

*Ledford, J. R., Gast, D. L., Luscre, D., & Ayres, K. M. (2008). Observational and incidental learning by children with autism during small group instruction. *Journal of Autism and Developmental Disorders, 38*, 86–103.

*Lee, S., Odom, S. L., & Loftin, R. (2007). Social engagement with peers and stereotypic behavior of children with autism. *Journal of Positive Behavior Interventions, 9*, 67–79.

*Liber, D. B., Frea, W. D., & Symon, J.B.G. (2008). Using time-delay to improve social play skills with peers for children with autism. *Journal of Autism and Developmental Disorders, 38*, 312–323.

*Licciardello, C. C., Harchik, A. E., & Luiselli, J. K. (2008). Social skills intervention for children with autism during interactive play at a public elementary school. *Education and Treatment of Children, 31*, 27–37.

Loveland, K. A., & Kelley, M. L. (1991). Development of adaptive behavior in preschoolers with autism or Down syndrome. *American Journal on Mental Retardation, 93*, 84–92.

*Lund, S. K., & Troha, J. M. (2008). Teaching young people who are blind and have autism to make requests using a variation on the picture exchange communication system with tactile symbols: A preliminary investigation. *Journal of Autism and Developmental Disorders, 38*, 719–730.

*MacDonald, R., Sacramone, S., Mansfield, R., Wiltz, K., & Ahearn, W. H. (2009). Using video modeling to teach reciprocal pretend play to children with autism. *Journal of Applied Behavior Analysis, 42*, 43–55.

Machalicek, W., O'Reilly, M. F., Beretvas, N., Sigafoos, J., Lancioni, G., Sorrells, A., et al. (2008). A review of school-based instructional interventions for students with autism spectrum disorders. *Research in Autism Spectrum Disorders, 2*, 395–416.

*Machalicek, W., Shogren, K., Lang, R., Rispoli, M., O'Reilly, M. F., Franco, J. H., & Sigafoos, J. (2009). Increasing play and decreasing the challenging behavior of children with autism during recess with activity schedules and task correspondence training. *Research in Autism Spectrum Disorders, 3*, 547–555.

*Marcus, A., & Wilder, D. A. (2009). A comparison of peer video modeling and self video modeling to teach textual responses in children with autism. *Journal of Applied Behavior Analysis, 42*, 335–341.

Mastropieri, M. A., Bakken, J. P., & Scruggs, T. E. (1991). Mathematics instruction for individuals with mental retardation: A perspective and research synthesis. *Education and Training in Mental Retardation and Developmental Disabilities, 26*, 115–129.

Matson, J., Dempsey, T., & Fodstad, J. C. (2009). The effect of autism spectrum disorders on adaptive independent living skills in adults with severe intellectual disability. *Research in Developmental Disabilities, 30*, 1203–1211.

*Murzynski, N. T., & Bourret, J. C. (2007). Combining video modeling and least-to-most prompting for establishing response chains. *Behavioral Interventions, 22*, 147–152.

National Council of Teachers of Mathematics. (2000). *Principles and Standards for School Mathematics*. Reston, VA: Author.

National Institute of Child Health and Human Development. (2000). *Report of the National Reading Panel. Teaching children to read: An evidence-based assessment of the scientific research literature on reading and its implications for reading instruction* (NIH Publication No. 00-4769). Washington, DC: Government Printing Office.

National Research Council (NRC). (1996). *National science education standards*. Washington, DC: National Academy Press.

National Research Council (NRC). (2001). *Educating children with autism*. Washington, DC: National Academy Press.

*Nelson, C., McDonnell, A. P., Johnston, S. S., Crompton, A., & Nelson, A. R. (2007). Keys to play: A strategy to increase the social interactions of young children with autism and their typically developing peers. *Education and Training in Developmental Disabilities, 42,* 165–181.

*Nikopoulos, C. K., Canavan, C., & Nikopoulou-Smyrni, P. (2009). Generalized effects of video modeling on establishing instructional stimulus control in children with autism: Results of a preliminary study. *Journal of Positive Behavior Interventions, 11,* 198–207.

*Okada, S., Ohtake, Y., & Yanagihara, M. (2008). Effects of perspective sentences in social stories on improving the adaptive behaviors of students with autism spectrum disorders and related disabilities. *Education and Training in Developmental Disabilities, 43,* 46–60.

*Olive, M. L., de la Cruz, B., Davis, T. N., Chan, J. M., Lang, R. B., O'Reilly, M. F., & Dickson, S. M. (2007). The effects of enhanced milieu teaching and a voice output communication aid on the requesting of three children with autism. *Journal of Autism and Developmental Disorders, 37,* 1505–1513.

*Paterson, C. R., & Arco, L. (2007). Using video modeling for generalizing toy play in children with autism. *Behavior Modification, 31,* 660–681.

Ramdoss, S., Lang, R., Mulloy, A., Franco, J., O'Reilly, M., Didden, R., & Lancioni, G. (2011). Use of computer-based interventions to teach communication skills to children with autism spectrum disorders: A systematic review. *Journal of Behavioral Education, 20,* 55–76.

Reagon, K. A., Higbee, T. S., & Endicott, K. (2006). Teaching pretend play skills to a student with autism using video modeling with a sibling as model and play partner. *Education and Treatment of Children, 29,* 517–528.

*Reeve, S. A., Reeve, K. F., Buffington Townsend, D., & Poulson, C. L. (2007). Establishing a generalized repertoire of helping behavior in children with autism. *Journal of Applied Behavior Analysis, 40,* 123–136.

*Reynhout, G., & Carter, M. (2008). A pilot study to determine the efficacy of a social story[TM] intervention for a child with autistic disorder, intellectual disability and limited language skills. *Australasian Journal of Special Education, 32,* 161–175.

Riesen, T., McDonnell, J., Johnson, J., Polychronis, S., & Jameson, M. (2003). A comparison of constant time delay and simultaneous prompting within embedded instruction in general education classes with students with moderate to severe disabilities. *Journal of Behavioral Education, 12,* 241–259.

*Rosenberg, N. E., Schwartz, I. S., & Davis, C. A. (2010). Evaluating the utility of commercial videotapes for teaching hand washing to children with autism. *Education and Treatment of Children, 33,* 443–455.

*Sansosti, F. J., & Powell-Smith, K. A. (2006). Using social stories to improve the social behavior of children with Asperger syndrome. *Journal of Positive Behavior Interventions, 8,* 43–57.

*Sansosti, F. J., & Powell-Smith, K. A. (2008). Using computer-presented social stories and video models to increase the social communication skills of children with high-functioning autism spectrum disorders. *Journal of Positive Behavior Interventions, 10,* 162–178.

Schepis, M., Reid, D., Behrmann, M., & Sutton, K. (1998). Increasing communicative interactions of young children with autism using a voice output communication aid and naturalistic teaching. *Journal of Applied Behavior Analysis, 31,* 561–578.

*Schneider, N., & Goldstein, S. (2010). Using social stories and visual schedules to improve socially appropriate behaviors in children with autism. *Journal of Positive Behavior Interventions, 12,* 149–160.

Sherer, M. R., & Schreibman, L. (2005). Individual behavioral profiles and predictors of treatment effectiveness for children with autism. *Journal of Consulting and Clinical Psychology, 73,* 525–538.

Sigafoos, J., O'Reilly, M., Seely-York, S., & Edrisinha, C. (2004). Teaching students with developmental disabilities to locate their AAC device. *Research in Developmental Disabilities, 25,* 371–383.

*Soares, D. A., Vannest, K. J., & Harrison, J. (2009). Computer aided self-monitoring to increase academic production and reduce self-injurious behavior in a child with autism. *Behavioral Interventions, 24,* 171–183.

*Soluaga, D., Leaf, J. B., Taubman, M., McEachin, J., & Leaf, R. (2008). A comparison of flexible prompt fading and constant time delay for five children with autism. *Research in Autism Spectrum Disorders, 2,* 753–765.

*Songlee, D., Miller, S. P., Tincani, M., Sileo, N. M., & Perkins, P. G. (2008). Effects of test-taking strategy instruction on high-functioning adolescents with autism spectrum disorders. *Focus on Autism and Other Developmental Disabilities, 23,* 217–228.

Taylor, B., & Harris, S. (1995). Teaching children with autism to seek information: Acquisition of novel information and generalization of responding. *Journal of Applied Behavior Analysis, 28,* 3–14.

Taylor, B., Hughes, C., Richard, E., Hoch, H., & Coello, A. (2004). Teaching teenagers with autism to seek assistance when lost. *Journal of Applied Behavior Analysis, 37,* 79–82.

Taylor, B. A., & Hoch, H. (2008). Teaching children with autism to respond to and initiate bids for joint attention. *Journal of Applied Behavior Analysis, 41,* 377–391.

Tekin-Iftar, E., & Birkan, B. (2010). Small group instruction for students with autism: General case training and observational learning. *Journal of Special Education, 44,* 50–63.

Thiemann, K., & Goldstein, H. (2004). Effects of peer training and written text cueing on social communication of school-age children with pervasive developmental disorder. *Journal of Speech, Language, and Hearing Research, 47,* 126–144.

*Tincani, M., Crozier, S., & Alazetta, L. (2006). The picture exchange communication system: Effects on manding and speech development for school-aged children with autism. *Education and Training in Developmental Disabilities, 41*, 177–184.

Volkmar, F. R., Sparrow, S. S., Goudreau, D., Cicchetti, D. V., Paul, R., & Cohen, D. J. (1987). Social deficits in autism: An operational approach using the Vineland adaptive behavior scales. *Journal of the American Academy of Child & Adolescent Psychiatry, 26*, 156–161.

Wang, P., & Spillane, A. (2009). Evidence-based social skills interventions for children with autism: A meta-analysis. *Education and Training in Developmental Disabilities, 44*, 318–342.

*West, E. A., & Billingsley, F. (2005). Improving the system of least prompts: A comparison of procedural variations. *Education and Training in Developmental Disabilities, 40*, 131–144.

Westling, D. L., & Fox, L. (2008). *Teaching students with severe disabilities* (4th ed.). Upper Saddle River, NJ: Prentice Hall.

*Whalon, K., & Hanline, F. M. (2008). Effects of a reciprocal questioning intervention on the question generation and responding of children with autism spectrum disorder. *Education and Training in Developmental Disabilities, 43*, 367–387.

Wichnick, A. M., Vener, S. M., Pyrtek, M., & Poulson, C. L. (2010). The effect of a script-fading procedure on responses to peer initiations among young children with autism. *Research in Autism Spectrum Disorders, 4*, 290–299.

Xin, Y. P., Grasso, E., Dipipi-Hoy, C. M., & Jitendra, A. (2005). The effects of purchasing skill instruction for individuals with developmental disabilities: A meta-analysis. *Exceptional Children, 71*, 379–400.

CHAPTER THREE

American Psychiatric Association. (1994). *Diagnostic and statistical manual of mental disorders* (4th ed.). Washington, DC: Author.

Arick, J. R., Young, H. E., Falco, R. A., Loos, L. M., Krug, D. A., Gense, M. H., & Johnson, S. B. (2003). Designing an outcome study to monitor the progress of students with autism spectrum disorders. *Focus on Autism and Other Developmental Disabilities, 18*, 75–87.

Ashburner, J., Ziviani, J., & Rodger, S. (2008). Sensory processing and classroom emotional, behavioral and educational outcomes in children with autism spectrum disorders. American Journal of Occupational Therapy, 62, 564–573.

Baer, D. M., Wolf, M. M., & Risley, T. R. (1968). Some current dimensions of applied behavior analysis. *Journal of Applied Behavior Analysis, 1*, 91–97.

Bettleheim, B. (1967). *The empty fortress: Infantile autism and the birth of the self.* New York: Free Press.

Boutot, E. A., & Dukes, C. (2011). Evidence-based practices for educating students with autism spectrum disorder. In E. A. Boutot & B. S. Myles (Eds.), *Autism spectrum disorders: Foundations, characteristics, and effective strategies* (pp. 77–101). Boston: Pearson.

Boutot, E. A., & Hume, K. (2010). Beyond time out and table time: Today's applied behavior analysis for students with autism. *Education and Training in Autism and Developmental Disabilities, 45*(4), 1–41.

Boutot, E. A., & Walberg, J. (2011). Working with families of children with autism. In E. A. Boutot & B. S. Myles (Eds.), *Autism spectrum disorders: Foundations, characteristics, and effective strategies* (pp. 166–189). Boston: Pearson.

Boyd, B. (2002). Examining the relationship between stress and lack of social support in mothers of children with autism. *Focus on Autism and Other Developmental Disabilities, 17*, 208–215.

Boyd, B., & Shaw, E. (2010). Autism in the classroom: A group of students changing in population and presentation. *Preventing School Failure, 54*, 211–219.

Campbell, S., Cannon, B., Ellis, J. T., Lifter, K., Luiselli, J. K., Navalta, C. P., & Taras, M. (1998). The May Center for Early Childhood Education: Description of a continuum of services model for children with autism. *International Journal of Disability, Development and Education, 45*, 173–187.

Cohen, H., Amerine-Dickens, M., & Smith, T. (2006). Early intensive behavioral intervention: Replication of the UCLA model in a community setting. *Journal of Developmental and Behavioral Pediatrics, 27*, 145–155.

Data Accountability Center. (2010). Individuals with Disabilities Education Act data. Available from www.ideadata.org/default.asp

Dawson, G. (2008). Early behavioral intervention, brain plasticity and the prevention of autism spectrum disorder. *Development and Psychopathology, 20*, 775–803.

Dawson, G., Rogers, S., Munson, J., Smith, M., Winter, J., Greenson, J., et al. (2009). Randomized, controlled trial of an intervention for toddlers with autism: The Early Start Denver Model. *Pediatrics, 125*, e17–e23.

Delprato, D. (2001). Comparisons of discrete trial and normalized behavioral intervention for young children with autism. *Journal of Autism and Developmental Disorders, 31*, 315–325.

DeMyer, M., Hingtgen, D., & Jackson, P. (1981). Infantile autism reviewed: A decade of research. *Schizophrenia Bulletin, 1*, 388–451.

Dillenburger, K. (2011). The emperor's new clothes: Eclecticism in autism treatment. *Research in Autism Spectrum Disorders, 5* (1119–1128).

Dingfelder, H., Shin, S., & Mandell, D. (2010). *The relationship between classroom climate and intervention fidelity.* Paper presented at the Annual Meeting of the International Society for Autism Research, Philadelphia.

Edelson, M. (2006). Are a majority of children with autism mentally retarded? A systematic evaluation of the data. *Focus on Autism and Other Developmental Disabilities, 21,* 66–83.

Eikeseth, S., Smith, T., Jahr, E., & Eldevik, S. (2007). Outcome for children with autism who begin intensive behavioral intervention between ages 4 and 7: A comparison controlled study. *Behavior Modification, 31,* 264–278.

Eldevick, S., Eikeseth, S. Jahr, E., & Smith, T. (2006). Effects of low-intensity behavioral treatment for children with autism and mental retardation. *Journal of Autism and Developmental Disorders, 36,* 211–224.

Fein, D., & Dunn, M. (2007). *Autism in your classroom: A guide for regular education teachers.* New York: Woodbine House.

Fenske, E., Zalenski, S., Krantz, P., & McClannahan, L. (1985). Age at intervention and treatment outcome for autistic children in a comprehensive intervention program. *Analysis and Intervention in Developmental Disabilities, 5,* 49–58.

Giangreco, M. F. (2009). *Critical issues brief: Concerns about the proliferation of one-to-one paraprofessionals.* Arlington, VA: Council for Exceptional Children, Division on Autism and Developmental Disabilities. Available from www.dddcec.org/positionpapers

Greenspan, S., & Weider, S. (1997). Developmental patterns and outcomes in infants and children with disorders in relating and communicating: A chart review of 200 cases of children with autism spectrum diagnoses. *Journal of Developmental and Learning Disorders, 1,* 87–141.

Gresham, F., & MacMillan, D. (1997). Autistic recovery? An analysis and critique of the empirical evidence on the early intervention project. *Behavioral Disorders, 22,* 185–201.

Gutstein, S., Burgess, A., & Montfort, K. (2007). Evaluation of the Relationship Development Intervention program. *Autism, 11,* 397–411.

Hart, B., & Risley, T. (1968). Establishing use of descriptive adjectives in spontaneous speech of disadvantaged preschool children. *Journal of Applied Behavior Analysis, 14,* 389–409.

Helt, M., Kelly, E., Kinsbourne, M., Pandey, J., Boorstein, H., Herbert, M., & Fein, D. (2008). Can children with autism recover? If so, how? *Neuropsychological Review, 18,* 339–366.

Hoyson, M., Jamieson, B., & Strain, P. S. (1984). Individualized group instruction of normally developing and autistic-like children: The LEAP curriculum model. *Journal of the Division for Early Childhood, 8,* 157–172.

Kanner, L. (1943). Autistic disturbances of affective contact. *Nervous Child, 2,* 217–250.

Kenworthy, L., Black, D., Wallace, G., Ahluvalia, A., & Sirian, L. (2005). Disorganization: The forgotten executive dysfunction in high functioning autism (HFA) spectrum disorder. *Developmental Neuropsychology, 3,* 809–827.

Koegel, R., & Koegel, L. (2006). *Pivotal response treatments for autism: Communication, social and academic development.* Baltimore: Brookes.

Koegel, R., O'Dell, M., & Koegel, L. (1987). A natural language paradigm for teaching nonverbal autistic children. *Journal of Autism and Developmental Disorders, 17,* 187–199.

Koegel, R., Schreibman, L., Good, A., Cerniglia, L., Murphy, C., & Koegel, L. (1989). *How to teach pivotal behaviors to children with autism: A training manual.* Santa Barbara: University of California.

Lerman, D., Tetreault, A., Hovanetz, A., Strobel, M., & Garro, J. (2008). Further evaluation of a brief, intensive training model. *Journal of Applied Behavior Analysis, 41,* 243–248.

Leyfer, O. T., Folstein, S. E., Bacalman, S., Davis, N. O., Dinh, E., Morgan, J., et al. (2006). Comorbid psychiatric disorders in children with autism: Interview development and rates of disorder. *Journal of Autism and Developmental Disorders, 36,* 849–861.

Lovaas, I. (1987). Behavioral intervention and normal educational and intellectual functioning in young autistic children. *Journal of Consulting and Clinical Psychology, 55,* 3–9.

Mandell, D., Listerud, J., Levy, S., & Pinto-Martin, J. (2002). Race differences in the age at diagnosis among Medicaid-eligible children with autism. *Journal of the American Academy of Child & Adolescent Psychiatry, 41,* 1447–1453.

McEachin, J., Smith, T., & Lovaas, I. (1993). Long-term outcome for children with autism who received early intensive behavioral intervention. *American Journal on Mental Retardation, 55,* 359–372.

Mesibov, G. B., & Shea, V. (2010). The TEACCH program in the era of evidence-based practice. *Journal of Autism and Developmental Disorders, 40,* 570–579.

Mesibov, G. B., & Shea, V. (2011). Evidence-based practices and autism. *Autism, 15,* 114–133.

National Autism Center. (2009). *The National Standards Project—Addressing the need for evidence based practice guidelines for autism spectrum disorders.* Randolph, MA: Author.

National Research Council. (2001). *Educating children with autism.* Washington, DC: National Academy Press.

Neitzel, J. (2010). Positive behavior supports for children and youth with autism spectrum disorders. *Preventing School Failure, 54,* 247–255.

Odom, S., Boyd, B., Hall, L., & Hume, K. (2010). Evaluation of comprehensive treatment models for individuals with autism spectrum disorders. *Journal of Autism and Developmental Disorders, 40,* 425–436.

Odom, S., Brantlinger, E., Gersten, R., Horner, R., Thompson, B., & Harris, K. (2004). *Quality indicators for research in special education and guidelines for evidence-based practices: Executive summary.* Arlington, VA: Council for Exceptional Children, Division for Research.

Odom, S., Collet-Klingenberg, L., Rogers, S., & Hatton, D. (2010). Evidence-based practices in interventions for children and youth with autism spectrum disorders. *Preventing School Failure, 54,* 275–282.

Offit, P. (2008). *Autism's false prophets: Bad science, risky medicine and the search for a cure.* New York: Columbia University Press.

Olive, M., Boutot, E. A., & Tarbox, J. (2011). Teaching children with autism using the principles of applied behavior analysis. In E. A. Boutot & B. S. Myles (Eds.), *Autism spectrum disorders: Foundations, characteristics, and effective strategies* (pp. 27–53). Boston: Pearson.

Panerai, S., Zingale, M., Trubia, G., Finocchiaro, M., Zuccarello, R., Ferri, R., & Elia, M. (2009). Special education versus inclusive education: The role of the TEACCH program. *Journal of Autism and Developmental Disorders, 39,* 874–882.

Prizant, B., Wetherby, A., Rubin, E., Laurent, A., & Rydell, P. (2006). *The SCERTS Model: A comprehensive educational approach for children with autism spectrum disorders.* Baltimore: Brookes.

Reed, P., Osborne, L., & Corness, M. (2007). Brief report: Relative effectiveness of different home-based behavioral approaches to early teaching intervention. *Journal of Autism and Developmental Disorders, 37,* 1815–1821.

Rimland, B. (1964). Infantile autism: The syndrome and its implications for a neural theory of behavior. Englewood Cliffs, NJ: Prentice Hall.

Rogers, S., Hayden, D., Hepburn, S., Charifue-Smith, R., Hall, T., & Hayes, A. (2006). Teaching young nonverbal children with autism meaningful speech: A pilot study of the Denver model and PROMPT interventions. *Journal of Autism and Developmental Disorders, 36,* 1007–1024.

Rogers, S., & Vismara, L. (2008). Evidence-based comprehensive treatments for early autism. *Journal of Clinical Child and Adolescent Psychology, 37,* 8–38.

Sallows, G., & Graupner, T. (2005). Intensive behavioral treatment for children with autism: Four-year outcome and predictors. *American Journal on Mental Retardation, 110,* 417–438.

Scheurmann, B., Webber, J., Boutot, E. A., & Goodwin, M. (2003). Problems with personnel preparation in autism spectrum disorders. *Focus on Autism and Other Developmental Disabilities, 1,* 197–206.

Schreibman, L., & Winter, J. (2003). Behavioral intervention strategies. *Exceptional Parent, 33*(11), 64–71.

Sheinkopf, S., & Siegel, B. (1998). Home-based behavioral intervention of young children with autism. *Journal of Autism and Developmental Disorders, 28,* 15–23.

Shin, S., Stahmer, A., Marcus, S., & Mandell, D. (2010). *Student, teacher and classroom-level mediators of outcomes for children with autism spectrum disorders.* Paper presented at the Annual Meeting of the International Society for Autism Research, Philadelphia.

Siklos, S., & Kerns, K. (2007). Assessing the diagnosis of a small sample of parents of children with autism spectrum disorders. *Research in Developmental Disabilities, 28,* 9–22.

Smith, T., Groen, A. D., & Wynn, J. W. (2000). Randomized trial of intensive early intervention for children with pervasive developmental disorder. *American Journal on Mental Retardation, 105,* 269–285.

Stahmer, A., Reed, S., Shin, S., & Mandell, D. (2010). *Fidelity of implementation of evidence-based practice in community classrooms.* Paper presented at the Annual Meeting of the International Society for Autism Research, Philadelphia.

Steege, M., Mace, F., Perry, L., & Longenecker, H. (2007). Applied behavior analysis: Beyond discrete trial teaching. *Psychology in the Schools, 44,* 91–99.

Stevens, M., Washington, A., Rice, C., Jenner, W., Ottolino, J., Clancy, K., & Whitney, J. (2007). *Prevalence of the autism spectrum disorders (ASDs) in multiple areas of the United States, 2000 and 2002.* Atlanta: Centers for Disease Control and Prevention.

Stoner, J., Bock, S., Thomson, J., Angell, M., Heyl, B., & Crowley, E. (2005). Welcome to our world: Parent perceptions of interactions between parents of young children with ASD and education professionals. *Focus on Autism and Other Developmental Disabilities, 20,* 39–51.

Volkmar, F., & Nelson, D. (1990). Seizure disorders in autism. *Journal of the American Academy of Child & Adolescent Psychiatry, 29,* 121–129.

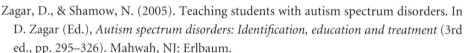

Wing, L., & Potter, D. (2009). The epidemiology of autism spectrum disorders: Is the prevalence rising? In S. Goldstein, J. Naglieri, & S. Ozonoff (Eds.), *Assessment of autism spectrum disorders* (pp. 18–54). New York: Guilford Press.

Zagar, D., & Shamow, N. (2005). Teaching students with autism spectrum disorders. In D. Zagar (Ed.), *Autism spectrum disorders: Identification, education and treatment* (3rd ed., pp. 295–326). Mahwah, NJ: Erlbaum.

CHAPTER FOUR

Adelman, H., & Taylor, L. (1998). Reframing mental health in schools and expanding school reform. *Educational Psychologist, 33,* 135–152. Available from doi: 10.1207/s15326985ep3304_1

Bauminger, N., & Shulman, C. (2003). The development and maintenance of friendship in high-functioning children with autism. *Autism, 7,* 81–97. Available from doi: 10.1177/1362361303007001007

Bauminger, N., Solomon, M., Aviezer, A., Heung, K., Brown, J., & Rogers, S. J. (2008). Friendship in high-functioning children with autism spectrum disorder: Mixed and non-mixed dyads. *Journal of Autism and Developmental Disorders, 38,* 1211–1229. Available from doi: 10.10007/s10803–007–0501–2

Bauminger, N., Solomon, M., Aviezer, A., Heung, K., Gazit, L., Brown, J., & Rogers, S. (2008). Children with autism and their friends: A multidimensional study of friendship in high-functioning autism spectrum disorder. *Journal of Abnormal Child Psychology, 36,* 135–150. Available from doi: doi 10.1007/s10802–007–9156–x

Bevill, A., Gast, L., Maguire, A., & Vail, C. (2001). Increasing engagement of preschoolers with disabilities through correspondence training and picture cues. *Journal of Early Intervention, 24,* 129–145. Available from doi: 10.1177/105381510102400207

Blakeley-Smith, A., Carr, E. G., Cale, S. I., & Owen-DeSchryver, J. S. (2009). Environmental fit: A model for assessing and treating problem behavior associated with curricular difficulties in children with autism spectrum disorders. *Focus on Autism and Other Developmental Disabilities, 24,* 131–145. Available from doi: 10.1177/1088357609339032

Brookman, L., Boettcher, M., Klein, E., Openden, D., Koegel, R. L., & Koegel, L. K. (2003). Facilitating social interactions in a community summer camp setting for children with autism. *Journal of Positive Behavior Interventions, 5,* 249–252. Available from doi: 10.1177/10983007030050040801

Butler, L. R., & Luiselli, J. K. (2007). Escape-maintained problem behavior in a child with autism: Antecedent functional analysis and intervention evaluation of noncontingent escape and instructional fading. *Journal of Positive Behavior Interventions, 9,* 195–202. Available from doi: 10.1177/10983007070090040201

Carr, E. G., Horner, R. H., Turnbull, A. P., Marquis, J., Magito-McLaughlin, D., McAtee, M. L., et al. (1999). *Positive behavior support for people with developmental disabilities: A research synthesis.* Washington, DC: American Association on Mental Retardation.

Carr, E. G., Ladd, M. V., & Schulte, C. (2008). Validation on the contextual assessment inventory for problem behavior. *Journal of Positive Behavior Interventions, 10,* 91–104. Available from doi: 10.1177/1098300707312543

Carter, E., O'Rourke, L., Sisco, L. G., & Pelsue, D. (2009). Knowledge, responsibilities, and training needs of paraprofessionals in elementary and secondary schools. *Remedial and Special Education, 30,* 344–359. Available from doi: 10.1177/0741932508324399

Cooper, M. J., Griffith, K. G., & Filer, J. (1999). School intervention for inclusion of students with and without disabilities. *Focus on Autism and Other Developmental Disabilities, 14,* 110–115. Available from doi: 10.1177/108835769901400207

Durand, V. M., & Carr, E. G. (1991). Functional communication training to reduce challenging behavior: Maintenance and application in new settings. *Journal of Applied Behavior Analysis* (Special issue: *Social Validity: Multiple Perspectives*), *24*, 251–264. Available from doi: 10.1901/jaba.1991.24–251

Durand, V. M., & Crimmins, D. B. (1988). Identifying the variables maintaining self-injurious behavior. *Journal of Autism and Developmental Disorders*, *18*, 99–117. Available from doi: 10.1007/BF02211821

Etscheidt, S. (2003). An analysis of legal hearings and cases related to individualized education programs for children with autism. *Research and Practice for Persons with Severe Disabilities*, *28*, 51–69. Available from doi: 10.2511/rpsd.28.2.51

Fisher, M., & Meyer, L. H. (2002). Development and social competence after two years for students enrolled in inclusive and self-contained educational programs. *Research and Practice for Persons with Severe Disabilities*, *27*, 165–174. Available from doi: 10.2511/rpsd.27.3.165

Frea, W., Koegel, L. K., & Koegel, R. L. (2004). *Understanding why problem behaviors occur: A guide for assisting parents in assessing causes of behavior and designing treatment plans.* Santa Barbara: University of California.

Frederickson, N., Warren, L., & Turner, J. (2005). "Circle of Friends"—an exploration of impact over time. *Educational Psychology in Practice*, *21*, 197–217. Available from doi: 10.1080/02667360500205883

Gardner, M. R. (2010). Understanding and caring for the child with Asperger syndrome. *Journal of School Nursing*, *17*, 178–184. Available from doi: 10.1177/10598405010170040201

Gengoux, G. (2009). *Priming for games and cooperative activities with children with autism: Effects on social interactions with typically developing peers* (Publication No. 3324042). Doctoral dissertation, University of California, Santa Barbara. Available from Dissertations & Theses @ University of California.

Ghaziuddin, M., Ghaziuddin, N., & Greden, J. (2002). Depression in persons with autism: Implications for research and clinical care. *Journal of Autism and Developmental Disorders*, *3*, 299–306. Available from doi: 10.1023/A:1016330802348

Gonzalez-Lopez, A., & Kamps, D. (1997). Social skills training to increase social interactions between children with autism and their typical peers. Focus on Autism and Other Developmental Disabilities, *12*, 2–14. Available from doi: 10.1177/108835769701200101

Greenway, C. (2000). Autism and Asperger syndrome: Strategies to promote prosocial behaviours. *Educational Psychology in Practice*, *16*, 469–486. Available from doi: 10.1080/713666112

Gus, L. (2000). Autism: Promoting peer understanding. *Educational Psychology in Practice, 16*, 461–468. Available from doi: 10.1080/02667360020006345

Harrower, J. K., & Dunlap, G. (2001). Including children with autism in general education classrooms: A review of effective strategies. *Behavior Modification, 25*, 762–784. Available from doi: 10.1177/0145445501255006

Hewitt, A. (1998). *Identification of competencies and effective training practices for direct support staff working in community residential services for people with disabilities.* Minneapolis: University of Minnesota.

Hewitt, A., & Larson, S. A. (1994). *Policy research brief: Training issues in direct support personnel working in community residential programs for persons with developmental disabilities.* Minneapolis: University of Minnesota, Research and Training Center on Community Living.

Hewitt, A., & O'Nell, S. (1998). People need people: The direct service workforce. *Impact, 10*(4), 3–4.

Howlin, P. (1998). *Children with autism and Asperger syndrome: A guide for practitioners and carers.* Hoboken, NJ: Wiley.

Howlin, P. (2000). Outcome in adult life for more able individuals with autism or Asperger syndrome. *Autism* (Special issue: *Asperger Syndrome*), *4*, 63–83.

Kalyva, E., & Avramidis, A. (2005). Improving communication between children with autism and their peers through the "Circle of Friends": A small-scale intervention study. *Journal of Applied Research in Intellectual Disabilities, 18*, 253–261. Available from doi: 10.1111/j. 1468–3148.2005.00232

Kamps, D. M., Kravits, T., Lopez, A. G., Kemmerer, K., Potucek, J., & Harrell, L. G. (1998). What do the peers think? Social validity of peer-mediated programs. *Education and Treatment of Children, 21*, 107–134.

Koegel, L., & LaZebnik, C. (2006). *Overcoming autism.* New York: Viking/Penguin.

Koegel, L., & LaZebnik, C. (2008). *Growing up on the spectrum: A guide to life, love, and learning for teens and young adults with autism and Asperger's.* New York: Viking/Penguin.

Koegel, L. K., Dunlap, G., & Koegel, R. L. (Eds.). (1996). *Community, school, family, and social inclusion through positive behavioral support.* Baltimore: Brookes.

Koegel, L. K., Koegel, R. L., Frea, W., & Green-Hopkins, I. (2003). Priming as a method of coordinating educational services for students with autism. *Language, Speech, and Hearing Services in Schools, 34*, 228–235. Available from doi: 10.1044/0161–1461(2003/019)

Koegel, L. K., Koegel, R. L., Hurley, C., & Frea, W. D. (1992). Improving social skills and disruptive behavior in children with autism through self-management. *Journal of Applied Behavior Analysis, 25*, 341–353. Available from doi: 10.1901/jaba.1992.25–341

Koegel, L. K., Koegel, R. L., & Smith, A. (1997). Variables related to differences in standardized test outcomes for children with autism. *Journal of Autism and Developmental Disorders, 27*, 233–243. Available from doi: 10.1023/A:1025894213424

Koegel, R. L., Klein, E., Koegel, L. K., Boettcher, M. A., Brookman-Frazee, L., & Openden, D. (2006). Working with paraprofessionals to improve socialization in inclusive settings. In R. L. Koegel & L. K. Koegel, *Pivotal response treatments for autism* (pp. 189–198). Baltimore: Brookes.

Koegel, R. L., Koegel, L. K., & Parks, D. (1995). "Teach the individual" model of generalization: Autonomy through self-management. In R. L. Koegel & L. K. Koegel (Eds.), *Teaching children with autism* (pp. 67–78). Baltimore: Brookes.

Koegel, R. L., Werner, G. A., Vismara, L. A., & Koegel, L. K. (2005). The effectiveness of contextually supported play date interactions between children with autism and typically developing peers, *Research and Practice for Persons with Severe Disabilities, 30*, 93–102. Available from doi: 10.2511/rpsd.30.2.93

Kohler, F. W., Anthony, L. J., Steighner, S. A., & Hoyson, M. (2001). Teaching social interaction skills in the integrated preschool: An examination of naturalistic tactics. *Topics in Early Childhood Special Education, 21*, 93–103. Available from doi: 10.1177/027112140102100203

Kozlowski, A., Wood, L., Gilligan, K., & Luiselli, J. K. (2009). Effects of nonverbal social disapproval on attention-maintained spitting and disruptive vocalizing in a child with autism. *Clinical Case Studies, 8*, 309–316. Available from doi: 10.1177/1534650109341840

Meyer, L., Fox, A., Schermer, A., Ketelson, D., Montan, N., & Maley, K. (1987). The effects of teacher intrusion on social play interactions between children with autism and their nonhandicapped peers. *Journal of Autism and Developmental Disorders, 17*, 315–332. Available from doi: 10.1007/BF01487063

Morrison, L., Kamps, D., Garcia, J., & Parker, D. (2001). Peer mediation and monitoring strategies to improve initiations and social skills for students with autism. *Journal of Positive Behavior Interventions, 3*, 237–250. Available from doi: 10.1177/109830070100300405

Myles, B., & Adreon, D. (2002). Message from the guest editors. *Assessment for Effective Intervention, 27*, 3–4. Available from doi: 10.1177/073724770202700102

Newton, C., Taylor, G., & Wilson, D. (1996). Circles of Friends: an inclusive approach to meeting emotional and behavioural needs. *Educational Psychology in Practice, 11*, 41–48.

Ormrod, J. E. (2006). *Educational psychology: Developing learners* (5th ed.). Upper Saddle River, NJ: Prentice Hall.

Ozdemir, S. (2008). The effectiveness of social stories on decreasing disruptive behaviors of children with autism: Three case studies. *Journal of Autism and Developmental Disorders, 38*, 1689–1696. Available from doi: 10.1007/s10803–008–0551–0

Reaven, J. A. (2009). Children with high-functioning autism spectrum disorders and co-occurring anxiety symptoms: Implications for assessment and treatment. *Journal for Specialists in Pediatric Nursing, 14,* 192–199. Available from doi: 10.1111/j. 1744–6155.2009.00197.x

Robinson, S. (2007). *Training paraprofessionals of students with autism to implement pivotal response treatment using a video feedback training package* (Publication No. AAT 3283763). Doctoral dissertation, University of California, Santa Barbara. Available from Dissertations & Theses @ University of California.

Rogers, S. (2000). Interventions that facilitate socialization in children with autism. *Journal of Autism and Developmental Disorders, 30,* 399–409. Available from doi: 10.1023/A:1005543321840

Rowe, C. (1999). Do social stories benefit children with autism in mainstream primary schools? *British Journal of Special Education, 16,* 12–14.

Santosh, P. J., Baird, G., Pityaratstian, N., Tavare, E., & Gringas, P. (2006). Impact of comorbid autism spectrum disorders on stimulant response in children with attention deficit hyperactivity disorder: A retrospective and prospective effectiveness study. *Child: Care, Health and Development, 32,* 575–583. Available from doi: 10.1111/j. 1365–2214.2006.00631.x

Scahill, L., & Pachler, M. (2007). Treatment of hyperactivity in children with pervasive developmental disorders. *Journal of Child and Adolescent Psychiatric Nursing, 20,* 59–62. Available from doi: 10.1111/j. 1744–6171.2007.00080.x

Scattone, D., Wilczynski, S., Edwards, R., & Rabian, B. (2002). Decreasing disruptive behaviors of children with autism using social stories. *Journal of Autism and Developmental Disorders, 32,* 535–543. Available from doi: 10.1023/A:1021250813367

Spencer, V. G., Simpson, C. G., & Lynch, S. A. (2008). Using social stories to increase positive behaviors for children with autism spectrum disorders. *Intervention in School and Clinic, 44,* 58–61. Available from doi: 10.1177/1053451208318876

Stichter, J. P., Randolph, J., Gage, N., & Schmidt, C. (2007). A review of recommended social competency programs for students with autism spectrum disorders. *Exceptionality, 15,* 219–232. Available from doi: 10.1080/09362830701655758

Test, D. W., Flowers, C., Hewitt, A., & Solow, J. (2004). Training needs of direct support staff. *Mental Retardation, 42,* 327–337. Available from doi: 10.1352/0047–6765 (2004) 422.0.CO;2

Velting, O. N., Setzer, N. J., & Albano, A. M. (2004). Update on and advances in assessment and cognitive-behavioral treatment of anxiety disorders in children and adolescents. *Professional Psychology: Research and Practice, 35,* 42–54. Available from doi: 10.1037/0735–7028. 35.1.42

Venter, A., Lord, C., & Shopler, E. (1992). A follow-up study of high-functioning autistic children. *Journal of Child Psychology and Psychiatry, 33*, 489–507.

Volden, J., Coolican, J., Garon, N., White, J., & Bryson, S. (2009). Brief report: Pragmatic language in autism spectrum disorder: Relationships to measures of ability and disability. *Journal of Autism and Developmental Disorders, 39*, 388–393. Available from doi: 10.1007/ s10803–008–0618-y

Wainscot, J. J. (2008). Relationships with peers and use of the school environment of mainstream secondary school pupils with Asperger syndrome (high-functioning autism): A case-control study. *International Journal of Psychology and Psychological Therapy, 8*, 25–38.

Whitehurst, T., & Howells, A. (2006). "When something is different people fear it": Children's perceptions of an arts-based inclusion project. *Support for Learning, 21*, 40–44. Available from doi: 10.1111/j. 1467–9604. 2006.00399.x

Wilkinson, L. A. (2005). Supporting the inclusion of a student with Asperger syndrome: A case study using conjoint behavioural consultation and self-management. *Educational Psychology in Practice, 21*, 307–326. Available from doi: 10.1080/0206673605003449l4

Wood, J. J., Drahota, A., Sze, K., Har, K., Chiu, A., & Langer, D. A. (2009). Cognitive behavioral therapy for anxiety in children with autism spectrum disorder: A randomized, controlled study. *Journal of Child Psychology and Psychiatry, 50*, 224–234. Available from doi: 10.1111/j. 1469–7610. 2008.01948.x

Zanolli, K., Daggett, J., & Adams, T. (1996). Teaching preschool age autistic children to make spontaneous initiations to peers using priming. *Journal of Autism and Developmental Disorders, 26*, 407–422. Available from doi: 10.1007/BF02172826

CHAPTER FIVE

Allen, K. D., & Fuqua, R. W. (1985). Eliminating selective stimulus control: A comparison of two procedures for teaching mentally retarded children to respond to compound stimuli. *Journal of Experimental Child Psychology, 39*, 55–71.

Burke, J. C., & Cerniglia, L. (1990). Stimulus complexity and autistic children's responsivity: Assessing and training a pivotal behavior. *Journal of Autism and Developmental Disorders, 20*, 233–253.

Creedon, M. P. (Ed.). (1975). *Appropriate behavior through communication: A new program in simultaneous language for nonverbal children* (2nd ed.; Dysfunctioning Child Center Publication). Chicago: Michael Reese Medical Center.

Delprato, D. J. (2001). Comparisons of discrete-trial and normalized behavioral intervention for young children with autism. *Journal of Autism and Developmental Disorders, 31*, 315–325.

Dube, W. V., & McIlvane, W. J. (1999). Reduction of stimulus overselectivity with non-verbal differential observing responses. *Journal of Applied Behavior Analysis, 32*, 25–33.

Gersten, R. (1983). Stimulus overselectivity in autistic, trainable mentally retarded, and non-handicapped children: Comparative research controlling chronological (rather than mental) age. *Journal of Abnormal Child Psychology, 11*, 61–75.

Humphries, T. L. (2003). Effectiveness of pivotal response training as a behavioral intervention for young children with autism spectrum disorders. *Bridges: Practice-Based Research Syntheses, 2*, 1–9.

Jones, E. A., Carr, E. G., & Feeley, K. M. (2006). Multiple effects of joint attention intervention for children with autism. *Behavior Modification, 30*, 782–834.

Koegel, L. K., Camarata, S. M., Valdez-Menchaca, M., & Koegel, R. L. (1998). Setting generalization of question-asking by children with autism. *American Journal on Mental Retardation, 102*, 346–357.

Koegel, L. K., Carter, C. M., & Koegel, R. L. (2003). Teaching children with autism self-initiations as a pivotal response. *Topics in Language Disorders, 23*, 134–145.

Koegel, L. K., Koegel, R. L., Harrower, J. K., & Carter, C. M. (1999). Pivotal response intervention I: Overview of approach. *Journal of the Association for Persons with Severe Handicaps, 24*, 174–185.

Koegel, R. L., O'Dell, M. C., & Koegel, L. K. (1987). A natural language teaching paradigm for nonverbal autistic children. *Journal of Autism and Developmental Disorders, 17*, 187–200.

Koegel, R. L., & Schreibman, L. (1977). Teaching autistic children to respond to simultaneous multiple cues. *Journal of Experimental Child Psychology, 24*, 299–311.

Koegel, R. L., Tran, Q. H., Mossman, A., & Koegel, L. K. (2006). Incorporating motivational procedures to improve homework performance. In R. L. Koegel & L. K. Koegel, *Pivotal response treatments for autism* (pp. 81–92). Baltimore: Brookes.

Kuhn, L. R., Bodkin, A. E., Devlin, S. D., & Doggett, R. A. (2008). Using pivotal response training with peers in special education to facilitate play in two children with autism. *Education and Training in Developmental Disabilities, 43*, 37–45.

National Research Council. (2001). *Educating children with autism*. Washington, DC: National Academy Press.

Laski, K. E., Charlop, M. H., & Schreibman, L. (1988). Training parents to use the natural language paradigm to increase their autistic children's speech. *Journal of Applied Behavior Analysis, 21*, 391–400.

Lovaas, O. I. (1987). Behavioral treatment and normal educational and intellectual functioning in young autistic children. *Journal of Consulting and Clinical Psychology, 55*, 3–9.

National Autism Center. (2009). *The National Standards Project—Addressing the need for evidence based practice guidelines for autism spectrum disorders.* Randolph, MA: Author.

Pierce, K., & Schreibman, L. (1995). Increasing complex social behaviors in children with autism: Effects of peer-implemented pivotal response training. *Journal of Applied Behavior Analysis, 28,* 285–295.

Reed, S., Stahmer, A. C., Schreibman, L., & Suhrheinrich, J. (2011). Examining the use of multiple cues as a necessary component of pivotal response training. Manuscript in preparation.

Rocha, M. L., Schreibman, L., & Stahmer, A. C. (2007). Effectiveness of training parents to teach joint attention in children with autism. *Journal of Early Intervention, 29,* 154–172.

Schreibman, L., Kaneko, W. M., & Koegel, R. L. (1991). Positive affect of parents of autistic children: A comparison across two teaching techniques. *Behavior Therapy, 22,* 479–490.

Sindelar, P. T., Brownell, M. T., & Billingsley, B. (2010). Special education teacher education research: Current status and future directions. *Journal of the Teacher Education Division of the Council for Exceptional Children, 33,* 8–24.

Stahmer, A. C. (1995). Teaching symbolic play skills to children with autism using pivotal response training. *Journal of Autism and Developmental Disorders, 25,* 123–141.

Stahmer, A. C. (2007). The basic structure of community early intervention programs for children with autism: Provider descriptions. *Journal of Autism and Developmental Disorders, 37,* 1344–1354.

Stahmer, A. C., Collings, N. M., & Palinkas, L. A. (2005). Early intervention practices for children with autism: Descriptions from community providers. *Focus on Autism and Other Developmental Disabilities, 20,* 66–79.

Stahmer, A. C., Suhrheinrich, J., Reed, S., Bolduc, C., & Schreibman, L. (2011). *Classroom pivotal response teaching for children with autism.* New York: Guilford Press.

Stahmer, A. C., Suhrheinrich, J., Reed, S., Schreibman, L., & Vattuone, C. (2011). A collaborative method for adapting an evidence-based intervention for classroom use. Manuscript in preparation.

Sze, K., Koegel, R. L., Brookman, L., & Koegel, L. K. (2003). *Rapid acquisition of speech in nonverbal children with autism: Developing typical, social, and communicative interactions in children with autism using pivotal response training and self-management.* Paper presented at the annual convention of the Association for Behavior Analysis, San Francisco.

Thorp, D. M., Stahmer, A. C., & Schreibman, L. (1995). Effects of sociodramatic play training on children with autism. *Journal of Autism and Developmental Disorders, 25,* 265–282.

Whalen, C., & Schreibman, L. (2003). Joint attention training for children with autism using behavior modification procedures. *Journal of Childhood Psychology and Psychiatry, 44,* 456–468.

CHAPTER SIX

Hanft, B. E., Rush, D. D., & Shelden, M. L. (2004). *Coaching families and colleagues in early childhood.* Baltimore: Brookes.

Horner, R., Carr, E., Halle, J., McGee, G., Odom, S., & Wolery, M. (2005). The use of single-subject research to identify evidence-based practice in special education. *Exceptional Children, 71,* 165–180.

Hume, K., & Smith, S. (2009). *Implementation checklist for visual supports.* Chapel Hill: National Professional Development Center on Autism Spectrum Disorders, Frank Porter Graham Child Development Institute, University of North Carolina.

Moran, M. R., Myles, B. S., & Downing, J. A. (1990). *PAIRS: Peer coaching for general and special educators.* Unpublished manuscript, University of Kansas, Lawrence.

Moran, M. R., Myles, B. S., & Downing, J. A. (1993). *TEAMS: Using peer coaching in rural schools to support professional development.* Unpublished manuscript, University of Kansas, Lawrence.

Moran, M. R., Myles, B. S., Downing, J. A., & Ormsbee, C. (1996). *Project PRIDE: Using coaching to support professional development: A train-the-trainer project.* Unpublished manuscript, University of Kansas, Lawrence.

Nathan, P., & Gorman, J. M. (2002). *A guide to treatments that work.* New York: Oxford University Press.

Odom, S. L., Brantlinger, E., Gersten, R., Horner, R. D., Thompson, B., & Harris, K. (2004). *Quality indicators for research in special education and guidelines for evidence-based practices: Executive summary.* Arlington, VA: Council for Exceptional Children, Division for Research.

Rinkel, P., & Myles, B. S. (1997). *TRIADS: Peer coaching among teachers, paraprofessionals, and parents.* Unpublished manuscript, Blue Valley Schools, Overland Park, KS.

Rogers, S. J., & Vismara, L. A. (2008). Evidence-based comprehensive treatments for early autism. *Journal of Clinical Child and Adolescent Psychology, 37,* 8–38.

Rush, D. D., & Shelden, M. L. (2011). *The early childhood coaching handbook.* Baltimore: Brookes.

Williams, C. M., Fan, W., & Goodman, G. (2011). Preliminary analysis of the "survey of educators' knowledge and value of research-based practices for students with autism." *Assessment for Effective Intervention, 38,* 113–130.

CHAPTER SEVEN

Anderson, T., Reinhart, J., & Slowinski, J. (2001). *A journey in virtual collaboration: Facilitating computer-mediated communication among pre-service teachers.* Paper presented at the 6th Annual Mid-South Instructional Technology Conference, Murfreesboro, TN.

Barab, S. A., Kling, R., & Gray, J. H. (Eds.). (2004). *Designing for virtual communities in the service of learning.* Cambridge, England: Cambridge University Press.

Blanchard, A. (2004). Virtual behavior settings: An application of behavior setting theories to virtual communities. *Journal of Computer-Mediated Communication, 9*(2). Available from http://jcmc.indiana.edu/vol10/issue1/porter.html

Blann, E. D., & Hantula, D. A. (2004). Design and evaluation of an Internet-based personalized instructional system for social psychology. In D. Monolescu, C. Schifter, & L. Greenwood (Eds.), *The distance education evolution* (pp. 286–314). Hershey, PA: Information Sciences.

Catagnus, R. M., & Hantula, D. A. (2011). The virtual individual education plan (IEP) team: Using online collaboration to develop a behavior intervention plan. *International Journal of e-Collaboration, 7*(1), 30–46.

Catania, C. N., Almeida, D., Liu-Constant, B., & Digennaro Reed, F. D. (2009). Video modeling to train staff to implement discrete-trial instruction. *Journal of Applied Behavior Analysis, 42*, 387–392.

Davis, E. S., & Hantula, D. A. (2001). The effects of download delay on performance and end-user satisfaction in an Internet tutorial. *Computers in Human Behavior, 17*, 249–268. Available from doi: 10.1016/S0747–5632(01)00007–3

DeWert, M. H., Babinski, L. M., & Jones, B. D. (2003). Safe passages: Providing online support to beginning teachers. *Journal of Teacher Education, 54*, 311–320.

Fjermestad, J. (2004). An analysis of communication mode in group support systems research. *Decision Support Systems, 37*, 239–263.

Gasson, S. (2005). The dynamics of sense-making, knowledge, and expertise in collaborative, boundary-spanning design. *Journal of Computer-Mediated Communication, 10*(4). Available from http://jcmc.indiana.edu/vol10/issue4/gasson.html

Geer, C. H., & Hamill, L. B. (2003). Using technology to enhance collaboration between special education and general education majors. *TechTrends, 47*(3), 26–29.

Hantula, D., & Pawlowicz, D. M. (2004). Education mirrors industry: On the not-so surprising rise of Internet distance education. In D. Monolescu, C. Schifter, & L. Greenwood (Eds.), *The distance education evolution* (pp. 142–162). Hershey, PA: Information Sciences.

Hawkes, M. (2000). Structuring computer-mediated communication for collaborative teacher development. *Journal of Research and Development in Education, 33*, 268–277.

Hawkes, M., & Romiszowski, A. (2001). Examining the reflective outcomes of asynchronous computer-mediated communication on inservice teacher development. *Journal of Technology and Teacher Education, 9*, 285–308.

He, W., Means, T., & Lin, G. Y. (2006). Field experience tracking and management in teacher development programs. *International Journal of Technology in Teaching and Learning, 2,* 134–147.

Hobbs, T., Day, S. L., & Russo, A. (2002). The virtual conference room: Online problem solving for first year teachers. *Teacher Education and Special Education, 25,* 352–361.

Holzer, E. (2004). Professional development of teacher educators in asynchronous electronic environment: Challenges, opportunities and preliminary insights from practice. *Educational Media International, 41,* 81–89.

Im, Y., & Lee, O. (2003/2004). Pedagogical implications of online discussion for pre-service teacher training. *Journal of Research on Technology in Education, 36,* 155–170.

Järvelä, S., & Häkkinen, P. (2002). Web-based cases in teaching and learning—the quality of discussions and a stage of perspective taking in asynchronous communication. *Interactive Learning Environments, 10,* 1–22.

Jones, C. (2001). Tech support: Preparing teachers to use technology. *Principal Leadership, 1*(9), 35–39.

Kilo, C. M. (1999). Improving care through collaboration. *Pediatrics, 103*(1 Suppl. E): 384–393.

Kochtanek, T. R., & Hein, K. K. (2000). Creating and nurturing distributed asynchronous learning environments. *Online Information Review, 24,* 280–293.

Kurtts, S., Hibbard, K., & Levin, B. (2005). Collaborative online problem solving with preservice general education and special education teachers. *Journal of Technology and Teacher Education, 13,* 397–414.

Lobel, M., Neubauer, M., & Swedburg, R. (2005). Comparing how students collaborate to learn about the self and relationships in a real-time non-turn-taking online and turn-taking face-to-face environment. *Journal of Computer-Mediated Communication, 10*(4). Available from http://jcmc.indiana.edu/vol10/issue4/lobel.html

Maurice, C., Green, G., & Fox, R. (2001). Making a difference: Behavioral intervention in autism. Austin, TX: PRO-ED.

McConnell, D. (2002). Action research and distributed problem-based learning in continuing professional education. *Distance Education, 23,* 59–83.

Ocker, R. J., & Yaverbaum, G. J. (1999). Asynchronous computer-mediated communication versus face-to-face collaboration: Results on student learning, quality, and satisfaction. *Group Decision and Negotiation, 8,* 427–440.

Reischl, U., & Oberleitner, R. (2009). Development of a telemedicine platform for the management of children with autism. *German Journal for Young Researchers, 1*(1). Available from www.nachwuchswissenschaftler.org/2009/1/3/ZfN-2009 –1–3.pdf

Rich, P. J., & Hannafin, M. (2009). Video annotation tools: Technologies to scaffold, structure, and transform teacher reflection. *Journal of Teacher Education, 60,* 52–67.

Rule, S., Salzberg, C., Higbee, T., Menlove, R., & Smith, J. (2006). Technology-mediated consultation to assist rural students: A case study. *Rural Special Education Quarterly, 25*(2), 3–7.

Scheeler, M. C., Congdon, M., & Stansbery, S. (2010). Providing immediate feedback to co-teachers through bug-in-ear technology: An effective method of peer coaching in inclusion classrooms. *Teacher Education and Special Education, 33,* 83–96.

Selwyn, N. (2000). Creating a "connected" community? Teachers' use of an electronic discussion group. *Teachers College Record, 102,* 750–778.

Simpson, M. G. (2002). *Managing the field experience in distance delivered teacher education programmes.* Paper presented at the 2nd Pan-Commonwealth Forum on Open and Distance Learning, Durban, South Africa. Available from www.col.org/pcf2 /papers/simpson.pdf

Winter, E. C., & McGhie-Richmond, D. (2005). Using computer conferencing and case studies to enable collaboration between expert and novice teachers. *Journal of Computer Assisted Learning, 21,* 118–129.

CHAPTER EIGHT

American Psychiatric Association. (2000). *Diagnostic and statistical manual of mental disorders* (4th ed., text rev.). Washington, DC: Author.

Board of Education of Hendrick Hudson Central School District v. Rowley. 458 U.S. 176 (1982).

Boutot, E. A., & Myles, B. S. (2011). *Autism spectrum disorders: Foundations, characteristics, and effective strategies.* Boston: Pearson.

Centers for Disease Control and Prevention (CDC). (2010). *Autism and developmental disabilities monitoring (ADDM) network.* Available from www.cdc.gov/ncbddd /autism/addm.html

de Boer, S. R. (2009). *Successful inclusion for students with autism: Creating a complete, effective ASD inclusion program.* San Francisco: Jossey-Bass.

DiPaola, M. F., & Walther-Thomas, C. (2003). *Principals and special education: The critical roles of school leaders* (COPPSE Document No. 1B-7). Gainesville: University of Florida, Center on Personnel Studies in Special Education.

Getty, L. A., & Summy, S. E. (2004). The course of due process. *TEACHING Exceptional Children, 36*(3), 40–44.

Hall, L. J. (2009). *Autism spectrum disorders: From theory to practice.* Upper Saddle River, NJ: Merrill.

Lake, J. F., & Billingsley, B. S. (2000). An analysis of factors that contribute to parent-school conflict in special education. *Remedial and Special Education, 21,* 240–251. Available from doi: 10.1177/074193250002100407

Minnesota Department of Education. (2010). *Special education litigation costs fiscal year 2009.* Available from http://archive.leg.state.mn.us/docs/2010/mandated/100532.pdf

National Autism Center. (2009). *Evidence-based practice and autism in the schools: A guide to providing appropriate interventions to students with autism spectrum disorders.* Randolph, MA: Author.

National Research Council. (2001). *Educating children with autism.* Washington, DC: National Academy Press.

Roberts, K. D. (2010). Topic areas to consider when planning transition from high school to postsecondary education for students with autism spectrum disorders. *Focus on Autism and Other Developmental Disabilities, 25,* 158–162. Available from doi: 10.1177/1088357510371476

Schillinger, M. (2010). *The administrator's guide to building and maintaining a comprehensive autism program.* Horsham, PA: LRP.

Stoner, J. B., Bock, S. J., Thompson, J. R., Angell, M. E., Heyl, B. S., & Crowley, E. P. (2005). Welcome to our world: Parent perceptions of interactions between parents of young children with ASD and education professionals. *Focus on Autism and Other Developmental Disabilities, 20,* 39–51.

Tomsky, J. E. (2010). The legal framework. In M. Schillinger, *The administrator's guide to building and maintaining a comprehensive autism program* (pp. 23–31). Horsham, PA: LRP.

Wilkinson, L. A. (2010). *A best practice guide to assessment and intervention for autism and Asperger syndrome in schools.* Philadelphia, PA: Jessica Kingsley.

Yell, M. L., Katsiyannis, A., Drasgow, E., & Herbst, M. (2003). Developing legally correct and educationally appropriate programs for students with autism spectrum disorders. *Focus on Autism and Other Developmental Disabilities, 18,* 182–191.

Zager, D., & Alpern, C. (2010). College-based inclusion programming for transition-age students with autism. *Focus on Autism and Other Developmental Disabilities, 25,* 151–157. Available from doi: 10.1177/1088357610371331

Zirkel, P. A. (2002). The autism case law: Administrative and judicial rulings. *Focus on Autism and Other Developmental Disabilities, 17,* 84–93.

CHAPTER NINE

Aldred, C., Green, J., & Adams, C. (2004). A new social communication intervention for children with autism: Pilot randomized controlled treatment study suggesting effectiveness. *Journal of Child Psychology and Psychiatry*, *45*, 1420–1430.

Aman, M. G., McDougle, C. J., Scahill, L., Handen, B., Arnold, L. E., Johnson, C., et al. (2009). Medication and parent training in children with pervasive developmental disorders and serious behavior problems: Results from a randomized clinical trial. *Journal of the American Academy of Child & Adolescent Psychiatry*, *48*, 1143–1154.

Arnold, L. E., Vitiello, B., McDougle, C., Scahill, L., Shah, B., Gonzalez, N. M., et al. (2003). Parent-defined target symptoms respond to risperidone in RUPP autism study: Customer approach to clinical trials. *Journal of the American Academy of Child & Adolescent Psychiatry*, *42*, 1443–1450.

Beaumont, R., & Sofronoff, K. (2008). A multi-component social skills intervention for children with Asperger syndrome: The Junior Detective Training Program. *Journal of Child Psychology and Psychiatry*, *49*, 743–753.

Boulware, G., Schwartz, I. S., Sandall, S. R., & McBride, B. J. (2006). Project DATA for toddlers: An inclusive approach to very young children with autism spectrum disorder. *Topics in Early Childhood Special Education*, *26*, 94–105.

Brookman-Frazee, L., Stahmer, A., Baker-Ericzén, M. J., & Tsai, K. (2006). Parenting interventions for children with autism spectrum and disruptive behavior disorders: Opportunities for cross-fertilization. *Clinical Child and Family Psychology Review*, *9*, 181–200.

Brookman-Frazee, L., Vismara, L., Drahota, A., Stahmer, A., & Openden, D. (2009). Parent training interventions for children with autism spectrum disorders. In J. Matson (Ed.), *Applied behavior analysis for children with autism spectrum disorders* (pp. 237–257). New York: Springer.

Callahan, K., Henson, R. K., & Cowan, A. K. (2008). Social validation of evidence-based practices in autism by parents, teachers and administrators. *Journal of Autism and Developmental Disabilities*, *38*, 678–692.

Charlop, M. H., & Trasowech, J. E. (1991). Increasing autistic children's daily spontaneous speech. *Journal of Applied Behavior Analysis*, *24*, 747–761.

Charlop-Christy, M. H., & Carpenter, M. H. (2000). Modified incidental teaching sessions: A procedure for parents to increase spontaneous speech in their children with autism. *Journal of Positive Behavior Interventions*, *2*, 98–112.

Dingfelder, H. E., & Mandell, D. S. (2011). Bridging the research-to-practice gap in autism intervention: An application of diffusion of innovation theory. *Journal of Autism and Developmental Disorders*, *41*, 597–609.

Dishion, T. J., Kavanagh, K., Schneiger, A., Nelson, S., & Kaufman, N. K. (2002). Preventing early adolescent substance use: *A* family-centered strategy for the public middle school. *Prevention Science, 3*, 191–201.

Drew, A., Baird, G., Baron-Cohen, S., Cox, A., Slonims, V., Wheelwright, S., et al. (2002). A pilot randomised control trial of a parent training intervention for pre-school children with autism: Preliminary findings and methodological challenges. *European Child & Adolescent Psychiatry, 11*, 266–272.

Forehand, R., & Kotchick, B. A. (2002). Behavioral parent training: Current challenges and potential solutions. *Journal of Child and Family Studies, 11*, 377–384.

Frankel, F., Myatt, R., Sugar, C., Whitham, C., Gorospe, C. M., & Laugeson, E. (2010). A randomized controlled study of parent-assisted children's friendship training with children having autism spectrum disorders. *Journal of Autism and Developmental Disorders, 40*, 827–842.

Green, J., Charman, T., McConachie, H., Aldred, C., Slonims, V., Howlin, P. et al. (2010). Parent-mediated communication-focused treatment in children with autism (PACT): A randomised controlled trial. *Lancet, 375*, 2152–2160.

Howlin, P., Goode, S., Hutton, J., & Rutter, M. (2004). Adult outcome for children with autism. *Journal of Child Psychology and Psychiatry, 45*, 212–229.

Hume, K., Bellini, S., & Pratt, C. (2005). The usage and perceived outcomes of early intervention and early childhood programs for young children with autism spectrum disorder. *Topics in Early Childhood Special Education, 25*, 195–207.

Ingersoll, B., & Dvortcsak, A. (2006). Including parent training in the early childhood special education curriculum for children with autism spectrum disorders. *Topics in Early Childhood Special Education, 26*, 179–187.

Ingersoll, B., & Gergans, S. (2007). The effect of a parent-implemented imitation intervention on spontaneous imitation skills in young children with autism. *Research in Developmental Disabilities, 28*, 163–175.

Iovannone, R., Dunlap, G., Huber, H., & Kincaid, D. (2003). Effective educational practices for students with autism spectrum disorders. *Focus on Autism and Other Developmental Disabilities, 18*, 150–165.

Kaiser, A. P., Hemmeter, M. L., Ostrosky, M. M., Alpert, C. L., & Hancock, T. B. (1995). The effects of group training and individual feedback on parent use of milieu teaching. *Journal of Childhood Communication Disorders, 16*(2), 39–48.

Kasari, C., Gulsrud, A. C., Wong, C., Kwon, S., & Locke, J. (2010). Randomized controlled caregiver mediated joint engagement intervention for toddlers with autism. *Journal of Autism and Developmental Disorders, 40*, 1045–1056.

Koegel, R. L., Bimbela, A., & Schreibman, L. (1996). Collateral effects of parent training on family interactions. *Journal of Autism and Developmental Disabilities, 26,* 347–359.

Koegel, R. L., Schreibman, L., Britten, K. R., Burke, J. C., & O'Neill, R. E. (1982). A comparison of parent training to direct child treatment. In R. L. Koegel, A. Rincover, & A. L. Egel (Eds.), *Educating and understanding autistic children* (pp. 260–279). San Diego, CA: College-Hill Press.

Koegel, R. L., Schreibman, L., Johnson, J., O'Neill, R. E., & Dunlap, G. (1984). Collateral effects of parent-training on families with autistic children. In R. F. Dangel & R. A. Polster (Eds.), *Behavioral parent-training: Issues in research and practice* (pp. 358–378). New York: Guilford Press.

Kratochwill, T. R., McDonald, L., Levin, J. R., Scalia, P. A., & Coover, G. (2009). Families and schools together: An experimental study of multi-family support groups for children at risk. *Journal of School Psychology, 47,* 245–265.

Laski, K. E., Charlop, M. H., & Schreibman, L. (1988). Training parents to use the natural language paradigm to increase their autistic children's speech. *Journal of Applied Behavior Analysis, 21,* 391–400.

Laugeson, E. A., Frankel, F., Mogil, C., & Dillon, A. R. (2008). Parent-assisted social skills training to improve friendships in teens with autism spectrum disorders. *Journal of Autism and Developmental Disorders, 39,* 596–606.

Mahoney, G., Kaiser, A., Girolametto, L., MacDonald, J., Robinson, C., Safford, P., & Spiker, D. (1999). Parent education in early intervention: A call for a renewed focus. *Topics in Early Childhood Special Education, 19,* 131–140.

Mahoney, G., & Perales, F. (2003). Using relationship-focused intervention to enhance the social-emotional functioning of young children with autism spectrum disorders. *Topics in Early Childhood Special Education, 23,* 77–89.

McConachie, H., & Diggle, T. (2007). Parent implemented early intervention for young children with autism spectrum disorder: A systematic review. *Journal of Evaluation in Clinical Practice, 13,* 120–129.

McConachie, H., Randle, V., Hammal, D., & Le Couteur, A. (2005). A controlled trial of a training course for parents of children with suspected autism spectrum disorder. *Journal of Pediatrics, 147,* 335–340.

Minjarez, M. B., Williams, S. E., Mercier, E. M., & Hardan, A. Y. (2011). Pivotal response group treatment program for parents of children with autism. *Journal of Autism and Developmental Disorders, 41,* 92–101.

Moes, D. R., & Frea, W. D. (2002). Contextualized behavioral support in early intervention for children with autism and their families. *Journal of Autism and Developmental Disorders, 32,* 519–533.

National Research Council. (2001). *Educating children with autism*. Washington, DC: National Academy Press.

Neef, N. A. (1995). Pyramidal parent training by peers. *Journal of Applied Behavior Analysis, 28*, 333–337.

Reid, M. J., Webster-Stratton, C., & Hammond, M. (2007). Enhancing a classroom social competence and problem-solving curriculum by offering parent training to families of moderate- to high-risk elementary school children. *Journal of Clinical Child and Adolescent Psychology, 36*, 605–620.

Salt, J., Sellars, V., Shemilt, J., Body, S., Coulson, T., & McCool, S. (2001). The Scottish Centre for Autism preschool treatment programme I: A developmental approach to early intervention. *Autism, 5*, 362–373.

Salt, J., Sellars, V., Shemilt, J., Body, S., Coulson, T., & McCool, S. (2002). The Scottish Centre for Autism preschool treatment programme II: The results of a controlled treatment outcome study. *Autism, 6*, 33–46.

Schreibman, L., & Koegel, R. L. (2005). In E. D. Hibbs & P. S. Jensen (Eds.), *Psychosocial treatments for child and adolescent disorders: Empirically based strategies for clinical practice* (2nd ed., pp. 605–631). Washington, DC: American Psychological Association.

Schwartz, I. S., Sandall, S. R., McBride, B. J., & Boulware, G. (2004). Project DATA (Developmentally Appropriate Treatment for Autism): An inclusive school-based approach to educating young children with autism. *Topics in Early Childhood Special Education, 24*, 156–168.

Seung, H. K., Ashwell, J. H., Elder, J. H., & Valcante, G. (2006). Verbal communication outcomes in children with autism after in-home father training. *Journal of Intellectual Disability Research, 50*, 139–150.

Sofronoff, K., Leslie, A., & Brown, W. (2004). Parent management training and Asperger syndrome: A randomized controlled trial to evaluate a parent based intervention. *Autism, 8*, 301–317.

Solomon, M., Goodlin-Jones, B. L., & Anders, T. F. (2004). A social adjustment enhancement intervention for high functioning autism, Asperger's syndrome, and pervasive developmental disorder NOS. *Journal of Autism and Developmental Disorders, 34*, 649–668.

Solomon, M., Ono, M., Timmer, S., & Goodlin-Jones, B. (2008). The effectiveness of parent-child interaction therapy for families of children on the autism spectrum. *Journal of Autism and Developmental Disorders, 38*, 1767–1776.

Stahmer, A., & Ingersoll, B. (2004). Inclusive programming for toddlers with autistic spectrum disorders: Outcomes from the Children's Toddler School. *Journal of Positive Behavior Interventions, 67*, 67–82.

Summers, J. A., Houlding, C. M., & Reitzel, J. M. (2004). Behavior management services for children with autism/PDD: Program description and patterns of referral. *Focus on Autism and Other Developmental Disabilities, 19,* 95–101.

Symon, J. B. (2001). Parent education for autism: Issues in providing services at a distance. *Journal of Positive Behavior Interventions, 3,* 160–174.

Tonge, B., Brereton, A., Kiomall, M., Mackinnon, A., King, N., & Rinehart, N. (2006). Effects on parental mental health of an education and skills training program for parents of young children with autism: A randomized controlled trial. *Journal of the American Academy of Child & Adolescent Psychiatry, 45,* 561–569.

Wheeler, J. J., Baggett, B. A., Fox, J., & Blevins, L. (2006). Treatment integrity: A review of intervention studies conducted with children with autism. *Focus on Autism and Other Developmental Disabilities, 21,* 45–54.

Whittingham, K., Sofronoff, K., Sheffield, J., & Sanders, M. R. (2009). Stepping Stones Triple P: An RCT of a parenting program of a child diagnosed with an autism spectrum disorder. *Journal of Abnormal Child Psychology, 37,* 469–480.

INDEX

Behavior management training, 209–211

Behavior Tracker Pro, 171

Behavioral Interventions, 37

Behavioral teaching strategies, 45–46

Behaviorimaging.com, 164

Bergen County, New Jersey, 81

BI-Capture technology, 164

BI-CARE technology (Behavior Connect), 164

BIE. *See* "Bug-in-ear" technology

Big Buddy programs, 91–95

Billingsly, B. S., 203

Bipolar disorder, 192

Bluetooth headset, 168

Blum-Dimaya, A., 50

Board Certified Behavior Analysts, 158, 161, 172

Board of Education of Hendrick Hudson Central School District v. *Rowley,* 195, 196

Boardmaker Share, 170

Bock, S. J., 204

Boettcher, M., 95

Boston, Massachusetts, 24

Boulware, G., 220

Bourgeois, B. C., 50

Boutot, E. A., 67, 71

Boyd, B., 80

Bristol Township School District (BTSD; Pennsylvania), 159–160_

Broad autism phenotype, 4–5

"Broad Autism Phenotype Questionnaire, The" (*Journal of Autism and Developmental Disorders, 37*), 4

Brookman, L., 95

Browder, D. M., 43

Brown, W., 209

Bucks County Intermediate Unit (BCIU; Pennsylvania), 157–159

Buffington Townsend, D., 38

"Bug-in-ear" (BIE) technology, 167–168

C

Campos, B. A., 50

Caregiver attachment, 10

Caregivers: attachment to, 10; physical play with, 13

Carpenter, M. H., 215

Carter, C. M., 109

Catagnus, R. M., 155, 162

CBI. *See* Computer-based intervention (CBI)

CBT. *See* Cognitive behavioral therapy (CBT) interventions

Center for Autism and Related Disorders, 69

Centers for Disease Control and Prevention (CDC), 7, 9, 183

Chaining procedures, 45–46

Charlop, M. H., 214

Charlop-Christy, M. H., 215

Child self-initiations, 109

Childhood Disintegrative Disorder, 188

Childrens Toddler School, 221–221

Children's Toddler Program, 69

Child with Autism" *(Behavioral Interventions)*, 37
Computer-aided instruction, 132
Computer-based intervention (CBI), 39–40, 47, 53
Conditional discriminations, 113–114
Congdon, M., 167
Conners, K., 25
Conners 3rd Edition (Conners 3), 25
Consequence-based interventions, 97
Contingent escape, 99
Conversational communication, 110
Cooper, M. J., 90–91
Cooperative arrangements, 93–94
Core cognitive difficulties, 6–7
Corness, M., 74–75
Courtade, G. R., 43
Crowley, E. P., 203, 204
Curricular modification, 98

D

Daggett, J., 94
Dawson, Geraldine, 10, 79
DDTrac Special Education Progress Monitoring, 171
Delprato, D., 76–77
Denver, Colorado, 81
Depression, 101, 192
Desktop videoconferencing, 167
Developmental, Individual Difference, Relationship-based (DIR or Floortime) Model, 69
Developmental social learning perspective, 14

Diagnostic and Statistical Manual of Mental Disorders (DSM-III; American Psychiatric Association), 13, 14; "technical revision," 13
Diagnostic and Statistical Manual of Mental Disorders (DSM-IV; American Psychiatric Association), 14, 63, 188
Diagnostic and Statistical Manual of Mental Disorders (DSM-V; American Psychiatric Association), 14
Differential reinforcement, 132
Dillenburger, K., 72
Dillon, A. R., 211, 216
Dingfelder, H., 19, 82
DIR (Floortime) model, 77
Disabilities Education Act (1990), 14
Disability, 4–5
Discrete trial behavioral intervention, 7; *versus* naturalistic behavior intervention, 76
Discrete trial training (DTT), 7, 72–74, 108–109, 132
Disorder, 4–5
Doodle, 170
Dotson, W. H., 48
Douglass program, 69
Down syndrome, 10, 12
Downing, Joyce Anderson, 147
Drahota, A., 102
Drasgow, E., 204
DSM-5, 14
DSM-III. *See* American Psychiatric Association); *Diagnostic and*

39–40, 43–44; and implications for practice, 52; and instructional interventions for targeted curricular areas, 36–42; and insufficient evaluation of interventions for older students, 49–51; and insufficient evaluation of interventions for students with severe autism, 51; overall findings from literature on, 42–44; and play and leisure skills, 41–42; summary of, 52–54; targeting academic skills in, 36–37

Evidence-based interventions, 26

Evidence-Based Practice and Autism in the Schools (National Autism Center), 192, 196–197, 205

Evidence-based practices, 139–146; components of training modules for, 140; process of assessment of, selection of, and monitoring outcomes of, 145

Executive Function hypothesis, 6

Exposure prevention, 102

Extinction, 132

Eyberg Child Behavior Inventory (ECBI), 209, 210

Eye contact, 10, 13, 16

F

Fein, Deborah, 61, 84

Fidelity, 139

Filer, J., 90–91

Floortime model, 77

Flores, M. M., 32, 50

Franco, J. H., 41, 50

Frankel, F., 211, 212, 216

Franzone, E. L., 131

Frea, W., 100

Freeman, S., 28

Functional communication training, 132

Functional life skills: and instructional interventions for targeted curricular areas, 39–40; and overall findings from literature, 42–44

G

Ganz, J. B., 32, 50

Garcia, J., 92

Gaze, following direction of, 10–11, 17

Gestures, use of, 10, 16

Goal attainment scale (GAS), 136, 138, 139, 151; and sample goal attainment scaling form, 137

Goodlin-Jones, B., 210, 212–214

Google, 170

Gorospe, C. M., 212

GoToMeeting, 169

Gray, L. H., 164

Greenson, J., 79

Greenspan, S., 77, 78

Greenway, C., 92

Griffith, K. G., 90–91

Groen, A. D., 73, 74

Guided noticing, 163

H

Hall, L., 80

Handen, B., 210

Hanft, B. E., 147

Hannafin, M., 163
Har, K., 102
Harrell, L. G., 90
Harris, Mary (special education
   teacher), 135, 137, 148
Harrison, J., 37
Harrower, J. K., 109
Hatton, D., 69
Hatula, D. A., 162
He, W., 172
Headsets, 167–168
Herbst, M., 204
Herr, C. M., 183
Heyl, B. S., 203, 204
Higbee, T., 167
Hoch, H., 50
Home Situations Questionnaire,
   211
Homework completion, 110
Howells, A., 90
Hoyson, M., 105
Human diversity perspective, 5
Hume, K., 71, 80
Hurley, C., 100

I

IDD. *See* Intellectual and
   developmental disabilities (IDD)
IDEA. *See* Individuals with Disabilities
   Education Act
IJA. *See* Joint attention: initiating
Imitation, 208
Impact of Targeting Joint Attention
   Skills in Preschool Interventions for
   Children with Autism, 26

Impairment, 4–5, 14; and impaired
   initiation, 14
Incidental teaching, 76
Inclusion, benefits of, 89–90
"Increasing Play and Decreasing the
   Challenging Behavior of Children
   with Autism during Recess with
   Activity Schedules and Task
   Correspondence Training"
   *(Research in Autism Spectrum
   Disorders)*, 41
"Increasing the Use of Empathic
   Statements in the Presence of a
   Non-Verbal Affective Stimulus in
   Adolescents with Autism"
   *(Research in Autism Spectrum
   Disorders)*, 38
Indiana, 208
Individualized education program
   (IEP), 112, 161, 183–184; use of, to
   develop goal attainment scale,
   135–138
Individualized family service plan
   (IFSP), 203
Individuals with Disabilities Education
   Act (IDEA), 7, 8, 19, 42, 65,
   186–188, 194, 196, 225–226;
   reauthorization of, 65
Infant sibling studies, 19
Ingersoll, B., 207, 217
Initiating, and responsiveness to,
   intervention, 23
Institute of Education Sciences (IES),
   7, 8
Instructional fading, 99

Instructional strategies, effective, across curricular areas: and antecedent manipulations: social stories and social scripts, 44–45; and behavioral teaching strategies: prompting and chaining procedures, 45–46; and one-to-one and small-group instruction, 47–49; and technologically enhanced strategies: video modeling and computer-based intervention, 47

Intellectual and developmental disabilities (IDD), 8–10, 12, 49, 51_, 52

Intelligence quotients (IQs), 9, 25, 27, 31, 33, 73, 79, 81

Intense Preschool Applied Behavior Analysis Intervention, Intervention Outcomes for, 27

Intense Preschool Developmental Intervention, Intervention Outcomes for, 27

Interactive Collaborative Autism Network (ICAN), 169

Interconnectivity hypothesis, 21

IQs. *See* Intelligence quotients

Irritability scale, 211

J

Jahr, E., 74, 81

Jahromi, L. B., 28

Johnson, C., 210

Johnson, Michael (special education teacher), 135

Joint attention, 12, 110; examples of, that develop in first nine to twelve months, 11; illustration of role of, in social learning, 18; initiating (IJA), 17, 22, 28; learning function of, 17–18; responding to (RJA), 16, 20, 22; role of, in typical development and in cases of autism, 14–24; social motivation hypothesis of, 22

Journal of Applied Behavior Analysis, 51

Journal of Positive Behavior Interventions, 50

Junior Detective Training Program, 213

K

Kamps, D. M., 90, 92

Kanner, L., 12, 61, 62

Kasari, C., 28

Katsiyannis, A., 204

Kemmerer, K., 90

Kid's Zone, National Center for Education Statistics, U.S. Department of Education, 171

Klein, E., 95

Kling, R., 164

Koegel, B. L., 87

Koegel, L. K., 31, 87, 95, 100, 109

Koegel, R. L., 31, 87, 95, 100, 109

Kohler, F. W., 105

Krantz, P., 51

Kravits, T., 90

Kucharczyk, S., 131

N

National Autism Center, 30, 70, 192, 196, 197, 205; Established Treatments, 196–197

National Center for Education Statistics, 171

National Council of Teachers of Mathematics, 43

National Health Service (United Kingdom), 218–219

National Institute of Child Health and Human Development, 42–43

National Professional Development Center model, 131–153; and assessing and evaluating data to inform decision making, 149–152; coach teachers and paraprofessionals in implementing, 146–148; and evaluating and strengthening overall program quality, 131–135; and facilitating use of evidence-based practices in classrooms, 131–153; and selecting evidence-based practices, 139–146; summary, 152–153; and using IEPs to develop goal attainment scaling, 135–138

National Professional Development Center on Autism Spectrum Disorders (NPDC on ASD), 69, 71, 131–153, 178

National Reading Panel, 42–43

National Research Council, 43, 52, 84–85, 207, 226

National Science Education Standards (National Research Council), 43

National Standards on Evidence Based Practices, 65

National Standards Project (National Autism Center), 30, 70, 71, 109

Natural Language Paradigm, 214–215

Naturalistic behavior intervention, 108, 132; discrete trials *versus,* 76

Neitzel, J., 75

Neural interconnectivity, 20–21

New Yorker, 23

No Child Left Behind Act (2002), 42, 187, 188, 225–226

Nonverbal communication, 13

O

Oberleitner, R., 164

Object manipulation, 10

Object permanence, 10

Obsessive-compulsive disorder, 192

Odom, S., 69, 80

Office of Special Education Programs (U.S. Department of Education), 133

Ohio Center for Autism and Low Incidence (OCALI), 140

Older students, 49–51

One-to-one instruction, 47–49

Online data reviews, 166

Online resources, 168–171

Online staff collaboration, 161–165; to develop intervention plans (case study), 162–163

Online training modules, 140

Ono, M., 210
Openden, D., 95
Oppeneheim, M. L., 48
Oppositional defiant disorder, 192
Oppositionality, 25
O'Reilly, M. F., 41, 50
Ormsbee, Chris, 147
Osborne, L., 74–75

P

Page, Tim, 23
Pagliaro, J., 155
Paparella, T., 28
Paraeducational standards, 104
"Parallel Play: A Lifetime of Restless
   Isolation Explained" (Page), 23
Paraprofessionals: role of, 65; training
   programs for, 104–106
Parent Child Interaction Therapy
   (PCIT), 210
Parent training: and behavior
   management training, 209–211,
   221–224; and implementation of
   school-based parent training
   programs, 221–224; incorporating,
   into school curricula for children
   with ASD, 207–227; and integrating
   parent training into school
   curricula, 217–221; and language
   development training, 214–217; and
   Project DATA (Developmentally
   Appropriate Treatment for
   Autism), 219–220; and Project
   ImPACT, 217–218; and Scottish
   Centre for Autism, 218–219; and

social skills training, 211–214;
   summary, 224
Parent training programs,
   implementing, 221–224; and
   determining who will provide
   parent training, 223; and identifying
   training format, 222; and increasing
   parent participation, 223; and
   making programs socially valid to
   parents, teachers, and other
   consumers, 223–224
Parent-child interactions, 208
Parent-implemented intervention, 132
Parker, D., 92
PDD. *See* Pervasive developmental
   disorders(PDD)
PDD-NOS. *See* Pervasive
   developmental disorders-not
   otherwise specified (PDD-NOS)
Peer groups, small, 92–93
Peer social interaction, 110
Peer-mediated intervention, 132
Pelicano, E., 6
Personal digital assistants (PDAs), 47
Personal FM system, 167–168
Pervasive Developmental Disorder-
   Not Otherwise Specified
   (PDD-NOS), 51, 63, 73,
   79, 188
Pervasive Developmental Disorders
   (PDD), 63
Pharmacological intervention, 210
Philadelphia, Pennsylvania, 81
Physical play with caregivers, 13
Picture cues, 95

Structured teaching (ST) model, 81

Structured work systems, 132

Student task engagement, 37

Sturmey, P., 38

Sugar, C., 212

Suhrheinrich, J., 107

Sullivan, L., 131

Symbolic play, 110

Sze, K., 102

Szidon, K., 131

T

Tapped In (online community), 164–165, 170

Task analysis, 132

Task completion, 37

Taylor, B. A., 155

TeacherTube, 170

Technologically enhanced strategies, 47

Technology use: and desktop videoconferencing (case study), 167; and email, video, and cell phone instruction for professional development (case study), 159–160; headsets and ear bugs (case study), 167–168; impediments to, 173–174; and Moodle and Podcasts (case study), 157–159; and online communities for collaboration (tool overview), 164–165; and online staff collaboration, 161–165; and Rethink Autism (tool overview),

160–161; for staff training, collaboration, and supervision in school-based programs, 155–175; summary, 174–175; and technology-based supervision and coaching, 165–170; and video annotation for self-reflection by practicing teachers (tool overview), 163–164; and Web- and video-based field experiences (case study), 172–173; and Web-based training and professional development, 156–159

Technology-based supervision, 165–173_

Test-taking skills, 37

Theory of mind hypothesis, 6

Thompson, J. R., 203, 204

Time delay, 132

Timmer, S., 210

Transitional supports (TS), 79

Treatment and Education of Autistic and Communication Related Handicapped Children (TEACCH), 69

Turn-taking, 114–115

U

Uniqueness, of each child, 190–191

University of California, Los Angeles, 28–29

University of California, Santa Barbara, 31

University of North Carolina, 70

UPSTREAM, 169